THE CENTURY PSYCHOLOGY SERIES

Richard M. Elliott, *Edi*

D0086846

SELECTED WRITINGS

FROM

A CONNECTIONIST'S PSYCHOLOGY

EDWARD L. THORNDIKE

SELECTED WRITINGS

FROM

A CONNECTIONIST'S PSYCHOLOGY

Edward L. Thorndike

Professor Emeritus

Teachers College

Columbia University

GREENWOOD PRESS, PUBLISHERS

NEW YORK

Preface

THIS volume is the result of a request that I collect some three hundred pages of my most important contributions to psychology, but I have not done that. The findings in disproof of the views of Romanes, Mills, and others of the anecdotal school concerning animal intelligence, the explorations of individual differences and their causes, and the application of scientific methods to problems of learning and teaching are now commonplace with only an historical interest. Facts about the intercorrelations of abilities and evidence of the importance of both wide and narrow group factors have served their purpose. The treatment of individual differences in communities in *American Cities and States*, and *Your City* is best regarded as a contribution to sociology rather than to social psychology. I also omit from this volume all work on tests, from the group tests devised in 1914 for the Metropolitan Life Insurance Company to the CAVD test constructed (in 1922–1925) as a sample of what a measuring instrument for a mental ability should be. This omission saves much space and the most important facts are readily available to students in *The Measurement of Intelligence*. In general, I have favored contributions which are not now readily available as references for a class because printed in journals or monographs, or in books likely to go out of print. I have, in fact, had in mind especially the needs of teachers who wish their students to know something of connectionist psychology at first hand, but find *Human Learning* and *Man and His Works* far too superficial, and my other books of recent date far too long and too burdened with evidential matter.

I have added comments freely, sometimes to show the significance of the material for psychology in general, sometimes to abbreviate a quotation.

E. L. T.

Contents

vii

SELECTED WRITINGS

FROM

A CONNECTIONIST'S PSYCHOLOGY

Edward Lee Thorndike *

I HAVE no memory of having heard .or seen the word *psychology* until in my junior year at Wesleyan University (1893–1894), when I took a required course in it. The textbook, Sully's *Psychology*, aroused no notable interest, nor did the excellent lectures of Professor A. C. Armstrong, though I appreciated and enjoyed the dignity and clarity of his presentation and admired his skill in discrimination and argument. These discriminations and arguments stimulated me very little, however, and this was later true also of the writings of Ward and Stout. There is evidently some lack in my equipment which makes me intolerant of critical studies unless fortified by new facts or decorated by a captivating style.

The candidates in a prize examination were required to read also certain chapters from James's *Principles*. These were stimulating, more so than any book that I had read before, and possibly more so than any read since. The evidence is threefold. I bought the two volumes (the only book outside the field of literature that I voluntarily bought during the four years of college) and read all save parts of the most technical chapters. Though not, I hope, more impertinent than the average collegian, I reproached Professor Armstrong for not having given us James in place of Sully as our text. When, a year later, circumstances permitted me to study at Harvard, I eagerly registered for the course available under James.

During the first semester at Harvard (1895–1896) my program was half English, one-fourth psychology, and one-fourth philosophy, the last at the suggestion or requirement of Pro-

° From A *History of Psychology in Autobiography*, Vol. III, (Worcester, Mass., Clark Univ. Press, 1936), pp. 263–270.

fessor Royce. The subtlety and dexterity of Royce's mind aroused admiration tinged with irritation and amusement. Most of the students saw him as a prophet, but to me then he seemed too much a performer. Under no circumstances, probably, could I have been able or willing to make philosophy my business. Its stars shone brightly at Harvard in those years (1895–1897); Royce and Santayana were at or near their full glory, and Palmer was, as ever, the perfect expositor, but what I heard from them or about them did not attract me. Later I read the *Life of Reason* with extraordinary interest and profit, and learned to value the integrity and sincerity and impartiality of Dewey's writings on philosophy as well as on psychology and education; but in general my acquaintance with philosophy has been superficial and casual. Work in English was dropped in favor of psychology in the course of the first graduate year, and, by the fall of 1897, I thought of myself as a student of psychology and a candidate for the Ph.D. degree.

Münsterberg was in Germany from the fall of 1895 to the fall of 1897. During the second half of the period from 1895 to 1896, Mr. Hackett and I had made experiments in a course under the direction of Professor Delabarre, who had charge of the laboratory. During 1896–1897 I first attempted to measure the responsiveness of young children (3–6) to facial expressions or movements made unconsciously as in mind-reading experiments. I would think of one of a set of numbers, letters, or objects (I cannot now recall which or how many.) The child, facing me across a small table, would look at me and guess. If he guessed correctly, he received a small bit of candy. The children enjoyed the experiments, but the authorities in control of the institution would not permit me to continue them. I then suggested experiments with the instinctive and intelligent behavior of chickens as a topic, and this was accepted. I kept these animals and conducted the experiments in my room until the landlady's protests became imperative. James tried to get the few square feet required for me in the laboratory, and then in the Agassiz Museum. He was refused, and with his habitual kindness and devotion to underdogs and eccentric aspects of science, he harbored my chickens in the cellar of his own home for the rest of the year. The nuisance to Mrs. James was, I hope, somewhat mitigated by the entertainment to the two youngest children.

During the two years of study at Harvard, I had supported myself by acting as tutor to a boy. We roomed together, and the incessant companionship and responsibility was burdensome, though he was cheerful, coöperative, and fonder of me than I deserved, and though I learned much practical psychology and pedagogy from the experience. A year free from such labor seemed desirable, so I applied for a fellowship at Columbia. I received the appointment, and upon inquiry was informed by Professor Cattell that an extension of my work on the mental life of animals would be suitable for a doctor's thesis. I continued these experiments with chickens at my parents' home during the summer. I tried white rats also, but I was stupid in handling them and the family objected to the smell, so I let them go.

I came to New York, bringing in a basket my two most educated chickens, from whom I expected in due time a family which would enable me to test the influence of acquired mental traits upon inherited capacity, a foolish project in view of the slow breeding-rate of fowls. I also expected to test the permanence of their learning over a long interval, but never did, the first of a regrettable list of enterprises left incomplete.

Cattell was not only kind, but highly efficient, providing a room in the attic which was ample for my purpose, and giving, as always, sound advice. The freedom from work and worry for money was a great boon. The present policy of universities is to reduce grants for scholarships and fellowships relatively to the number of students, replacing them by loan funds, and this may be wise. But, so far as I can judge, scholarships at Harvard and a fellowship at Columbia increased my productive work in science by at least two years and probably improved its quality.

The motive for my first investigations of animal intelligence was chiefly to satisfy requirements for courses and degrees.

Any other topic would probably have served me as well. I certainly had no special interest in animals and had never taken a course in biology until my last year of graduate work, when I worked hard at it and completed a minor for the doctor's degree. The work with monkeys, from 1899 to 1901, was done from the mixture of duty, interest, and desire for good repute which motivates most scientific work. The extension of the fruitful experimental method to representative primates was obviously important. I would have gladly continued the work with the higher apes, but could not afford to buy or maintain them.

In the spring of 1898, I was offered two positions, one as a teacher of psychology in a normal school, the other at a much lower salary as a teacher of education in the College for Women of Western Reserve University. I chose the latter, partly because my brother expected to go there and partly because of the repute of Western Reserve. I spent the summer in reading the facts and important theories about education and teaching. This could then be done if the history of educational practices was omitted. After a year at Cleveland, I was given a trial at teaching psychology and child study at Teachers College, and there I have spent the past thirty-one years.

I have recorded my beginning as a psychologist in detail because it illustrates what is perhaps the most general fact about my entire career as a psychologist later; namely, its responsiveness to outer pressure or opportunity rather than to inner needs. Within certain limits set by capacity and interest I did in those early years and have done since what the occasion seemed to demand. Thus for various courses taught at Teachers College I wrote the *Elements of Psychology*, *Notes on Child Study*, *Educational Psychology* (in three editions, from 1903 to 1914), *An Introduction to the Theory of Mental and Social Measurements*, and *The Psychology of Arithmetic*. It has always seemed to me better for an instructor to present his contributions in black and white than to require the labor and risk the errors of note-taking. Thus I have made somewhat laborious researches on mental inheritance, individual and sex differences, memory, work, fatigue, interest, the interrelations of abilities, the organization of intellect, and other topics in educational psychology, because in each case the matter seemed important for theory or practice or both. I planned and directed the psychological work of the New York State Commission on Ventilation, prepared tests for the selection of clerical employees, and served on the Committee on Classification of Personnel in the Army and in various other enterprises because I was told by persons in whom I had confidence that it was in the line of duty. I have written textbooks for children to show that psychology does apply in detail to the work of the classroom. Thus, in 1919, at the request of the faculty of Columbia College, I undertook the responsibility of preparing annually an intelligence examination suitable for use in the selection and placement of freshmen; and in 1922, at the request of Justice Stone, then Dean of the Columbia Law School, I conducted a three-year investigation which resulted in the Capacity Test adopted in 1928 as a part of the system of selection of entrants to the Columbia Law School.

Obviously I have not "carved out my career," as the biographers say. Rather, it has been a conglomerate, amassed under the pressure of varied opportunities and demands. Probably it would have been wiser to plan a more consistent and unified life-work in accord with interest and capacity, but I am not sure. Even in the case of great men, there is considerable evidence that the man's own interests and plans may not cause a better output than his responses to demands from outside. Under pressure, James wrote the *Principles* with wailing and gnashing of teeth to fulfill a contract with a publishing firm. *Pragmatism* and *The Will to Believe* were done when he was free to choose. An ordinary man of science has probably less reason to put his own plans above those which the world makes for him. So I do not complain of the restrictions imposed by the necessity of earning a living by various drudgeries to which I have been assigned. And I reproach myself only moderately for not having looked and thought longer before leaping to this, that, and the other job.

In the last dozen years I have been enabled by grants from the Carnegie Corporation to carry on two investigations which I did choose and plan, one on the fundamentals of measurement of intellect and capacity, the results of which appeared as *The Measurement of Intelligence,* the other on the fundamentals of learning, the results of which have appeared in *The Fundamentals of Learning* and in *The Psychology of Wants, Interests, and Attitudes.* These do seem to me by far the best work that I have done and I cannot help wondering what would have happened if similar support had been available in 1905 or 1915.

The impetuosity to which I have referred has influenced my work in detail. I often have to do corrective and supplementary experiments and discard work because in its course a better way is found.

Another weakness has been an extreme ineptitude and distaste for using machinery and physical instruments. Presumably my work would have been better, and certainly it would have *seemed* better, if I had been at home with apparatus for exposing, timing, registering, and the like.

The training which I have most keenly missed has been a systematic course in the use of standard physiological and psychological apparatus and extended training in mathematics. Perhaps the first would not have profited me much in view of my extreme incapacity. I did not lack capacity for mathematics and tried to remedy the second deficiency by private study, but something else always seemed more important. I managed to learn the essentials of statistical method somehow, and have handled some fairly intricate quantitative problems without, I think, making more than one mistake (which I was able to correct promptly at the suggestion of Dr. T. L. Kelley). I feel incompetent and insecure, however, in the abstract algebraic treatment of a quantitative problem and I am helpless when the calculus is necessary.

Young psychologists who share one or more of my disabilities may take comfort in the fact that, after all, I have done useful experiments without mechanical ability or training and have investigated quantitative relations with very meager knowledge of mathematics.

As personal features on the other side of the ledger I may put intelligence, good health, strong eyes, the interest in work and achievement which Veblen has called the "instinct of workmanship," impartiality, and industry. As environmental features I may note home life with parents of superior intelligence and idealism, many profitable courses at Wesleyan, Harvard, and Columbia, especially those in abnormal psychology with James, statistical methods with Boas, and neurology with Strong, university colleagues eminent in psychology and other fields, and the great body of published work in science.

The last is, of course, the most important. Though an investigator rather than a scholar, I have probably spent well over 20,000 hours in reading and studying scientific books and journals.

I have tried to make two lists, one of authors all or nearly all of whose writings I have read, and another of authors not included in the above to whom I owe valuable facts or suggestions. But the first list of thirty or so names grades off into the names of many more, much of whose writing I have read, and the second list, which is very long, cannot be accurate because of faults of memory. Therefore, I may note only that the writings of James and Galton have influenced me most, and that factual material seems to benefit me more than what is commonly called discussion and criticism. Although, as has been stated, my tendency is to say "Yes" to persons, my tendency seems to have been to say "No" to ideas. I have been stimulated to study problems to which Romanes, Wesley Mills, Stanley Hall, Alexander Bain, Kraepelin, Spearman, and others seemed to me to give wrong answers, more often than to verify and extend work which seemed sound. Of late years this negative or critical tendency seems to have weakened and given place to an interest in questions to which the answers are conflicting or inadequate, and in questions which have not even been faced.

Until the first World War I was able to keep fairly well informed of the findings of psychologists in respect to animal psychology, individual psychology, and educational psychology, but since 1917 I have been able only to follow specially important work and that which I had to know about in connection with my own researches. In spite of the saving of time due to the Psychological Abstracts, my reading is now less and less adequate each year.

I have a suspicion that our scientific code, which demands that an investigator should acquaint himself with everything, good, bad, and indifferent, that has been done on the problem which he is investigating, should be somewhat relaxed. Personally, I seem to have profited more from reading important books outside of the topics I had to investigate, and even outside of psychology, than from some of the monographs and articles on animal learning, intelligence tests, and the like, which our code required me to read.

We are especially urged in these psychological autobiographies to describe our methods of work, but I seem to have little or nothing useful to say in this regard. In the actual work of advancing knowledge of human nature we may use three methods. We may observe and think about the facts that come our way; we may deliberately gather by observation or experiment facts which we see can be got and which seem likely to be instructive; we may pose a question that we know is important and then do our best to get facts to answer it. I have done all three; most often the last. The most fruitful methods often come to mind late in the course of an investigation. When one does everything that he can think of, the doing often makes him think of something else. So the idea of the delayed-reaction experiment (which has proved the most valuable of my methods of studying animal mentality) came to me after two years of work with animals. So the idea that the difficulty of a task for intellect (or any other ability) can be measured only in the case of a task composed of enough elements to involve all of intellect (or of the ability, whatever it may be), and nothing but it, came only after thirty years of study of intellect, and over a year of special investigation of means of measuring difficulty for intellect.

Concerning conditions favorable and unfavorable to scholarly and productive work in science, I have little or nothing instructive to report. Peaceful successful work without worry has rarely tired me, though if I drop below a certain minimum amount of sleep, a headache results. Noise does not disturb me unless it is evidence of distress, as of a person or animal in pain. Surety of freedom from interruption is of course beneficial. Social intercourse except with intimate friends is fatiguing, and all forms of personal conflict, as in bargaining, persuading, or rebuking, are trebly so. Physical exercise is enjoyable, but not, so far I know, beneficial. A general background of freedom from regret and worry is almost imperative, and I early decided to spend so little and earn so much as to keep free from financial worries. In order to reduce one cause for worry, it has been my custom to fulfill my contractual obligations as a professor before doing anything else. The good opinion of others, especially those whom I esteem, has been a very great stimulus, though I have come in later years to require also the approval of my own judgment.

Since my own history is so barren of interest and instruction I may add a few notes of general observation. Excellent work in psychology can surely be done by men widely different in nature or training or both. James and Hall were essentially literary men, one with an extraordinary sense of fact, the other with extraordinary imagination and prophetic zeal. On the other hand, some of our present leaders were first trained in physics or engineering.

Excellent work can surely be done by men with widely different notions of what psychology is and should be, the best work of all perhaps being done by men such as Galton, who gave little or no thought to what it is or should be.

Excellent results have come from the successive widenings of the field of observation to include the insane, infants, and animals, and from the correlation of mental events with physiological changes. Should we not extend our observations to include, for example, history, anthropology, economics, linguistics, and the fine arts, and connect them with biochemistry and biophysics?

The above covers my work till 1934 or age 60. I now (1948) add notes about some activities since then which may be of interest to students of psychology.

It seemed to me that psychology should strive to become a basic science on which Anthropology, Sociology, Economics, Political Science, Law, Criminology, and Philanthropy could count for certain fundamental facts and principles, especially concerning human abilities and wants. With generous aid from the Carnegie Corporation, I spent much time from 1934 to 1940 working with a group of students of history and political science, lawyers, and psychologists who already had doctor's degrees and were given fellowships for two or more years. It was hoped that some of them would become leaders in making psychology a basic part of these special sciences: and perhaps some of them yet will. So far they have done many excellent things, but not that.

I myself wrote *Human Nature and the Social Order* (1940), stating some of the facts of psychology which students of these special sciences, especially of Economics, Political Science, Law, and Philanthropy, seemed to me to need to know. This book may yet be used by such students, but so far it has not. Their neglect of it does not seem to be due to any distrust of me; for articles by me on topics strictly within the fields of economics, political science, and law have been accepted by the *Quarterly Journal of Economics,* the *Harvard Business Review,* the *Public Administration Review,* and the *Columbia Law Review.* The distrust seems to be of psychology.

It seemed to me probable that sociology would profit by studying the differences of communities in the same way that psychology studies the differences of individuals. Therefore I collected nearly 300 items of fact concerning each of 310 cities, studied their variations and intercorrelations, computed for each city three scores for the general goodness of life for good people for each city (G), for the personal qualities of its residents (P), and for their per capita income (I), and studied the causes of the differences among cities in G. The resulting book, *Your City* (1939), has been welcomed by leaders in many cities and used as an aid to community improvement, but has had little influence upon either research or teaching by sociologists. However, I still think that a college course in sociology may profitably include the measurement of individual differences among communities and the causation of these differences as revealed by suitable correlational methods.

It had long seemed to me that both the science and the teaching of language deserved more attention from psychology than they were receiving. I had begun with the humble task of counting the frequencies of occurrence of English words, publishing the facts for a ten-million count in 1921 and an extension of it in 1931. Dr. Irving Lorge and I brought out a greatly extended and improved count in 1944, and a count of meanings (*A Semantic Count of English Words*) in 1938. From 1937 on I published ten articles reporting work on euphony, semantics, and other features of language.

Apart from these three divagations I continued to work on learning, interests, and individual differences and their causes, especially heredity, as previously.

It should perhaps be noted that I have spent much time and thought on educational science proper, as shown in various monographs and articles, most of them factual.

CHAPTER I

The Law of Effect

[The Law of Effect, that the immediate consequence of a mental connection (in particular, a satisfying state of affairs following a connection and belonging to it) can work back upon it to strengthen it, is now accepted by most psychologists. It is unnecessary to report here any of the experiments by myself or my pupils which helped to change a heresy into orthodoxy. Samples can be found in Chapters IX to XI of *The Fundamentals of Learning,* in *The Experimental Study of Rewards,* in Chapter 14 of the *Psychology of Wants, Interests, and Attitudes,* and in various articles in *The Journal of Experimental Psychology.* I report here the simple (perhaps too simple) explanation of the facts which I believe is true, and some facts first published in the Michotte memorial volume.]

A THEORY OF THE ACTION OF THE AFTER-EFFECTS OF A CONNECTION UPON IT [*]

One of the objections to the hypothesis that a satisfying after-effect of a mental connection works back upon it to strengthen it is that nobody has shown how this action does or could occur. It is the purpose of this article to show how a mechanism which is as possible physiologically as any of the mechanisms proposed to account for facilitation, inhibition, fatigue, strengthening by repetition or other forms of modification, could enable such an after-effect to cause such a strengthening. I shall also report certain facts and hypotheses concerning the work which this mechanism has to do and the

[*] *Psychological Review,* Vol. 40, (Sept., 1933), pp. 434–439.

way in which it seems to do it. These are of value regardless of the correctness of my identification of the mechanism itself.

For convenience we may use symbols as follows:

N = the neurones of an animal.
B = the rest of the animal's body.
C = any activity, state, or condition of N.
S = any situation or state of affairs external to N considered as a cause of some C.
R = any response or state of affairs external to N, considered as a result of some C.

By a satisfying state of affairs or satisfier is meant one which the animal does nothing to avoid, often doing things which maintain or renew it. By an annoying state of affairs is meant one which the animal does nothing to preserve, often doing things which put an end to it.

A satisfier exerts an influence that strengthens any modifiable C upon which this influence impinges. Not knowing what Cs are made of, or how a strong C differs from a weaker form of the same C, one must speak in figures and analogies. The influence may thus be thought of as like an addition of current or potential, or a decrease of resistance, or an intimacy of connection, or a continuance for a longer time.

The Cs upon which it impinges most will be among those which have recently been active or will shortly be active. That is, the action of a satisfier is conditioned by its place in the succession of Cs.

The Cs upon which it impinges will be preferentially those situated in the part or feature or pattern or system or organization of N in which the satisfier occurs. When an animal that runs about seeking food attains it, the strengthening will be more likely to influence the Cs concerned with its locomotion, its hunger, and its ideas about food and eating, than those concerned with contemporaneous casual scratchings of an itching ear, or stray thoughts about Shakespeare's sonnets or Brahms's symphonies.

More narrowly the influence will impinge preferentially upon the C (or Cs) to which the satisfier "belongs" as a part of a more or less unitary group of Cs, or larger C. In the animal just mentioned, the satisfier will strengthen the C between reaching the doorway to the food-box and going in, more than the C between reaching that doorway and pausing to inspect it. The excess strengthening will be far more than the slight difference in time can account for. If, in an exercise in completing a word, say oc·re, by supplying a missing letter, a person tries first a, then e, then i, then o, and then h, being rewarded by "Right" for the last, and then at once proceeds to look at the next word, the satisfier will strengthen the C with h enormously more than the next preceding or following C, far more than the removal by one step and a second or so could account for.

Its influence will not, however, pick out the "right" or "essential" or "useful" C by any mystical or logical potency. It is, on the contrary, as natural in its action as a falling stone, a ray of light, a line of force, a discharge of buckshot, a stream of water, or a hormone in the blood. It will strengthen not only the C which is the most preferred according to the principles stated above, but also to some extent Cs which are wrong, irrelevant, or useless, provided they are close enough to the satisfier in the succession of Cs.

One naturally asks first whether the action of a satisfier may be by stimulating the general circulation and thus causing the Cs which happen to be in a state of excitement at or near the time of occurrence of the satisfier to be preferentially strengthened by some metabolic process. The facts seem to deny this possibility. The strengthening influence of a satisfier is probably in the form of a reaction of the neurones themselves. It is too rapid to be via an increase or decrease in the general circulation, or by the liberation of a hormone. When a series $S \rightarrow R \rightarrow$Reward or Punishment, $S \rightarrow R \rightarrow$Reward or Punishment, $S \rightarrow R \rightarrow$Reward or Punishment is run at the rate of 3 seconds per unit, the action of each satisfier is localized at and around its point of application in the series with almost perfect clearness. And this is approximately true with rates of $1\frac{1}{2}$ seconds or even 1 second per unit. Moreover, remoteness in steps seems (though the data are not yet adequate) very much more important than remoteness in time in restricting its application.

This unknown reaction of neurones which is aroused by the satisfier and which strengthens connections upon which it impinges I have called the "Yes" reaction, or "O.K." reaction, or confirming reaction. Though its intimate histological basis and physiological nature are no better known than those of facilitation, inhibition, fatigue, strengthening by repetition, or any other forces causing temporary or permanent modifications in N, certain facts about it are known in addition to those already stated concerning its causes and results.

The confirming reaction is independent of sensory pleasures. A pain may set it in action, as Tolman, Hall, and Bretnall have recently demonstrated in a striking experiment.[1] The confirming reaction, though far from logical or inerrant, is highly selective. It may pick out and act upon the words one is saying, leaving uninfluenced one's posture and gross bodily movements and all that one is seeing.

The confirming reaction seems often to issue from some overhead control in N, the neural basis of some want or "drive" or purpose or then active self of the animal. This overhead control may be rather narrow and specific, as when a swallow of liquid satisfies thirst, and the satisfaction confirms the C which caused the swallowing, and makes the animal continue or repeat that C. This may happen while the main flow of his purposes concerns the work he is doing or the game he is playing or the book he is reading. It may be very broad and general, as when the purpose is to do well and win a game or to pass the time pleasantly, and is satisfied by any one of many movements in response to some play of one's adversary or by attentiveness to any one of many sights and sounds. It may be stimulated to send forth its confirming reaction by a rich sensory satisfier, such as freedom, food, and companionship for an animal escaping from a cage, or by a purely symbolic

[1] E. C. Tolman, C. S. Hall, & E. P. Bretnall, *J. Exper. Psychol.*, 15, (1932), 601–614.

satisfier, such as the announcement of "Right" in an experiment in learning. If what the overhead control wants is the announcement of "Right," that is what will most surely lead it to make the confirming reaction.

As suggested by the preceding paragraph, several wants or purposes or controls may be operative at the same time or in close alternation.

Arrangements may be made whereby certain events acquire power to cause the confirming reaction in the absence of anything that would ordinarily be called an overhead control. The reward or satisfier may then exert the confirming reaction directly upon the C.

If a $S \rightarrow R$ connection has a satisfying after-effect which causes some control in the N to send forth a confirming reaction, and if the S continues, the confirming reaction tends to cause a continuance or continued repetition of the R then and there, and often with more vigor and shorter latency. If the situation has vanished, the strengthening of the C can only manifest itself when S recurs, which may be in a few seconds or only after months. There will then be an increased probability of repetition over what there would have been if no confirming reaction had affected the C in question. In either case the strengthening causes the repetition, not the repetition the strengthening.

The potency of a confirming reaction may bear little relation to the intensity of the satisfier. A "want" or "purpose" or "self" may be as well satisfied, and so issue as full and adequate a confirming reaction, by a moderate reward as by one much larger. There seems to be an upper point beyond which increases in a reward add only excitement. Toward the low end there is a range where the reward fails more and more frequently to arouse an adequate confirming reaction. There seems to be a point below which a confirming reaction is not evoked. A state of affairs below this degree of satisfyingness is satisfying to the extent of being tolerated, and nothing is done to abolish or evade it, or to replace the C which caused it by some other C; but also nothing is done to strengthen the C

and continue it longer than it would otherwise have been continued, or to repeat it in the future more frequently than it would otherwise have been repeated.

At the other end of this neutral zone begin states of affairs which are annoying to the animal and stimulate him to do whatever his repertory provides as responses to the annoyance in question. His repertory does not provide a general destructive or weakening reaction which is comparable and opposite to the confirming reaction, and which subtracts from the C upon which it acts. Any apparent subtraction is due to the increased strength of competing tendencies. The annoyer does not then and there destroy or weaken the connection of which it is the after-effect, but only causes the animal to make a different response to the S in question.

I do not think that this tendency to do something different in response to an S the first response to which has resulted in an annoying state of affairs, is a unitary tendency applicable to any C, and replacing it indifferently by any other C than it. The confirming reaction set in action by a satisfier, has, if my observations are correct and adequate, no comparable altering reaction set in action by an annoyer. The reactions in the latter case seem specialized and closely dependent on what the annoyer is and what state the N is in.

Whether or not this is so, an annoying after-effect of a certain $S \rightarrow R$ has very different possibilities *according as the S remains or vanishes*. If it vanishes, the annoyer can do nothing, because it cannot change the response to an S which is not there. So, in multiple-choice learning in which each S vanishes as soon as it is responded to, punishments have zero influence upon learning and punished connections may do more harm to learning by occurring than they do good by being punished. If the S remains and the response to it is changed, the animal may benefit from the fact of changing, and from the occurrence and the after-effects of the $S \rightarrow R_2$ which has replaced $S \rightarrow R_1$.

What sort of force acting through what sort of process or mechanism can be and do what the confirming reaction is and does? The answer which seems to me to fit all or nearly all the facts is that the force and mechanism of the confirming reaction are the force and mechanism of reinforcement, applied to a connection.

All explanations of reinforcement agree that one part of N can exert a force to intensify activities elsewhere in N, and that processes or mechanisms exist whereby this force can be directed or attracted to one activity rather than promiscuously; and that is all that is required to explain the fundamental physiology of the confirming reaction. It is distinguished from other sorts of reinforcement by the fact that satisfaction sets the force in action and that the force acts on the connection which was just active in intimate functional association with the production of the satisfier, or on its near neighbors.

THE INFLUENCE OF OCCURRENCE, REWARD AND PUNISHMENT UPON CONNECTIONS THAT HAD ALREADY CONSIDERABLE STRENGTH [2]

As one result of an investigation of the pleasantness of English words to English-speaking persons, I had over a thousand words rated by educated adults (usually by 64 such) providing approximate values from 10 (for such words as *blossom, Hercules, serene,* and *sonata*) down to 1 (for such as *asexual, clack, hank,* and *sewage*). 800 of these words were arranged in 20 sets of 40 words each, 4 of value 10, 4 of value 9, 4 of value 8, etc., the 40 words in each set being arranged in a random order.

These were used in an experiment (BBB of the Thorndike series) in which eighteen educated adults responded to hearing a word by stating the value they thought a consensus of adults would attach to it. They were instructed as follows:

"I shall say a word. You will say a number from 1 to 10 representing your opinion concerning the pleasantness of the

[2] *Miscellanea Psychologica, Albert Michotte,* 1947, pp. 308–322. Reprinted here only in part.

sound of the word to people in general. 1 will mean that it is extremely unpleasant, like *squangunk* or *brishrashpunk;* 10 will mean that it is very pleasant sounding, like *melody* or *adora.* 2, 3, 4, or 5 will be less and less degrees of unpleasantness; 9, 8, 7, and 6 will be less and less degrees of pleasantness. You will have to make very quick judgments to keep up with the timer. You will have no chance to stop to think about the matter but will just have to blurt the first number that seems appropriate."

The experimenter first gave the subject enough practice with a practice series to accustom him to saying a number from 1 to 10 quickly enough to keep up with the timer, which was set at 2½ seconds. He then used set 1 of 40 words and recorded the subject's responses. He then used set 1 in the same way a second time.

Then he said, "This time I shall say 'Right' if the number you give does represent the degree of pleasantness or unpleasantness of the sound of the word in the average judgment of 64 educated adults of good taste. I shall say 'Close' if the number that you give is within one of the judgment of this group. I shall say 'Wrong' if your number is more than one step away from the general judgment. For example, if the average judgment of the 64 gives 8 for the sound of 'cluster,' I would say 'Right' if you said 8, 'Close' if you said 7 or 9, and 'Wrong' if you said any other number. Be sure to say your number very promptly so as to keep up with the timer, since I am using up a half-second to make the announcement." He then used set 1, recorded each response, and announced "Right" or "Close" or "Wrong" after each.

After this third trial with the words of set 1, the experimenter said, "We will go through the series again and in just the same way. I will later tell you how much you have improved in the sense of making your judgments more like those of the average of the 64 persons of good taste."

After this fourth trial the experimenter said "This time you will make the judgments just as before, trying to be near what people of good taste think, but I will say nothing." He then used the words of set 1 a fifth time, recording each response, but making no announcement. . . . [There follow in the original certain further facts concerning the use of the 20 sets of 40 words each. In all cases rounds 1, 2, and 5 were with no announcements; but in rounds 3 and 4 the subject was told "Right," "Close" or "Wrong" after each of his guesses.]

I report first the facts for cases where a word evoked the same response in all of trials 1 to 4. Using r to represent one occurrence announced as "Right," c to represent one occurrence announced as "Close," w to represent one occurrence announced as "Wrong," and o to represent one occurrence with no announcement, we have the three following histories:

oorr, followed in trial 5 by the r connection in 87 per cent of the cases.

oocc, followed in trial 5 by the c connection in 73 per cent of the cases.

ooww, followed in trial 5 by the w connection in 52 per cent of the cases.

For cases where a word evoked the same response in trials 3 and 4 and in either trial 1 or trial 2 we have the three following histories (using n to represent the occurrence of some other response to the word in question):

onrr or *norr*, followed in trial 5 by the r connection in 78 per cent of the cases.

oncc or *nocc*, followed in trial 5 by the c connection in 65 per cent of the cases.

onww or *noww*, followed in trial 5 by the w connection in 50 per cent of the cases.

For cases where a word evoked the same response in trials 3 and 4 but in neither trial 1 nor trial 2 we have:

nnrr, followed in trial 5 by the r connection in 71 per cent of the cases.

nncc, followed in trial 5 by the c connection in 55 per cent of the cases.

nnww, followed in trial 5 by the w connection in 39 per cent of the cases.

The number of cases in these nine categories are, in order,

761, 949, 911, 556, 821, 970, 355, 484, and 680. Hence the percentages are fairly reliable.

The facts for cases where an *r*, *c*, or *w* connection occurred in trial 4, but not in trial 1, 2, or 3, will be reported later.

It is clear from the facts listed above that *cc* is intermediate between *rr* and *ww* in influence. It is also clear that an occurrence in trial 1 or trial 2, though not announced as "Right," "Close," or "Wrong," either adds strength to a connection or is a sign that the connection already had more than average strength prior to trial 1.

Consider next the facts for the influence on the response in trial 4 of histories where the response in trial 3 was *r*, *c*, or *w*. When the response was the same in trials 1, 2 and 3 we have:

oor, followed in trial 4 by the *r* connection in 76 per cent of the cases.

ooc, followed in trial 4 by the *c* connection in 60 per cent of the cases.

oow, followed in trial 4 by the *w* connection in 43 per cent of the cases.

When the response was the same in trials 1 and 3 or in trials 2 and 3 we have:

onr or *nor*, followed in trial 4 by the *r* connection in 60 per cent of the cases.

onc or *noc*, followed in trial 4 by the *c* connection in 49 per cent of the cases.

onw or *now*, followed in trial 4 by the *w* connection in 38 per cent of the cases.

For cases where the response made in trial 3 was not made in either trial 1 or trial 2 we have:

nnr, followed in trial 4 by the *r* connection in 50 per cent of the cases.

nnc, followed in trial 4 by the *c* connection in 37 per cent of the cases.

nnw, followed in trial 4 by the *w* connection in 28 per cent of the cases.

The numbers of cases involved in these nine categories

were, in order, 986, 1614, 2104, 902, 1665, 2561, 694, 1346, and 2499. (29 of the 14,400 histories could not be used because of the absence or illegibility of some number.)

In these histories again c is midway between r and w in influence; and occurrences in trials 1 and 2 though with no announcement of "Right," "Close," or "Wrong," are important either as adding strength or as signs of its presence.

For convenience in making certain comparisons the eighteen varieties of histories are listed together in Table I, together with certain differences.

The general facts found in earlier experiments with multiple-choice learning seem to be corroborated in this experiment with connections already existing in considerable strength. The mere occurrence of a connection strengthens it. The addition of a satisfying state of affairs strengthens it much more. The addition of an annoying state of affairs does not weaken it enough to counterbalance the influence of mere occurrence. The satisfying state of affairs or "reward" acts not only by giving the learners information which may cause useful memories, but also and much more, by a direct and immediate action on the connection. Thus the announcement of "Close" (which is satisfying, though not so surely or strongly satisfying as "right") strengthens mainly the connection to which it is attached, not the connection between the word and the number just above or just below that announced to be "Close."

The significance of the direct influence of "Close" as a satisfier is of so much importance for general theories of learning that I have made a special, and probably crucial, test of it in the case of connections of the form *word x———>response 1, announcement "Close,"* and *word x———>response 10, announcement "Close."* In proportion as being nearly right satisfies the learner and arouses the "confirming reaction" the next trial with the word in question will tend to evoke that same connection. In proportion as learning consists in the learner being informed by the experiences in question that 2 is right and 9

TABLE I

Percentages of recurrence in trial 5 or 4 of connections having histories as specified in trials 1-4 or 1-3.				Differences in frequency of recurrence related to differences in history.			
				rr-r	rr-cc	cc-ww	oo-o
oorr	87	oor	76	11	14, 13, and 16	21, 15, and 16	9
onrr		onr					
or	78	or	60	18			8
norr		nor					2
nnrr	71	nnr	50	21			16
				cc-c	r-c	c-w	
oocc	73	ooc	60	13	16, 11, and 13	17, 11, and 9	11
							5
oncc		onc					
or	65	or	49	16			0-n
nocc		noc					
nncc	55	nnc	37	18			7
				ww-w			
ooww	52	oow	43	9			10
							11
onww		onw					
or	50	or	38	12			10
noww		now					12
nnww	39	nnw	28	11			10

Average Differences

rr-r, 16.7;   rr-cc, 14.3;   cc-ww, 17.3;   oo-o, 8.5;
cc-c, 16.3;   r-c, 13.3;   c-w, 12.3;   o-n, 10.0;
ww-w, 10.7

is right, the next trial with the word in question will tend to evoke 2 rather than 1, or 9 rather than 10. I have tabulated the facts for all cases of 1c and 10c in trial 3 in the records of ten of the eighteen subjects. The same 1 (or 10) recurs in trial 4 almost exactly three times as often as does the 2 (or 9). Cases of 2 "Close," 3 "Close," 4 "Close," 5 "Close," 6 "Close," 7 "Close," 8 "Close," and 9 "Close," in trial 3 recur in trial 4 a little less than three times as often as the number one below, or as the number one above. . . .

It is remarkable how closely the total effect of any one of the eighteen histories can be predicted from a reasonable assignment of potencies to (1) the initial strength of the connections involved, (2) the occurrence of a connection in trial 1 or trial 2 without any announcement, (3) the occurrence of a connection in trial 3 or trial 4 followed by the announcement of "Right," (4) the occurrence of a connection in trial 3 or 4 followed by the announcement of "Close," and (5) the occurrence of a connection in trial 3 or 4 followed by the announcement of "Wrong." If these assignments are, in order,

TABLE II

Comparison of the observed facts with those predicted (A) by the formula .28 for initial strength, .10 for each occurrence with no announcement, .21 for each occurrence announced as "Right," .13 for each occurrence announced as "Close," and .01 for each occurrence announced as "Wrong," and (B) those predicted from the formula .27, .10, .22, .13 and .02 for the same facts in order.

	Predicted frequencies of recurrence. In trial 5		Observed frequencies of recurrence.	Differences, predicted minus observed.	
	By formula A	By formula B	Observed in trial 5	By formula A	By formula B
oorr	.90	.91	.87	+.03	+.04
onrr or norr	.80	.81	.78	+.02	+.03
nnrr	.70	.71	.71	−.01	.00
oocc	.74	.73	.73	+.01	.00
oncc or nocc	.64	.63	.65	−.01	−.02
nncc	.54	.53	.55	−.01	−.02
ooww	.50	.51	.52	−.02	−.01
onww or noww	.40	.41	.50	−.10	−.09
nnww	.30	.31	.39	−.09	−.08

	Predicted in trial 4		Observed in trial 4	By formula A	By formula B
	By formula A	By formula B			
oor	.69	.69	.76	−.07	−.07
onr or nor	.59	.59	.60	−.01	−.01
nnr	.49	.49	.50	−.01	−.01
ooc	.61	.60	.60	+.01	.00
onc or noc	.51	.50	.49	+.02	+.01
nnc	.41	.40	.37	+.04	+.03
oow	.49	.49	.43	+.06	+.06
onw or now	.39	.39	.38	+.01	+.01
nnw	.29	.29	.28	+.01	+.01
			Average	.030	.028

.28, .10, .21, .13, and .01, the predicted values differ from the observed by only .03 on the average, as shown in Table II. If they are .27, .10, .22, .13 and .02, the predicted values differ from the observed by even less (.028).

The estimate of .28 for the average probability that the same number would be given in response to a word apart from any tuition could be checked empirically by having a group of subjects comparable to the 18 used in the experiment respond to an adequate sampling of words twice with so long a time between the two trials that any influence from the first occurrence would be nearly or quite zero. But I have not been able to do that.

[There follows in the original article a statement of the evidence justifying approximately .28 as an estimate of average initial strength of the connection between one of the words and one of the numbers, and also a statement of the facts for 4135 histories of the forms *ooxr, onxr, noxr, ooxc*, etc. in which *x* represents an occurrence of any other than the *r, c,* or *w* connection operating in trial 4.]

CHAPTER II

The Spread or Scatter Phenomenon *

[Whether or not we accept the *Confirming Reaction* described above as the agent whereby a satisfying consequence of a connection strengthens it, we must, I think, accept the fact that such a "reward" acts biologically rather than logically in the sense that it sometimes misses its logical mark and strengthens connections that are nearby. The phenomenon described in the following excerpt was verified by both American and European observers. There are a few recent dissenters, but if they will repeat the original experiments in full I prophesy that they will be convinced.]

We provide in an experiment a long series of situations to each of which several responses are possible, one of which is arbitrarily followed by a reward, any other being followed by a punishment. For example, a series of 40 words is said by the experimenter to each of which the subject may respond by any number from 1 to 10. If he says the number that has been chosen to be "right," he is rewarded; if he says any other, he is punished. So we have a long sequence of connections and after-effects, in the form Word 1→number, reward or punishment; Word 2→number, reward or punishment; Word 3→ number, reward or punishment; Word 4→number, reward or punishment; Word 5→number, reward or punishment; and so on.

This series is repeated again and again. A sample record is shown in Appendix I, from which we quote here the results for the first ten words in trials 1 to 4.[1]

* From "An Experimental Study of Rewards," *Teachers College Contributions to Education*, No. 580 (1933), pp. 1–72.
[1] In this experiment the series of words, each with its "right" number, was

	Trial or Round 1	Trial or Round 2	Trial or Round 3	Trial or Round 4
catnip	2	4	10	2
cedar	3	3	6	2
chamber	1	2	9	8
chorus	8	10	7	6
dally	4	8	5	4
dazzle	C2	6	9	1
debate	9	7	2	5
deduce	5	2	2	2
early	4	C5	C5	C5
effort	3	6	C7	C7

The time-intervals were as follows: One unit of the series from word to word or number to number took about 2.2 seconds. The time from the announcement of "Right" or "Wrong" to the approximate mid-point of the word→number connection to which it belonged was about 0.5½ seconds. The time to the mid-point of the next preceding connection was about 2.8 seconds; to the next, 5.0 seconds; to the next 7.2 seconds; and so on. The time to the mid-point of the next word→number connection following the announcement of "Right" or "Wrong" was 1.7 seconds. The time to the next following was 3.9 seconds; to the next, 6.1 seconds; and so on.

In such a series the rewarded connections are strengthened, but that fact is not our present concern. The fact to which I invite attention now is that the punished connections do not behave alike, but that the ones that are nearest to a reward are strengthened most. The strengthening influence of a reward spreads to influence positively not only the connection which it directly follows and to which it may be said to belong, but also any connections which are near enough to it. We may measure nearness in terms of time or in terms of number of connections or steps. Thus the punishment connection *catnip*→2 in trial 1 preceded the reward for *dazzle*→2 by about 11.6 seconds and by 5 connections or steps. The punished connection *cedar*→3 in trial 1 preceded the reward of *dazzle*→2 by about 9.4 seconds and by 4 connections or steps.

read to the subject first, so that correct choices even in the first round would be a matter of ability [to remember] plus chance rather than of chance alone.

The punished connection *dally*→4 in trial 1 preceded *dazzle*→2 by about 2.8 seconds and by one connection or step.

The amount of strengthening is measured by the percentage of repetitions in the following trial. For example, for the ten subjects of the experiment chosen as an illustration we find the following for punished connections alike in all respects save their proximity to a reward: [2]

	N	Percentage of repetitions in the following trial
One step removed	4136	26.4
Two steps removed	2250	23.6
Three steps removed	1211	20.0
Four steps removed	722	22.0
Five or more steps removed	1228	20.8
Three or more steps removed	3161	20.7

From the results of this and twelve other experiments, we conclude that a satisfying after-effect strengthens greatly the connection which it follows directly and to which it belongs, and also tends to strengthen by a much smaller amount any connections in close enough proximity to it.

If we compare punished connections next to a rewarded connection (but not just between two rewarded connections) with those so remote as to be probably uninfluenced by the reward, the average difference in our main experiments (F to M) is 4.2 with a probable error of 0.36. The average is then surely above 2.6. If we included the connections occurring just after one rewarded connection and just before another (i.e., those just "between two"), the average would be raised. The inclusion of the other experiments would also raise the average.

A second important fact is that the reward or satisfying state of affairs spreads backward as well as forward. This disposes once and for all of the objection that an after-effect can-

---

[2] Here, as elsewhere, the terms one step removed, two steps removed, three steps removed, etc., will mean next to the rewarded connections, separated from it by one intervening connection, separated from it by two intervening connections, etc.

not cause learning because to do so it would have to act upon a connection which preceded it. It demonstrably acts upon connections one or more steps further back than that.

In the detailed results presented in Section II we may compare the strengthening of connections preceding a reward with those following it. In every experiment the connection which immediately precedes it and which is rewarded by it is strengthened much more than any other. In every experiment the total amount of strengthening of connections preceding the reward is, consequently, much greater than the total amount of strengthening of connections following the reward. Among the punished connections one or two steps removed from the rewarded connection, those preceding are strengthened about five-sixths as much as the comparable ones following it. The comparability is not perfect because a preceding connection is a little more remote in time from the reward than the succeeding connection the same number of steps away from the rewarded connection, and because the rewarded connection itself intervenes between the preceding punished connections and the reward.

[The above is from pp. 2–6 of "An Experimental Study of Rewards," *Teachers College Contributions to Education*, No. 580, (1933). Pp. 7–46 present detailed evidence from fifteen experiments. What follows is from pp. 47 to 58 of this same monograph.]

Table 21 presents a summary of the evidence proving the influence of proximity.

The strengthening of a rewarded connection by its sequent reward may be complicated by inner repetitions of the connection or some equivalent of it, or later by conscious expectation of the reward, but the strengthening of a neighboring punished connection is entirely free from any such complications, any accessory processes which occur in the learner being such as would weaken it. The satisfier acts upon it unconsciously and directly, much as sunlight acts upon plants, or an electric current upon a neighboring current, or the earth upon

TABLE 21

The influence of proximity to a satisfying after-effect upon connections which were themselves punished, that is, followed immediately by an annoying after-effect.

Column I gives the difference in strengthening of a punished connection which, at its first occurrence, was just before or just after a rewarded connection, over the strengthening of comparable punished connections two or more steps removed from a rewarded connection. The difference in strengthening was measured by the difference in the percentages of repetition (in the following trial of the series) for the near and the more remote punished connections. Column II gives the differences in strengthening between punished connections within one step or steps of a rewarded connection and comparable punished connections three or more steps removed from a rewarded connection. n (1), n (2 or >), n (1 + 2), and n (3 or >) = the numbers of connections involved in the comparison.

Experiment	I	n (1)	n (2 or >)	II	n (1 + 2)	n (3 or >)
A	6.7	2411	2413	7.3	3658	1166
B	0.9	1863	2260	0.2	2766	1357
C	2.0	521	1355 *			
D	—0.7	1480	2167	0.5	2304	1343
E	8.6	311	309	15.8	456	164
F	2.1	3053	3700	2.7	4644	2109
G	1.6	465	631	2.8	753	343
Ha + Hl	4.5	4136	5411	4.7	6386	3161
Hb	0.7	1024	1597	3.6	1596	1025
Hc	2.5	1147	1556	2.6	1723	980
I	2.4	7774	14592	2.8	12799	9837
J	3.7	2085	8509	2.5	3718	6873
K	0.8	2263	3566	0.9	3692	2137
L	0.9	809	3017	—0.1	1465	2361
M	4.7	1088	1988	4.9	1762	1314

* In Experiment C, punished connections occurring after one rewarded connection and before another were included. [In all the other experiments they were not. If they had been, the reported influence of proximity would have been greater.]

the moon. Presumably it acts upon the connection which is psychologically nearest to it of all, the connection whose after-effect it is felt to be, primarily in this same immediate and direct manner. A satisfying after-effect can strengthen its connection with no paraphernalia to help it, as easily as frequency of occurrence can. Probably it does.

Beneath all deliberate choice, prior to all conscious selection, is the fundamental fact in nature that a satisfier strengthens tendencies which are "at hand," as it were, when the satisfier happens. From it issues a strengthening force, which they absorb. Which of them will absorb it depends upon laws of nature, not of logic or teleology. . . .

THE EXTENT OF THE SPREAD OF A SATISFIER'S INFLUENCE

It is obviously important to measure the extent of the spread both in terms of steps or connection-units and in terms of time. This will require an enormous body of data, since the extent of spread may vary with the kinds of learning, and the learners.

From the experiments so far made, it is certain that the influence can spread farther than one step, though it does not always do so. It is fairly certain that the influence can spread farther than 10 seconds if the number of steps is small enough. It is fairly certain that when the influence spreads beyond one step, it weakens, but our data are not extensive enough to give reliable differences for individuals. Consequently we cannot distinguish surely between a genuine gradual weakening of the influence with remoteness and a possible mixture of individuals in whom the influence spreads to different extents, stopping abruptly in each. . . .

We have plotted the amount of strengthening of a connection due to its being rewarded, that is, occurring just before a reward which belongs to it, and to its being in various degrees of proximity to a rewarded connection, though itself punished, for Experiments F, G, Ha, Hl, Hb, Hc, I, J, K, L, and M, first against time and second against number of steps.

In no case are the data adequate to provide smooth or reliable curves. They demonstrate beyond question that proximity is influential, but they do not reveal at all exactly the relative potencies of proximities of 1, 2, and 3 steps, or of proximities of n, 2n, and 3n seconds.

We present an unweighted average curve for Experiments F, Ha plus Hl and I, which are enough alike in the material learned, the learners, and the time-relations to make an instructive mongrel. We do the same for Experiments K and M, in which the material learned was of the same general nature, the learners were adult students, and time per connection was 1.5 seconds always. (See Figs. 4 and 5.). . . .

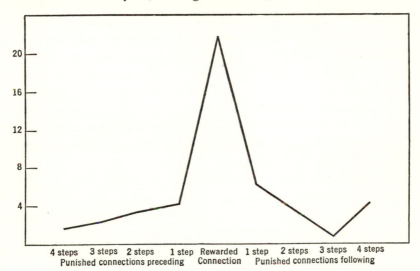

Fig. 4.

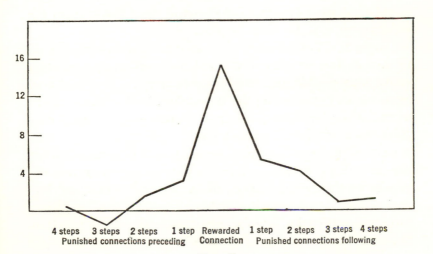

Fig. 5.

THE COMBINATION OF INFLUENCES FROM TWO
OR MORE SATISFIERS

It is of interest to learn whether the influence of a reward beyond the connection to which it belongs coöperates with that of other rewards or is exclusive. If, for example, a punished connection X occurs in such sequences as $X_1X_2X_3X_4X_5C_1$-$X_6C_2X_7X_8X_9X_{10}X_{11}$ or $X_1X_2X_3X_4X_5C_1C_2X_6X_7X_8X_9X_{10}X_{11}$, will the influences of the two rewarded connections C_1 and C_2 combine or will the action of one inhibit the action of the other? If they do combine, how does the combined influence of the two compare with the sum of the two separate influences?

The facts for an X between two C's are shown in Table 23. The strengthening is unquestionably greater than that for an X before or after a C but not between two, but less than the sum of the two strengthenings. Using only the comparisons in which there were at least 100 punished connections equidistant from two rewarded connections, the unweighted median $\dfrac{Bet}{B + A}$ is .74. Using all comparisons it is .81. Using weights in proportion to the number of punished connections equidistant from two rewarded connections involved in the comparison, it is .80 (P.E. $\pm$ .05).

[Pages 58–72 of the original present facts concerning the influence of two or more rewarded connections in sequence, concerning double and treble occurrences of punished connections, and concerning the time relations in certain experiments. There are also a few paragraphs of theoretical considerations, of which I quote a part.]

One simple hypothesis may be adequate to explain many of the facts. Suppose that in animals possessed of a certain degree of cerebral organization, the acceptability or satisfyingness of any status arouses what we may call the "confirmatory" reaction, or the "let it be" reaction, or the "O.K." reaction. Suppose that the nature of this confirmatory reaction is such that it strengthens whatever connections it acts upon. Suppose

TABLE 23

Experiment	Distance from the nearest rewarded connection In steps	Excess over the strengthening due to one punished occurrence remote from any reward			Bet. / Bef.	Bet. / Aft.	Bet. / Bef. + Aft.	Number of cases of Bet.
		Bet.	Bef.	Aft.				
A1	1	21.1	16.3	15.7	1.29	1.34	.66	151
	2	14.9	7.9	13.8	1.89	1.08	.69	192
	3	6.4	12.6	3.1	.51	2.06	.41	140
	4	21.7	5.7	6.4	3.81	3.39	1.79	48
B	1	9.5	—0.9	4.3	high	2.21	2.30	381
C	1	13.6	0.3	8.1	high	1.68	1.62	205
	2	5.0	3.6	5.1	1.39	.98	.57	115
D	1	3.9	—1.6	1.1	high	3.55	high	266
E	1	9.2	5.6	2.9	1.64	3.17	1.08	79
F	1	7.6	2.7	6.7	2.81	1.13	.81	316
	2	5.1	3.7	4.4	1.38	1.16	.63	210
G	1	—1.2	1.4	7.1	low	low	low	29
	2	7.7	3.7	3.8	2.08	2.03	1.03	44
Ha and Hl	1	9.2	6.3	7.6	1.46	1.23	.67	816
	2	6.2	3.3	4.1	1.88	1.51	.84	370
	3	7.8	0.3	—0.7	26.00	high	high	174
	4	4.8	0.5	2.0	9.60	2.40	1.92	87
Hb	1	8.1	4.1	3.6	1.98	2.25	1.05	206
	2	15.3	5.4	4.9	2.83	3.12	1.49	83
Hc	1	7.5	4.4	5.8	1.70	1.29	.74	202
	2	2.7	4.1	5.6	.66	.48	.28	81
I	1	8.4	4.7	5.8	1.79	1.45	.80	1291
	2	5.5	4.4	4.3	1.25	1.28	.63	854
	3	2.8	6.0	2.2	.47	1.27	.34	323
	4	3.4	2.9	4.5	1.17	.76	.46	198
J	1	4.5	5.0	0.3	.88	15.00	.83	123
K	1	8.4	2.4	2.2	3.50	3.82	1.83	356
	2	0.7	1.0	3.2	.70	.22	.17	174
	3	4.6	3.1	—0.6	1.48	high	1.84	114
L	1	1.3	3.4	—1.6	.38	high	.72	44
M	1	7.3	3.8	7.7	1.92	.95	.63	107
	2	7.1	1.7	4.7	4.18	1.51	1.11	93
	3	3.7	—4.9	2.0	high	1.85	high	45

that it acts upon the connections that belong with the acceptability, putting its pressure or influence upon this system of connections as they are at the time when it reaches them. Suppose it to have a very short latency, so that it follows the

satisfier promptly and its influence reaches the system of connections in 0.1 to 0.2 seconds. Of this system of connections,
the one it will most likely influence will be the one that has
just been acting, but, being a biological, not a logical or mystical force, it will not always strike just that one, but sometimes
one preceding, or one succeeding, or one contemporaneous,
but off the main chain of the system. The rewarded connections will then in the long run receive many strengthenings,
the neutral or punished connections some, in proportion to
their proximity to the reward. A somewhat less simple hypothesis may serve better. Each confirmatory reaction may be
diffuse, spreading its influence out upon the connections of
the system, and influencing one most, its nearest neighbors
next most, and so on. We may call the first the "scatter"
hypothesis and the second the "spread" hypothesis.

Concerning the constitution of the confirmatory reaction, I
shall not theorize at this time, beyond noting three facts. The
rapidity and focalization of its activity seem to preclude an
indirect action by way of the blood stream, and require a
direct neural action. The confirmatory reaction probably is set
up and controlled by large fractions of the "higher" levels of
the cortex, often by whatever corresponds to the general "set"
and purpose of the animal at the time. Under the ordinary
conditions of life the confirmatory reaction will not merely,
as in our experiments, make the animal more likely to repeat
the connection when the situation recurs; it will make the
animal repeat or continue the connection then and there.

CHAPTER III[*]

The Influence of Punishments

IN THE early statements of the Law of Effect, the influence of satisfying consequences of a connection in the way of strengthening it was paralleled by the influence of annoying consequences in the way of weakening it.[1] As was stated near the beginning of the previous chapter, [Chapter X of *The Fundamentals of Learning*], I now consider that there is no such complete and exact parallelism.

In particular, the strengthening of a connection by satisfying consequences seems, in view of our experiments and of certain general considerations, to be more universal, inevitable, and direct than the weakening of a connection by annoying consequences. The latter seems more specialized, contingent upon what the annoyer in question makes the animal do, and indirect. For example, if an animal in a certain situation pulls a loop and gets food, or freedom, or praise, or any consequence then satisfying to it, the connection is likely

[*] The first few pages of this chapter are from pp. 276–280 of *The Fundamentals of Learning*, 1932. Then follow selections from *Reward and Punishment in Animal Learning*, 1932, and from pp. 75–80 and 147–152 of *The Psychology of Wants, Interests and Attitudes*, 1935.

[1] An early statement by the writer was as follows: "The Law of Effect is that: Of several responses made to the same situation, those which are accompanied or closely followed by satisfaction to the animal will, other things being equal, be more firmly connected with the situation, so that when it recurs, they will be more likely to recur; those which are accompanied or closely followed by discomfort to the animal will, other things being equal, have their connections with that situation weakened, so that, when it recurs, they will be less likely to occur. The greater the satisfaction or discomfort, the greater the strengthening or weakening of the bond. . . . By a satisfying state of affairs is meant one which the animal does nothing to avoid, often doing such things as attain and preserve it. By a discomforting or annoying state of affairs is meant one which the animal commonly avoids and abandons." ['11, pp. 244, 245.]

37

to be strengthened (if it is modifiable at all) every time. But if an animal in the same situation pulls a loop and either (a) gets a shock in its paw at contact with the loop, or (b) gets a blow on the back, or (c) gets a sudden pain in the bowels, the weakening of the connections is likely to vary. In (a) there will probably be much weakening by way of the strengthening of the connection between the situation and the response of drawing back from the loop. In (b) there will probably be weakening, but less, because the reaction will probably be jumping away from the place, which is not so inconsistent with pulling at the loop. If the animal in (c) reacts by screaming without letting go of the loop, there may be no weakening at all.

The contrast may be put in another way, as follows: Rewards and punishments alike will teach by virtue of the conditions and activities which they produce in the animal. Rewards in general tend to maintain and strengthen any connection which leads to them. Punishments often but not always tend to shift from it to something else, and their educative value depends on what this something else is. They weaken the connection which produced them, when they do weaken it, by strengthening some competing connection.

It is the purpose of this chapter to present the facts which have led to these conclusions and, in particular, to demonstrate the existence of cases where punishment does not weaken the connection leading to it at all—does not strengthen the tendency to any other connection than that in the slightest degree.

Ordinarily, in the interplay of rewards and punishments we cannot tell to what extent the reward strengthens and to what extent the punishment weakens connections X_1, X_2, X_3, X_4, and so on. The learning may be due to either alone or to both in various combinations. In multiple-choice learning, however, a suitable technique will enable us to decide whether C comes to prevail because it has been made stronger, and so displaces X_1, X_2, X_3, and so on, or because X_1, X_2, X_3, and so on have been made weaker and so have left the field free for C.

What this technique is will be clear from the accounts of its operation which follow.

Experiment 71

Nine subjects were given training in choosing the right meaning for a Spanish word from five in a series of two hundred lines like the five shown below. At each trial the subject chose a word and underlined it. If it was right the experimenter "rewarded" him by the announcement of *Right*. If it was wrong, the experimenter "punished" him by the announcement of *Wrong*.

1. abedul   ameer....birch....couch....carry....punch
2. abrasar   oaf....walk....fill....alienate....burn
3. aceite   oil....copper....acerbity....crab....ferment
4. acometer   calculate....asteroid....escort....attack....credit
5. adefesio   defenceless....relief....nonsense....support....obstruct

The series was repeated each week-day (with some exceptions and with occasional double series on the later days), until there had been twelve or more repetitions of it.

We take, on the one hand, all the cases where the response was right in the second trial but not in the first, and, on the other hand, all the cases where the response was wrong in the second trial but was not that same wrong response in the first.[2] We compute how often in the former the next response is right, and how often in the latter the next response is any save that particular wrong. We subtract 20 per cent from the former and 80 per cent from the latter to free the measures from the responses of the sort specified which mere chance would produce. These computations are shown in Table 114. The *Right* produces a substantial difference from what chance would give. The *Wrong* does not.

[The failure of punishment to weaken the connection which it follows and to which it belongs has been shown in many

---

[2] The reason for not using cases where the same response had occurred in trial 1 as in trial 2 is that we wish to exclude from the experiment all records with words whose meanings were known to the subject by reason of experiences prior to the experiment, and all records with words that may have had specially strong connections with some one response, right or wrong.

TABLE 114

THE INFLUENCE OF ANNOUNCEMENTS OF *Right* AFTER EACH RIGHT RESPONSE AND OF *Wrong* AFTER EACH WRONG RESPONSE

Experiment 71. The numbers 1, 2, 3, 4, 5, 6, 7, 8, and 9 refer to the individual subjects.

	1	2	3	4	5	6	7	8	9	Av.
Number of cases where a right response in the second trial, but not before, was followed in the next trial										
(a) by a right response	6	10	8	9	28	15	20	7	9	
(b) by a wrong response	8	31	19	15	24	12	16	15	21	
Per cent which (a) is of (a + b)	43	24	30	38	54	56	56	32	30	
Per cent due to chance	20	20	20	20	20	20	20	20	20	
Strengthening due to one connecting in trial 2 followed by *Right*	.23	.04	.10	.18	.34	.36	.36	.12	.10	.20
Number of cases where a wrong response in the second trial, but not before, was followed in the next trial										
(c) by any other response than it	62	93	76	70	60	54	89	106	87	
(d) by the same wrong response	24	23	22	30	33	26	20	20	30	
Per cent which (c) is of (c + d)	72	80	78	70	65	68	82	84	74	
Per cent due to chance	80	80	80	80	80	80	80	80	80	
Weakening of that response (or strengthening of responses other than it) due to one connecting in trial 2 followed by *wrong*	−.08	0	−.02	−.10	−.15	−.12	.02	.04	−.06	−.05

other experiments. I quote from the monograph, *Reward and Punishment in Animal Learning.*[3]]

In all of the six experiments to be described in this section . . . the animal was put in a small box leading to a large choice-chamber at the end of which were six alleys, or doors, or hurdles, or openings, three of which were always shut off from any possibility of response, leaving three which he might go into, or push against, or jump upon, or try to squeeze through. (The intention was to have as many alternatives as would be consistent with fairly rapid learning by young chicks, but more than three alternatives were not used.) The six situations were differentiated for the animal by the shape and appearance of the choice-chamber and by the appearance of the end where the three alleys, doors, hurdles or openings were. Figure 1 shows the arrangement for each of the six. The three choices are denoted as 1, 2 and 6 or 1, 5 and 6 according to their position from left to right of an animal facing them.

In Experiment AA the hurdles were pieces of wood 12 inches high and ¼ inch thick with a space cut out 6 inches by 2½ inches. The chick thus had to jump up to an opening 6 inches by 2½ inches, at a level 6 inches above the floor.

In Experiment AA, if the animal jumped upon hurdle 2 and down into alley 2, a wooden slide at the food-pen end of the alley was opened allowing him to escape to the food-pen where he had freedom, food and company for 60 seconds.[4] If he jumped upon hurdle 1 and down into alley 1, a wooden slide was inserted behind him and he was left confined in the alley for 30 seconds. Similarly for hurdle 6. If he did not himself jump down into alley 1 or 6 after jumping on the hurdle, he was knocked down from behind and left confined as before. AA then has as reward 60 seconds freedom, food and company, and, as punishment, 30 seconds of confinement. An animal had ten trials in immediate succession, being put into

[3] *Comparative Psychology Monographs,* Serial No. 39, (March, 1932), pp. 1–65.
[4] Two or more chicks, usually four or five, were always present in the food-pen to provide the feature of company.

a pen with no food after the confinement of trial 10, if that was a 1 or 6. After eleven days, he had ten more trials in immediate succession. In the case of some animals there was a third set of ten trials after a further interval of four days. A similar time arrangement (7 to 14 days between trial 10 and trial 11, and 2 to 5 days between trial 20 and trial 21) holds good for experiments BB, CC, DD, EE, and FF, also, save for a very few irregularities due to some special circumstances.

In Experiment BB the three acts were simply going into alley 1, 5, or 6 to a distance of 2 or 3 inches. In the case of 1, a wooden slide at the food-pen end was lifted, allowing the animal to go on to the food-pen and have 60 seconds of freedom, food, and company. In the case of 5 and 6, a wooden slide was inserted behind the animal, leaving him confined in the alley for 30 seconds. The reward and punishment were thus the same in BB as in AA.

Experiment FF was like BB, except that the act consisted not only of entering alley 1, 2, or 6 but also of going along the alley 10 or 12 inches, and up an inclined plane, or block, or flight of steps in the alley. The three alleys differed markedly in appearance, the plane in 1 being long and ending in a platform and hurdle (4 inches tall) with a platform on the farther side also, the steps in 2 being short and low (2¼ inches tall in all), the block in 6 being narrow and ending in a 4-inch hurdle. Six was rewarded; 1 and 2 were punished by confinement. Each of AA, BB, and FF is thus a simplified case of choice among three acts alike in general nature but different in the location where the act is performed and (in FF) in its particular nature. The reward and punishment are identical for AA, BB, and FF. The punishment is confinement (to which, it may be noted, the chicks reacted by typical signs of discomfort, such as loud cheeps and jumping).

In Experiment CC, the choice was between three doors each 4¾ inches high and 2⅝ inches wide hung from the top in a space 5¾ inches by 3½ inches. One (6) would swing back letting the animal into the alley if he pushed against it stead-

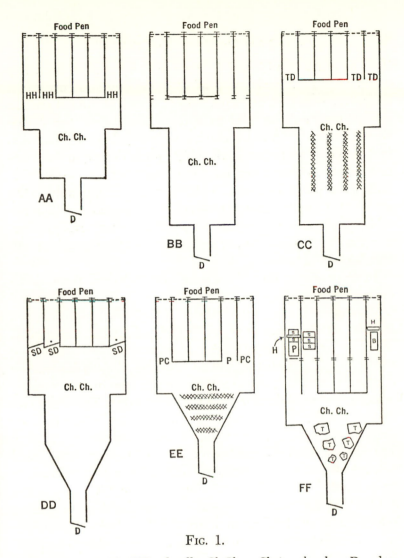

FIG. 1.

AA. Apparatus AA. HH = hurdle. Ch.Ch. = Choice chamber. D = door at which chick was put in.

BB. Apparatus BB. Ch.Ch. and D as in AA.

CC. Apparatus CC. TD = door hinged at the top. Ch.Ch. and D as in AA. On the floor of the choice chamber there was laid a board with four wide black stripes, shown here as cross-hatchings.

DD. Apparatus DD. SD = door hinged at the side. Ch.Ch. and D as in AA.

EE. Apparatus EE. P = tissue paper. PC = tissue paper backed by cardboard. Ch.Ch. and D as in AA. On the floor of the choice chamber there was laid a board with black stripes, shown here by cross-hatching.

FF. Apparatus FF. H = hurdle. P = inclined plane. S = step. B = block. T = red tile to aid identification of the apparatus. Ch.Ch. and D as in AA.

43

ily. The other two (1 and 2) were held by pegs so that they could be pushed back not at all at the center and only about an eighth of an inch at either side. If, then, the animal pushed against 6 steadily or tried to squeeze under 6 vigorously, he would enter alley 6, in which case a glass slide at the food-pen end of alley 6 was opened allowing him to escape to the food-pen, where he had freedom, food, and company for 60 seconds. If he pushed against 1 or 2, he was punished only to the extent that any tendency to escape from the choice-chamber which may have led to the act was thwarted.[5] His confinement in the choice-chamber continued, but nothing else punitive happened to him.

In Experiment DD, the choice was between three doors each 3¾ inches high by 2½ inches wide set in an opening 5 by 3, hung by hinges at the left side. All were set partway open so as to leave a space of about ¾ inches between the edge of the door and the edge of the alley. One (1) would swing further back letting the animal into the alley if he pushed against it or tried to squeeze through the opening (¾ inch by 5 inches) at its right side with sufficient vigor. The other two doors (2 and 6) were prevented from moving further back by pegs. If the animal pushed door 1 open and went into alley 1, a glass slide at the food-pen end was lifted, and the usual reward of 60 seconds freedom, food and company ensued. If he pushed at 2 or 6, he was punished, as in CC, only to the extent that any tendency to escape from the choice-chamber which may have led him to do so was thwarted.[6] His confinement in the choice-chamber continued, but nothing else punitive happened to him.

In Experiment EE, the choice was between trying to squeeze through a rectangular opening 4 inches tall by ¾ inch wide cut in a white expanse 7 inches tall and 4 inches wide which covered the entrance to alley 1, or 2, or 6, re-

[5] Too feeble pushing at 6 was, in general, punished similarly. A squeezing under 6 which was not continued long enough was followed by similar punishment plus also occasionally the discomfort of having one's head caught for a second or so.

[6] Too feeble pushing or squeezing at 1 was punished similarly.

spectively. This cut was made in soft tissue paper in the case of 5 and in soft tissue paper backed up by stiff cardboard in the case of 1 and 6. In the case of 5 the paper would easily give or tear permitting entrance to alley 5. In the case of 1 and 6, the cardboard prevented entrance. In the case of squeezing through 5, a glass slide at the food-pen end of alley 5 was lifted, allowing the chick exit to the usual reward. In the case of attempts to squeeze through 1 or 6, the punishment was only whatever the failure to get out of the choice-chamber involved.

Each of CC, DD, and EE is thus a case of choice among three acts alike in nature, but differing in the location where the act is performed. The reward and the punishment are identical for CC, DD, and EE. The reward is the same as for AA, BB, and FF. The punishment is very different. In CC, DD, and EE it consists in a continuance of the confinement in the choice-chamber, with the possibility at any second of escape by attack on the "right" door or opening, and in the thwarting of whatever tendencies to escape from the choice-chamber led to the act. In AA, BB, and FF it consisted in a much narrower confinement, with no possible escape, for 30 seconds, followed by readmission to the confinement of the choice-chamber.

The punishments of CC, DD and EE differ from those of AA, BB, and FF also in the behavior to which they lead. In CC, DD, and EE, the failure of the pushing or squeezing at the "wrong" door or opening may lead to withdrawal from it, and, indirectly, to attack upon one of the other two doors or openings. It may lead to looking at it without pushing it or trying to squeeze through it. But in AA, BB, and FF the confinement in the alley prevents the animal for 30 seconds from forming *directly* any connection whatever with anything in the choice-chamber. He cannot withdraw from the choice-chamber side of the hurdle or alley entrance. He cannot even see any of these. The actual situation has vanished.

In AA, BB, and FF the punishment and the reward are comparable in that by the time they arrive, the situation and response, the connection between which is punished or rewarded, are inaccessible in reality. In CC, DD, and EE this is true only of the situation and response whose connection is rewarded. In the case of punishment, the external situation persists, and the animal may be led to back away from the door, or turn aside from it, or neglect it, and so on.

This is true when the technique is carried out perfectly. Unfortunately, at times a chick will jump back or run back out of an alley in AA, BB or FF before the slide can be inserted behind him. Consequently the learning is to a slight extent influenced by retreats from the "wrong" alleys in AA, BB, and FF.

Besides the three acts with which we are primarily concerned an animal may respond in any of the six choice-chambers by running around the chamber, cheeping, jumping at the confining walls, pecking at various objects, voiding urine or excrement, squatting down and other acts within its repertory. Its behavior was observed and in some cases various instructive features of it were recorded. But the records to be used here for any chick consist simply of the time it was put into the entrance-box, the fact and time of occurrence of the specific "right" and "wrong" acts during the day's experiment until ten had occurred, or until two (in some series, 1 or 3) periods of failure to do any one of them in 300 seconds had been spent in the choice-chamber or until eight had occurred plus two such periods of failure, or until nine had occurred plus one such period of failure.

[Pages 9–21 of the original article present the individual records of the 64 chicks and determinations of the amount of initial favoritism of each chick for certain alleys.]

METHODS OF COMPARING THE EFFECT OF REWARD WITH THAT OF PUNISHMENT

Having thus an approximate measure of the initial strength of the tendency to choose act 1, 2 or 6 and 1, 5, or 6 for each chick, we may use any or all of the following methods:

A. Let the external situation of presence in the choice

chamber be called S. Let the rewarded act be called C and the two punished acts X_1 and X_2. The connections acting in the next trial after a sequence consisting exclusively of C may be compared with their initial strengths; and the connections acting in the next trial after a sequence consisting exclusively of X_1 (or X_2) may be compared with their initial strengths. . . .

B. Let C, X_1 and X_2 mean as before. The connections acting in the next one or two (or three, or more) trials after a sequence rich in C's may be compared with their initial strengths, and similarly after a sequence rich in X_1 (or in X_2). . . .

We have applied Method B to the data, but do not report all the results, since Method C seems preferable.[7]

C. Let C, X_1 and X_2 mean as before. A rough estimate of the average increase in the strength (that is, the percentile frequency) of the connection S→C in any experiment due to any one rewarded occurrence of S→C is made from a general study of the records of that experiment. Call this R. Various estimates of the average decrease in strength of S→X_1 or S→X_2 due to one punished occurrence of it are made. Call this P. For example, P may be 0, or .1R, or .4R, or .7R, or 1.0R or 1.5R. The first 8 or 10 or 15 or 20 or 25 trials in an experiment may be used for a chick. We compute the changes in the strength of S→C, S→X_1 and S→X_2 which would result from the addition of 1R to the initial strength of S→C in the chick for each occurrence of C, and from the subtraction of 1P from the initial strength of S→X_1 for each occurrence of X_1 in that chick, and from the subtraction of 1P from the initial strength of S→X_2 in that chick for every occurrence of X_2. This is done for each chick separately, and the resulting strengths at the end of trial 8 or 10 or 15 or 20 or 25 by each estimate of the strengthening and weakening effects are compared with the actual strengths as indicated by the frequencies of C, X_1 and X_2 in trials 11 to n, or 16 to n, or 20 to n, or 25 to n.

That ratio of P to R is truest which shows the smallest diver-

---

[7] The results are in entire harmony with those obtained by Method A and Method C.

gences of the calculated later strengths (in per cents) from the actual observed later strengths.

[Pages 24–58 of the original study present the facts about rewards and punishments found by using these methods in experiments BB, CC and DD and also in a further experiment (G).]

The results of all comparisons by all methods tell the same story. Rewarding a connection always strengthened it substantially; punishing it weakened it little or not at all.

Using Method A . . . there was an average strengthening for each rewarded connection amounting to 19.5 in BB, 28.5 in CC and 24 in DD. The change due to one punished connection averaged —1.2 in BB, +4.3 in CC, and —1 in DD, being on the whole a little on the plus side of zero.

Using Method C the results were as shown in Table 20. In every one of the ten comparisons there is evidence that punished occurrences of a connection weaken it very slightly if at all.

[A better fit to the observed facts is obtained in every case by crediting a punished occurrence with zero influence or a slight positive influence than by crediting it with a negative influence, no matter how slight. The detailed records for the 64 chicks have now been available for sixteen years, as have my analyses of the learning of the rats, crows, pigs, monkeys, and canaries of Kuo, Yerkes, Coburn, and Sadovinkova.[8] No psychologist has explained them by assigning to a punished connection a negative influence even one tenth as great as the positive influence of a rewarded connection. It therefore seems advisable to scrutinize the influence of punishments in general with care. I quote some statements from pages 75–80 of *The Psychology of Wants, Interests and Attitudes* (1935).]

. . . On the whole, it now seems certain that annoying after-effects influence behavior only in specialized ways. Whereas attaining what satisfies an active want directly strengthens any connection which the attainment follows and to which it belongs, failure to attain such satisfaction or the

[8] *The Fundamentals of Learning,* pp. 571–593.

TABLE 20

Summary of comparisons by method C

Experiment	Method of estimating initial status	Trials the effects of which are prophesied	Trials used to test the prophecies	A Scheme of additions for C, X₁ and X₂ with close fit	Sum of divergences of prophecy from actual, by A	B Scheme of additions with weakening for punishment	Sum of divergences of prophecy from actual, by B
BB	Combined	1 to 15	16 to 20 *	+25, 0, 0	3,680	+25, −2, −2	3,690
CC	"	"	"	+40, 0, 0	2,208	+40, −2, −2	2,280
DD	"	"	"	+15, 0, 0	3,420	+15, −1, −1	3,452
BB	Av. for group	1 to 8, 11 to 18	9 and 10, 19 and 20	+30, 0, 0	212.6	+30, −2, −2	226.8
CC	"	1 to 8, 11 to 18	9 and 10, 19 and 20	+60, +1, +1	245.0	+60, −4, −4	305.0
				+60, 0, 0	250.4		
DD	"	1 to 8, 11 to 18	9 and 10, 19 and 20	+15, 0, 0	432.4	+15, −1, −1	455
G		1 to 8	9 to 13	+30, 0, 0	1,990	+30, −4, −4	2,332
BB	Pure indiv.	1 to 25	26 to 30	+25, 0, 0	1,800	+25, −2, −2	1,888
CC	"	"	"	+20, 0, 0	1,832	+20, −2, −2	2,046
CC	"	"	"	+20, 0, 0	1,320	+20, −2, −2	1,450
DD	"	"	"	+30, 0, 0	1,308	+30, −2, −2	1,538
DD	"	"	"	+5, 0, 0	2,770	+5, −1, −1	2,812

* Checked by the use of 16 and 17.

49

occurrence of something definitely annoying certainly does not weaken the corresponding "punished" connection directly. Nor does it do so by strengthening whatever connections other than the punished connection are capable of being made under the conditions effective at that time. An annoying after-effect simply makes the animal do what is in his repertory as a consequence of that particular annoyance in those conditions. This may be useful, as in retreat from a blind alley which thwarts, or avoidance of an object which shocks or burns, or spitting out what tastes nasty. It may be of zero or nearly zero value, as in sulking at failure or crying at a shock. It may be actually harmful, as in paralysis, negativism, or extreme terror.

The utility of an annoying state of affairs may be by causing the animal to do something useful in the premises, as when confinement evokes struggles to escape. It may be by counteracting a satisfying after-effect of undesirable behavior and so reducing the net total after-effect to zero or to annoyingness, as when a child who grabs another's toy has the satisfaction of success and possession counterbalanced by the pain of being spanked and deprived of the toy. Roughly speaking, the former sort of utility is predominant in learning matters of intellect and skill, and the latter in matters of moral conduct.

If the person or animal has the capacity to get and make use of the information that such and such responses to such and such situations produce such and such consequences, an annoying after-effect is potentially useful as a giver and impresser of information, but this informative value may bear little relation to the amount of annoyance. A mere "Wrong" after $3 \times 9 = 28$ may be as useful in teaching a child that $3 \times 9 = 27$ as a severe beating; and when he has learned that $3 \times 9 = 27$ he may be no more likely to revert to $3 \times 9 = 28$ if it once produced the gentle annoyance than if it once produced the severe beating. Doubtless the latter will be more memorable, but memories of the tragic consequences of an error concerning 3×9 may not recall what the error was, much less what the right connection was. Inducing the child to think $3 \times 9 = 27$ and rewarding that connection will be at least as good informatively and much better for learning as a whole.

It would be useful to have an inventory of the commonest annoyers, and of their results, temporary and lasting, on the strands of behavior along with which the annoyer occurs and on the subject's total nature or personality, for persons of both sexes, various ages, and various sorts of mentality. Such an inventory would aid us in choosing annoyers as incitements to change a connection to one more suitable or as counter-balances to the satisfying after-effect of an undesirable connection.

As a provisional beginning of such an inventory, I suggest the list shown below. It is neither logical nor biological, but it does cover the common annoyers in a way convenient for memory and discussion.

A. Injuries to the body
B. Diseases and imperfect functioning of bodily organs (including excessive stimulation of any sense organ)
C. Work without rest
D. Certain sensory stimuli, such as bitter tastes
E. Deprivations of:
    1. Food
    2. Water
    3. Movement
    4. Sleep
    5. Society
    6. Attention
    7. Affection
    8. Sex activity
    9. Parental activity
F. Thwartings of any purpose
G. Social treatment by:
    1. Dislike, enmity, hate
    2. Disapproval, scorn, derision
    3. Aversion, repugnance, loathing
    4. Domination, bullying
H. Conditions, variously caused, of:
    1. Fear, dread, anxiety
    2. Disgust or repugnance
    3. Shame

4. Inferiority
5. Sadness
6. Irritation
7. General ill-being

It is obvious that the influence of many annoyers varies greatly among individuals in the immediate reaction produced and in the wider and more lasting effect on the person. But the nature of these differences is not well enough known to justify an attempt to describe them here. I will only give two illustrations.

Suppose that we have chambers built with four slits all of the same size, but identifiable by their positions and marks of one sort or another. Each of them is wide enough for the animal in question (chick, child of three, man) to insert his head, but not to pass his body through. All but one are backed by an immovable wall. One (call it slit C) has in place of the wall a perfect imitation of it (to vision) which will easily give way if the chick, child, or man pushes against it vigorously. Beyond the wall are freedom, food, and other chicks, children, or men. The animal is put in the chamber when in a state such that solitary confinement there without food will annoy him and freedom, food, and society will satisfy him.

Consider the result when connection is made with the act of trying to push through slit A (or B or D), the connection being followed by thwarting of the effort and continuance of S. The influence on the chick will be substantially zero. If it ever learns to escape from S, it will learn because, in the chance up-and-down in strength of the tendencies to try to push through slit A, slit B, slit C, slit D, and so on, the tendency to push through C becomes temporarily the strongest. The thwarting in and of itself will not weaken S→push at A (or B or D). It may evoke harder pushes, irritation, and peeping. The child may be moved by the thwarting to harder pushing, angry behavior, kicks at the wall, screams, and the like. A specially intelligent one may be moved to try the other slits in order. A specially hysterical one may be prejudiced against slits for a long time. The man presumably will try the other slits. But he will probably have a modicum of anger or irritation at each failure. Only in so far as the punishment leads child or man to try sooner or later slit C will it benefit the special learning. It may have a share in teaching general lessons of considering all possibilities of the possible differences among things that look alike, and so on.

Compare next the results of food swung down behind in easy reach when the face enters slit C versus a blow on the face when it enters slits A, B, D, etc. The influence of the food will be much the same as that of escape. But the blow will probably cause surprise, retreat, and fear behavior in the chick and in timid children, and surprise, temporary or partial retreat, and angry behavior in the man or in an aggressive child. A psychologist employing this experiment with certain subjects would find the bar that delivered the blow torn from its fastenings. The retreat will be beneficial if it is attached to slit A, B, D, etc., and not to all the slits. The tendency to pull the head out of A indirectly weakens the tendency to put the head in at A. The value of the fear and anger for the immediate task at hand is probably negative. For the general task of life it is also probably negative, fear and anger being inappropriate responses to most of the mechanical contrivances of civilization.

The best results are obtained from punishments when the annoying state of affairs then and there causes or encourages or at least permits the animal to operate a right connection and receive satisfaction therefor. So in the experiments of Warden and Aylesworth the annoyance of receiving a shock in the wrong alley may provoke the animal to run back out of it and enter the right alley. So in *Umweg* experiments the annoyance of being thwarted in efforts to go through an obstacle may provoke the profitable response of running around it. So if a child after being punished by a "Wrong" for spelling *red* "r-e-d-e," may be led to try "r-e-d" and win success. So a player whose shots fall short may be led by the failure plus the special information to use more force and get the satisfaction of hitting the mark.

In much learning in which the annoyingness due to a certain connection causes the person to change to a more successful connection, there is an element of special information besides the information that the first connection had bad results. Thus, in the simplest case of all, if there are only two responses possible, one learns from the failure of one that the other is right. One often learns something about the direction and magnitude of one's error, which gives his next trial a greater probability of success.

In all cases the benefit of the punishment lies in its power to provoke a change to or toward the desired behavior. I venture the prediction that with sufficient ingenuity ways can usually be found to evoke the desired behavior more directly and economically.

There are two cases of the use of punishment which are so common as to deserve special discussion. In the first the punishment is simply the failure to attain a want, occurring typically in learning by trial and error (better named learning by trial and success). In the second the punishment acts by associating fear, repulsion, shame, or some other strong negative attitude with certain responses to certain situations.

As things now are, an enormous amount of learning in homes, schools, and shops consists in doing one thing after another with some guidance from physical circumstances, models, explanations, and directions. Each item is a case of multiple-choice learning with usually very many possible choices. The learning progresses by the selection of the connections which have satisfying after-effects. The connections which fail to do so may vary from neutrality to a very annoying degree of failure and frustration and may have various punishments *ab extra* attached to them in the form of disapproval, ridicule, physical pain, and so on. The child flounders in this way and that until he learns to swim. The scholar makes this, that, and the other sound until he attains a tolerable pronunciation of the French *u*. The writer does this and that to his essay or story until it seems fit. All is largely on the basis of "Try, try again," with expectation that out of the welter of wrongs and rights improvement will somehow manifest itself. Improvement will come from the rights if they are rewarded, but the less confidence we put in the utility of the wrongs the wiser we shall be in most cases.

Teachers have sought to reduce the waste from the "Try, try again" procedure, but they have too often tried to cure it by some doctrinaire method or one-sided set of exercises based on erroneous psychology. One after another of such methods is tried and found little or no better than the haphazard self-education it was supposed to eliminate. What is needed is a method which will get learners to make the right connections and be satisfied thereby with a minimum of practice in error and with due regard for other educational desiderata.

The most striking case of the use of punishment is our second case where a certain response to a certain situation is punished by pain, ignominy, ridicule, or some other consequence which attaches a potent negative tendency to that connection. If the situation recurs, the idea of making that response or the impulse to make it then tends to arouse a memory of the punishment and fear, repulsion, or shame. This is relieved by making no response to the situation (more properly speaking, by responding to it by neglect) or by making a response that is or seems opposite to the original punished response. Whatever the original attractiveness was in the punished behavior, it is submerged or neutralized by the unattractive prospect of a repetition of the punishment.

A very important variant of it, much used in schools and industry, is the one in which the failure to make a certain response to a certain situation or to attain a certain status is punished. Unless a child knows his lesson, he is beaten. Unless the slave does his work, he is not fed. In such cases the person concerned may well have a pronounced satisfaction at learning his lesson or doing his work. The absence of the punishment may be psychologically as positive a reward as words of praise or a money payment. When anything but a certain specified behavior is punished, that behavior is in a true and important sense rewarded.

[The last two statements may sound evasive and doctrinaire, but they are not. Sudden relief from pain or fear is as truly a satisfier capable of evoking a confirming reaction as is food to a hungry man. To a child who is customarily nagged or derided, the absence of blame or ridicule may be as truly a satisfier as is praise to ordinary children, and may strengthen connections causing him to efface himself. If a calamity is expected, its failure to occur may cause intense satisfaction. There is every reason to believe that the absence of an x may act as a reward as truly as the presence of a y.]

Punishment by pain, blame, disgrace, ridicule, and so on, is an almost universal feature of most human societies, and perhaps of many animal groups. It has been a pillar in family life, was until recently the corner-stone of school discipline and industrial management, permeates law and penology, and is essential to most religions. It deserves study in all its aspects, including its origin (of which vengeance is only a minor fraction), its kinship with other social consequences of behavior, its theoretical justifications, and its obvious misuses.

[For the sake of readers who are interested in the practical uses of punishments I include here some comments from pages 147–152 of *The Psychology of Wants, Interests, and Attitudes*.]

. . . In general, punishment compares very unfavorably with reward in dependability. Unless it is a means of inducing the person to shift then and there to a right connection which is then and there rewarded, it may involve waste or worse. In particular (1) the attainment of active rather than passive learning at the cost of practice in error may often be a bad bargain. Refusal to supply information on the ground that the learner will be more profited by discovering the facts by himself runs the risk not only of excessive time-cost but also of strengthening of wrong habits. The learner's self-punishment when he makes a mistake may sometimes be no better than the punishment in our experiments. (2) The almost universal tolerance of imperfect learning in the early treatment of a topic, leaving it to be improved by the gradual elimination of errors in later treatments, is probably unsound, and certainly risky. What removes the errors in later treatments is the rewarding of the right connections, and such rewarding might better be put to work earlier. (3) The widespread limitation of guidance in oral and written composition, handwriting, drawing, and the like to designating errors is a sign of weakness in the techniques of teaching. With sufficient investigation and ingenuity, education should devise methods which would systematically make good work satisfying. . . .

Society makes habitual use of pain, ignominy, ridicule, or other consequences which attach, fear, shame, or repulsion to ideas of, or impulses to, the punished behavior.

The practical uses of these procedures deserves fuller treatment than can be given here. We shall neglect entirely the effects on the punisher, and treat very inadequately the effects on the person punished beyond the particular behavior punished, though both are of great importance. We shall also not develop the detailed consequences of any of the facts and principles discussed.

These attachments of fear, shame, and the like, to certain tendencies have a natural origin in the instinctive tendencies of man. To respond to a blow by a blow, to respond to the seizure of what is in one's hands or nest or sphere of control by grabbing it back, to respond to a person who interferes with one's progress by shoving him away—these are unlearned punitive tendencies. Such are to be found in the animal kingdom long before man. They occur in even the most kindly relations, that of mother and mothered. "Whom he loveth, he chasteneth" applies to human, canine, and feline parents as well as to the Hebrew and Christian gods.

In so far as they spring from man's original nature, they are natural social consequences just as falls, scratches, and bumps are natural physical consequences. Just as the latter are fairly well adapted to guide conduct in a world of trees, bushes, and rocks, so the former are fairly well adapted to family life in the wild.

Such instinctive punishments by parents, playmates, and

other community members are, however, only a small fraction of the elaborate system of scoldings, blame, scorn, ridicule, ostracism, pains, and deprivations which have been developed from them by acquired customs. The family, the schools, government, and the church have all shared in inventing and popularizing new punishments. Any behavior whatsoever that annoyed any person in authority was likely to be treated by him as a punishable offense. To the punishments given by men were added those which gods and demons might be expected to give. A hell after death was invented to supply more, and offenses against the gods increased the need for punishments in this world and the next. With and supporting all this was the dogma, accepted as axiomatic, that he who does wrong should be made to suffer. The doctrine also prevailed that the memory of past, and expectation of future, suffering would prevent the recurrence of the offense.

This doctrine had and has a substantial basis in fact. In proportion as virtue is unrewarded by the social system, pleasant vices can be diminished only by some unpleasant consequences. Fear and shame are potent. Workers do work partly because of fear of losing their jobs. Men do avoid breaking the laws partly because of fear of being put in jail. Children do study their lessons partly for fear of being laughed at by other pupils, or scorned at home for failure to be promoted. Many of our habitual moralities have roots in the fear of punishments. Certainly even the best of men act in part in fear of the punishments which their own consciences may inflict. . . . In the factual discussion of Chapter 8, it appeared that "Any form of expectation of an annoying after-effect tends to evoke the particular behavior which experience has attached to it." The punishments with which we are concerned will by this principle often have a preventive value.

In the important cases where these punishments are used to secure a certain positive behavior by punishing anything other than it, they may have the effect of rewarding that positive behavior. It may be the satisfying of security from fear and shame that makes a workman do his work, a soldier maintain his post, a student attend to his lesson. In all cases where the choice is between two alternatives, what originated as an expectation of annoying consequences due to a punishment of behavior A may easily shift to a sense of comfort after behavior B. The relief from, or absence of, the annoying consequence or the expectation of it may cause as real, though not as intense, a satisfaction as success, praise, or sensory pleasure.

The conventional system of punishments is, however, beset by difficulties and dangers.

(1) It tends to work best where it is least needed, and least well where it is most needed. Individuals who are sensitive to moral issues and to the feelings of others and who will probably in any case approximate what is right and proper, are influenced markedly by punishments. Those more callous and base in nature, who are not easily stimulated by nobler means, are not easily improved by punishments.

(2) The punishments sometimes do not prevent or lessen the punished behavior but only make the person more miserable, frightened, and ashamed. The fear and shame occur, but they do not prevent recurrence. He continues to sin, but he is more remorseful and unhappy.

(3) The essential service of the punishments is to thwart or repress certain impulses by adding counterbalancing negative impulses. This conflict of impulses is supposed by most psychiatrists to be an unhealthy and irritating state of affairs.

(4) A person can weaken, or even nullify, the force of all save the purely physical pains and deprivations by choosing as the social group whose opinions he will value one that is to any degree liberal, unorthodox, eccentric, low, or vicious. This is very commonly done. Indeed the action of the law of effect requires that individuals favor and select a social milieu in which they are comfortable. So traders are not much annoyed by the scorn of communistic idealists. Politicians are not punished by the attacks of reformers. Many college boys feel little dissatisfaction at being disesteemed by their professors. They

would be much more disturbed if they were accused by their cronies of "being like the profs." A crook lives in a crook's world.

(5) There is danger of arousing more fear or shame than is needed to counteract some pleasant minor sin, and so of dulling the person's sensitiveness to punishment. It is easy to scold violently, give harsh sentences, or exact cruel deprivations— much easier than to provide adequate and steady satisfactions for well-doers. In certain schools of the not so remote past there was so much and so heavy punishment that a little more or less did not seem to matter, and many pupils probably gave up their attempts to avoid it.

(6) There is danger of cruel atrocities which no reasonable or humane society should tolerate. This has happened so often in schools, in the treatment of slaves and child laborers, in armies, and in religious persecutions that it must be reckoned as an almost necessary feature of the punitive system.

(7) What little evidence is available suggests that the influence of customary punishments as actually administered has been inferior to that of customary rewards.

IMPROVEMENTS IN THE ADMINISTRATION OF PUNISHMENTS

Psychology suggests five ways of improving the results from punishments.

The first is to try to make sure in each case that the punishment belongs to the behavior in question. If it cannot be its direct after-effect, means should be taken to recall the occurrence and to make clear and emphatic connection in the punished person's mind between the impulse to that behavior and the expectation of the punishment.

The second is to forestall the punishment in cases where the want which led to the offense can be satisfied innocently. A large fraction of punishments is used to counteract the otherwise satisfying consequences of certain behavior. Some of this behavior is really innocent and desirable and should not be punished at all. It was, for example, sheer folly to make children of five to ten sit still for hours in school and to punish them if they fidgeted. Some of it can be obviated by the provision of an innocent outlet. So children who steal jam may in some cases be cured by providing sufficient sweets in the diet, and athletic clubs may prevent hooliganism.

The third is to shift the emphasis from the discomfort of A to the relief, security, and comfort of not-A, when it is prudent to do so, as it usually is.

The fourth is to search for ingenious ways of using the sure and almost fool-proof method of arousing the confirming reaction by attaching relevant satisfiers to the desired connections, in place of punishments for wrong connections. There are now homes in which the ratio of rewards to punishments for children from birth to fifteen years or later has been as high as 20 to 1, perhaps 50 to 1, with apparently excellent results. The motivation to learning in the primary grades of schools has changed in a half-century from pain to pleasure, to the great advantage of all concerned. If weakness and sentimentality can be avoided and sufficient ingenuity can be exercised, the management of men in all lines by the selection of their good tendencies rather than the repression of bad ones is a hopeful prospect.

The fifth is to arrange in a scientific, or at least a reasonable, manner the punishments which, even after the fullest use of rewards, will still remain as important means of human control. Much of the use of punishments in the past has been doctrinaire, haphazard, fantastic, and perverted. . . .

CHAPTER IV

The Influence of Repetition of a Connection

I. BELONGINGNESS

. . . BELIEF in the potency of repetition has been almost universal in psychology, but the evidence to prove it has been somewhat unsatisfactory. In most cases there have been not only repetitions of the connection, but also certain after-effects of a more or less satisfying nature. The connections learned by repetition have usually been such as were right and proper. I have tried to discover what happens when we keep the influence of frequency of occurrence of the connection free from any chance for such satisfying after-effects to operate.

The orthodox view of the potency of repétition of a connection has recently been attacked by various adherents to Gestalt principles, who would limit the efficacy of repetition to cases where the things connected possessed some inherent unity or *Zugehörigkeit*. It has also been attacked on the basis of experimental findings, especially by Lewin, who found that two hundred or more repetitions of nonsense syllables in a certain sequence left only a very weak tendency for one of them to call up its sequent. Our experiments will, I hope, clear up these disagreements.

The first to be described concern the coöperation of temporal sequence and what I shall call "belonging."

The term mental connection has meant different things to different psychologists and at different times. One clear-cut and important possible meaning is mere sequence in time of two events in the mind, or in a man's behavior. And we

---

[*] Sections I and II are from *The Fundamentals of Learning*, pp. 64–72 and 78–114 *passim*. Section III is from the *Proceedings of the National Academy of Sciences*, Vol. 19, (July, 1933), pp. 734–745.

shall first study the influence of repetition of a temporal sequence of events in the mind, though perhaps no psychologist ever meant only such temporal sequence when he wrote of "association by contiguity" or of "the mere association" or of "one event going with another in the mind," or of "a certain response being connected with a certain situation."

If two events, A and B, occur in the mind in that sequence with nothing but a very brief interval of time as an interruption, and do so repeatedly, what results which would not have resulted if they had both occurred, but days apart with an infinitude of interrupting events? In particular, what results in respect of the probability that A thereafter will evoke B?

The answer to which the evidence (with one very important possible exception) [1] points is that such mere sequence does little or nothing in and of itself. Ten or twenty or a hundred such repetitions of B after A do not appreciably increase the probability that A will evoke B.

Experiment 29

Consider the following experiment: The paragraph printed below is read ten times to persons who are instructed to "listen to what I read with moderate attention, as you would listen to a lecture."

Belonging A

Alfred Dukes and his sister worked sadly. Edward Davis and his brother argued rarely. Francis Bragg and his cousin played hard. Barney Croft and his father watched earnestly. Lincoln Blake and his uncle listened gladly. Jackson Craig and his son struggle often. Charlotte Dean and her friend studied easily. Mary Borah and her companion complained dully. Norman Foster and his mother bought much. Alice Hanson and her teacher came yesterday.

As soon as the tenth reading is completed the subjects of the experiment are required to answer the following questions, ten seconds being allowed for answering each one of them.

1. What word came next after rarely?
2. "   "   "   "   " Lincoln?

[1] [The conditional reflex in its pure Pavlovian form is possibly an exception.]

3. What word came next after gladly?
4.   "   "   "   "   " dully?
5.   "   "   "   "   " Mary?
6.   "   "   "   "   " earnestly?
7.   "   "   "   "   " Norman Foster and his mother?
8.   "   "   "   "   " and his son struggle often?

Questions 1, 3, 4, 6, and 8 test the influence of ten moderately attentive repetitions of a sequence with very, very little belongingness. Questions 2 and 5 test the influence of ten such with the belongingness which attaches to the first and last name of the same person. Question 7 tests the influence of ten such with the belonging which attaches to the subject and predicate in a sentence.

Two series of experiments were carried out with 100 and 140 subjects, respectively. The frequency of right responses to questions 1, 3, 4, and 6 testing the strength of the connection between the last word of one and the first word of the next, was 2¾ per cent in one series of experiments and 2¼ per cent in another. The percentages should be as high as these by mere chance guessing of some first name of the ten heard. The frequency of right responses to questions 2 and 5, testing the strength of the connection between first and last name was 21½ per cent in one series of experiments and 19½ in another. These rise to 81 and 73 for question 7. The connection between "and his son struggle often" and the immediately following "Charlotte" was not strengthened at all by the ten occurrences of the sequence. The per cent of correct responses was 2 for one series and 1 for the other. Guessing at random would produce as high per cents as these.

Consider the following experiment in which the same general issue is studied but with different material and with a change in the instructions designed to equalize attentiveness throughout by a method different from that of the previous experiment.

Experiment 30

The series of sentences shown below under *Belonging B* was read six times to 200 college and university students.

They were instructed as follows: "Please listen to what I read just attentively enough so that you can say that you have heard it and understood it." As soon as the sixth reading was completed the subjects were asked to write answers to the questions listed below which were read at the rate of one every ten seconds in the order shown here.

Questions 1 to 4 test the strength of the connection from the end of the one sentence to the beginning of the next. Each of these had a frequency of 6 but with very little belonging —only so much as would be due to the few persons who may have considered the series of sentences as something to be memorized as a total. With a possibility of 800 correct responses there were only 5, or 6 tenths of one per cent. This number may be accounted for by mere guessing of any given name remembered as having been heard, or even by mere guessing of any common given name.

Questions 21 to 24 test the strength of the connections from verb to adverb in the same sentence. Each verb was followed six times by each of four adverbs. The two terms belonged together closely. With a possibility of 3200 correct responses (if each subject had written four for each question) there were 265 or 8.3 per cent. Guessing from adverbs remembered would give only 80 plus or minus a small chance variation, even if each subject wrote 16 words. As a matter of fact, few of the subjects wrote more than half that number, so that 30 is a generous allowance.

A less extreme contrast between little and much belonging is given by questions 5 to 8 and questions 9 to 12. In the former, there were 24 occurrences for each of the four connections, but the degree of belonging was only that due to inclusion of the two names in the same sentence. In the latter there were only six occurrences of each connection but the belonging was of first and last name of the same person in the same sentence. The correct responses numbered 55 for the former and 94 for the latter. With only a fourth as many repetitions the greater belongingness results in much greater strengthening, producing nearly twice as many correct responses. In both of these comparisons position in the test series favors the connections with less belonging.

Belonging B

Alfred   Duke and Ronald Barnard worked sadly.
Edward   "   "   "   Foster   "   lightly.
Francis   "   "   "   Hanson   "   here.
Barney   "   "   "   Curtis   "   today.

Lincoln   Davis and Spencer Lamson argued rarely.
Jackson   "   "   "   Evans   "   singly.
Charlotte "   "   "   Landis   "   yesterday.
Mary   "   "   "   Noble   "   slowly.

Norman Bragg and Truman Astor   played hard.
Alice   "   "   "   Dennis   "   gently.
Daniel   "   "   "   Mason   "   there.
Janet   "   "   "   Napier   "   apart.

Martha Croft and Roscoe Bentley watched earnestly.
Norah   "   "   "   Hunter   "   brightly.
Andrew   "   "   "   Podson   "   much.
Ellen   "   "   "   Conant   "   late.

Kenneth Blake and Thomas Rollins listened gladly.
Orville   "   "   "   Durant   "   everywhere.
Arthur   "   "   "   Roper   "   then.
Henry   "   "   "   Nichols "   long.

Maxwell Craig and Richard Allen   struggled often.
David   "   "   "   Franklin "   up.
Laura   "   "   "   Travis   "   always.
Patrick   "   "   "   Custer   "   quickly.

Bertram Dean and Vincent Ellis   studied easily.
Norris   "   "   "   Golden   "   fiercely.
Horace   "   "   "   Wilder   "   little.
Lewis   "   "   "   Sackett "   easily.

Peter   Borah and Sarah Alden   complained dully.
Edgar   "   "   "   Hogan   "   never.
Rachel   "   "   "   Morris   "   now.
Randolph "   "   "   Bishop   "   together.

1. What word came next after rarely?
2.   "   "   "   "   "   much?
3.   "   "   "   "   "   up?
4.   "   "   "   "   "   fiercely?
5.   "   "   "   "   "   Blake and?
6.   "   "   "   "   "   Borah and?

7. What word came next after Bragg and?
8.   "   "   "   "   "   Craig and?
9.   "   "   "   "   "   Alfred?
10.   "   "   "   "   "   Bertram?
11.   "   "   "   "   "   Kenneth?
12.   "   "   "   "   "   Lincoln?
13.   "   "   "   "   "   Astor?
14.   "   "   "   "   "   Allen?
15.   "   "   "   "   "   Alden?
16.   "   "   "   "   "   Barnard?
17. What words or words came after Richard?
18.   "   "   "   "   "   "   Ronald?
19.   "   "   "   "   "   "   Roscoe?
20.   "   "   "   "   "   "   Sarah?
21.   "   "   "   "   "   "   argued?
22.   "   "   "   "   "   "   complained?
23.   "   "   "   "   "   "   listened?
24.   "   "   "   "   "   "   played?

Experiment 31

A more conclusive experiment may be arranged as follows: Let a long series of pairs of words followed by numbers be arranged in which also certain of the numbers are always followed by certain of the words. We announced to the subjects "I shall read you a long list of pairs of words and numbers like *bread 29, wall 16, Texas 78.* You will listen as I read them. Pay about as close attention as you would in an average class. Be sure that you hear each pair as I read it." The series of 1304 pairs contained, among other pairs, four pairs (*dregs 91, charade 17, swing 62,* and *antelope 35*) each occurring 24 times, and so placed that *dregs* always came just after 42, *charade* always came just after 86, *swing* always came just after 94, and *antelope* always came just after 97.

After the series had been read, the subjects were asked to write which numbers came just after certain words and also which words came just after certain numbers, namely, 42, 86, 94, 97.

The average percentage of correct responses for the numbers following words in pairs occurring 18 or 21 times each scattered throughout the series was 37½ (median 38). The average percentage of correct responses for the words following the numbers 24 times each was one half of one per cent, which is no more than mere chance guessing would give.

The nature of the instructions, the way in which the pairs were read and the habits of life in general, led the subjects to consider each word as belonging to the number that followed it, and each number as belonging to the word that preceded it. In this experiment, the temporal contiguity of a number with the word following it, the mere sequence without belonging, does nothing to the connection. . . .

The belonging which is always or nearly always necessary in order that the repeated occurrence of a sequence may strengthen the connection between the first term of the sequence and the second need not be more than the least which the word implies. There need be nothing logical, or essential, or inherent, or unifying in it. Any "this goes with that" will suffice. Each nonsense syllable in a series which is read as a series "belongs" to the one before it in the series. 1492 belongs to Mr. Jones as his telephone number as truly as to Christopher Columbus as an auspicious year. In an experiment, 1492 may truly belong to 65 or to 7843 or to *sig nop*.[2]

[Even a small amount of "belongingness" of *E 2* with *E 1* will enable repeated occurrences of *E 1* followed by *E 2* to increase appreciably the probability of certain future behavior by the person concerned. Thus the belongingness of numbers from 10 to 99 with three-place numbers such as 942, 176, 325, and so on in a series of over 7000 pairs is only that of being in pairs as stated in the instructions, as follows:

I shall read you a long list of three-place numbers like 726 or 939 and two-place numbers like 68, 21, or 47, in pairs. I shall read, say, four ninety-seven twenty-one, three eighty-five sixty-four, nine thirteen

---

[2] [As a convenient zero of "belongingness" we may take that of *Event 1* in *your* brain to *Event 2* in *my* brain. The probability that *Event 1* will evoke *Event 2* if both occurred in the same brain is greater than this zero. And the probability will be still greater if *Event 2* followed closely upon *Event 1* in the same brain than if they occurred years apart. Indeed if all of a person's dreams, deliriums, and insanities were available for study, a positive value, perhaps of the order of 1 chance in 1,000,000,000,000,000,000,000, might be found for the recurrence of such sequences in which the one event belonged with the other no wise save by proximity in time in the same brain.]

twenty-seven, five eighteen twenty-four. The first number will always be a three-figure number, that is, one from 100 to 999. The second number will always be a two-figure number, that is, one from 10 to 99. The same three-place number may or may not be always followed by the same two-place number. You are to listen to the pairs of numbers as I read them, without making any effort to remember them or think about them. Just listen comfortably and with equal attention throughout.

Yet the subjects of the experiment had records of success far above chance when required to "write the number that came after 942," and so on. Chance would, of course, give 1.1 per cent of correct guesses. The percentages for pairs with 96, 84 and 72 occurrences were respectively 28, 20 and 11. However, a score of 28 per cent right after 96 occurrences means only a slight strengthening compared to what occurrence plus rewarding after-effects would give. It would be foolish to try to teach $13^2 = 169$, $14^2 = 196$, $15^2 = 225$, and so on, by repeating these pairs over and over to persons who were not set to try to learn them, and did not in the least care whether they learned them or not.]

II. OCCURRENCE WITHOUT REWARD

In the ordinary experiments upon learning the individual knows what he is to learn. He is consequently satisfied by what makes, or seems to make, progress toward it. It is then difficult to obtain any measurements of the potency of repetition alone. In memorizing lists or pairs, for example, the subject is better satisfied when he holds the material in mind for a second or so after hearing or seeing it than when he loses it. If, on hearing the first member of a pair, he anticipates the second member, he is notably satisfied when his anticipatory reaction is correct. So "number of repetitions" in the ordinary experiments means in part also "number of opportunities for satisfying or annoying after-effects to operate."

We have sought to obtain closer approximations to the activity of repetition plus belonging without the influence of the consequences of the connection, by using a different form of presentation of the connected pairs, by instructing the subjects in certain ways, and by concealing or disguising the learning which we later test.

The most usual plan of our experiments to this end is to present long series of pairs (from about 500 to 4000) in which certain pairs recur often, with instructions to the subjects to listen comfortably without any effort to remember and without thinking about what is heard, just experiencing what is provided. A second plan is to have the subjects copy the pairs or write them from dictation, the experiment being described as a means of obtaining data on fatigue, or on speed and accuracy, or on lapses. . . .

Series *Number Number 3586* consisted of 3586 pairs, each consisting of a three-place and a two-place number. Its constitution was as follows:

```
 8  pairs occurring 48 times
 8    "        "    42   "
 8    "        "    36   "
 8    "        "    30   "
 8    "        "    24   "
 8    "        "    18   "
 8    "        "    12   "
 8    "        "     6   "
12    "        "     6   "  in sequences
24    "        "     3   "
10  meaningful pairs occurring 3 times
```

There were also pairs in which the same three-figure number was followed in half the cases by one two-figure number and in the other half by a different two-figure number. Of these "doubles" there were 8 with 24 repetitions with one two-figure number and 24 with another, 8 with 21 and 21 repetitions, 8 with 18 and 18, 8 with 15 and 15, 8 with 12 and 12, 8 with 9 and 9, and 8 with 6 and 6. There were four extra pairs making 3586 in all. [The "doubles" were to prevent subjects from thinking that the same first three figures were always followed by the same last two.]

Experiment 35

Series *Number Number* 3586 was used with fourteen university students in an experiment ostensibly on fatigue. The instructions were as follows:

I shall read a long series of five-figure numbers like 218 97, 432 16, 874 53. You will write each one as I read it making as clear and legible figures as you can in the time available. Try not to miss any, and have each one correct. I shall read each number in two parts like two eighteen ninety-seven, four thirty-two sixteen, eight seventy-four fifty-three. Write the numbers in columns. Begin a new column when I say "Begin at the top."

The numbers were then read at the rate of 2½ seconds for each three-figure two-figure pair, with a rest of 2 minutes after each 320 pairs, and with rests of ten minutes at the end of 1280 pairs and of 2560.

There was just barely time for some of the subjects to write the numbers.

As soon as the entire series had been read, each individual was given Test Sheet S and required to write the two-figure number which came after each three-figure number on sheet S and, with it, made the five-figure number written, in case the individual remembered what it was. In case he did not at once remember it, he was required to copy the three-figure number on Sheet S and to add to it the first two figures that came to his mind.[3]

After this had been done he was instructed as follows:

Mark any that you are sure were right with an *s*.
Answer these questions on the back of the sheet.
1. Did you make any effort to remember any of the numbers while you were writing them or after you had written them?
2. Did you form special associations about any of the numbers?
3. If so, what were they? . . .

All answered "No" to the first question. Twelve answered "No" to the second. The two having special associations noted

[3] Test Sheet S is not shown here. It consisted of 90 three-figure numbers. . . . [It included none of those used in the doubles, only 8 of the 12 used in the sequences, and only 8 of the 24 used in the 24 non-meaningful pairs.]

in one case that in 444 44 all the figures were the same, and in the other that 120 25 had a certain rhythm.

The results for the various pairs arranged according to the number of occurrences of each appear in Table 64.

TABLE 64

RESULTS OF EXPERIMENT 35, WITH SERIES NUMBER
NUMBER 3586

Copied once from dictation. 14 university students.
Only pairs in which each 3-place number always
had the same sequent were used in the test.

Number of Pairs	Occurrences	Number Correct
8	48	10
8	42	3
8	36	5
8	30	5
8	24	2
8	18	0
8	12	1
8	6	0
8	6s	1
8	3	1

and 10 meaningful pairs occurring 3 times each
produced 26 correct responses.

Since there were 14 individuals, the expectation by chance is .156 right per pair or 1.24 per eight pairs. This is exceeded by those pairs having 48, 42, 36, and 30 occurrences (the sums correct being 10, 3, 5, and 5, respectively).

Such an experiment measures the force of sheer frequency plus belonging with as near a minimum of satisfying after-effect of the connection as is perhaps obtainable. The individuals had no interest in remembering any of the five-figure numbers longer than to write them. If in late learnings of, say, *one twenty* the subject occasionally anticipated the *twenty-five* and found his anticipation correct, the satisfyingness thereof was only such a very mild satisfyingness as perhaps attaches to any exercise of power without thwarting. If, in late hearings of, say, *eight hundred one twenty four*, the subject recognized it as a number that had occurred before, the satisfyingness of such recognition could have been only the very mild satisfyingness of a state of recognition versus ignorance. . . .

Taken along with our other experiments this one seems nearly crucial against those theorists who have declared that association by contiguity [in time] has zero power.

[However, it is also nearly crucial against those who set the power of temporal contiguity much above zero. The 1800 occurrences of meaningless numbers cause hardly any more right responses than 30 occurrences of meaningful numbers (28 versus 26). The main power of close temporal sequence is to enable other forces to act.]

For efficient learning of such pairs it is not enough to have them occur together and attend to them as they occur. The mind should also have the attitude or "set" toward forming and preserving the connection; it should itself make the response; and it should be satisfied by success in so doing either as an immediate result of the trace left by an occurrence or as an anticipatory response to hearing the first member of a pair.

If a person wished to strengthen the connections between, say, the three-place numbers and the two-place numbers as much as possible in two hours, he would not rely on repetition and attention alone. He would try to arouse interest in the learning, and would recall each pair from within after he heard it and before the trace left by the hearing had become ineffective, and would be pleased when he so recalled them and when later he could evoke the second term upon hearing or seeing the first.[4]

III. EVIDENCE FROM THE REPETITION OF PUNISHED CONNECTIONS [5]

. . . In *The Fundamentals of Learning* evidence was reported showing that the mere occurrence of a connection does

---

[4] He would, of course, also reduce the interference due to the chaotic arrangement of the pairs, and would make the connections meaningful where it was useful to do so.

[5] This section consists of parts of an article entitled "The Influence of Use or Frequency of Occurrence Upon the Strength of Mental Connections" pub-

strengthen it, in the shape of the strengthening found where after-effects of any sort were at a minimum, and also in the shape of the strengthening of connections which were punished. The latter evidence was not treated fully or critically in that volume. It has been extended by Lorge and the writer, and will be the topic of the present report.

Consider first the facts from an experiment (Q) in learning one response out of six for each of 960 situations, the response being the numbers 1 to 6 and the situations 960 words, divided into 24 sets of 40. A word was read by the experimenter; the subject said 1 or 2 or 3 or 4 or 5 or 6; the experimenter said "Right" or "Wrong," and then read the next word, and so on through a series of 40, and through the same series four times more. Each "Right" signified a money payment which was of real importance to the learner. There were 24 subjects.

The influence of one rewarded occurrence in Experiment Q is such that the connection which occurs and is rewarded occurs again in the following trial or round in 4029 out of 9751 cases, or in 43.6 per cent. The influence of one punished occurrence is such that the connection which occurs and is punished occurs in the following trial or round in 9868 out of 43,915 cases, or in 22.5 per cent.

If we assume that, apart from the occurrences, rewards and punishments, the subject would at any occasion be as likely to choose any one number as any other, the rewarded occurrence has increased the probability of reoccurrence by 0.269 (from 0.167 to 0.436) and the punished occurrence has increased it by 0.058 (from 0.167 to 0.225).

Some of the latter increase is, however, probably due to the "spread" or "scatter" action of rewards, and some of it may be due to favoritism in the choice of numbers. We will consider the latter first.

The percentage of repetitions which there would have been if the punishment and occurrence had had a net influence of zero would be 100 divided by the number of different responses (here 6), if the subject was as likely to select one response as another. But if he favored certain responses it would not. In any trial (call it II) the probability of repetition of a response made in the preceding trial (call it I) apart from all influence from the learning itself, is aI aII + bI bII + cI cII ...... nI nII where aI, bI, cI, etc., are the probabilities of occurrence in trial I and aII, bII, cII, etc., are the probabilities of occurrence in trial II. Favoritism for certain numbers can lower the probability of repetition to 0 or raise it to 1.00. For example, in a case where the subject must respond by any number from 1 to 6, we could have such cases as A, B, C and D below (the occurrences total 1000 in each trial).

Case A:
| Trial I | 1, | 400; | 2, | 300; | 3, | 200; | 4, | 100; | 5, | 0; | 6, | 0. |
| Trial II | 1, | 0; | 2, | 0; | 3, | 0; | 4, | 0; | 5, | 400; | 6, | 600. |

Probability of repetition, 0.000.

Case B:
| Trial I | 1, | 1000; | 2, | 0; | 3, | 0; | 4, | 0; | 5, | 0; | 6, | 0. |
| Trial II | 1, | 1000; | 2, | 0; | 3, | 0; | 4, | 0; | 5, | 0; | 6, | 0. |

Probability of repetition, 1.00.

Case C:
| Trial I | 1, | 400; | 2, | 300; | 3, | 200; | 4, | 100; | 5, | 0; | 6, | 0. |
| Trial II | 1, | 400; | 2, | 300; | 3, | 200; | 4, | 100; | 5, | 0; | 6, | 0. |

Probability of repetition, 0.300.

Case D:
| Trial I | 1, | 350; | 2, | 250; | 3, | 200; | 4, | 100; | 5, | 50; | 6, | 50. |
| Trial II | 1, | 360; | 2, | 240; | 3, | 180; | 4, | 100; | 5, | 60; | 6, | 60. |

Probability of repetition, 0.238.

Favoritism of a similar sort in both trials will raise the probability of repetition above 0.1667. Reversal of favoritism in the second trial will lower it below 0.1667.

We therefore proceed to investigate the favoritism, if any, shown by each of the twenty-four subjects in choosing among 1, 2, 3, 4, 5 and 6 as responses. The responses of each are tabulated in successive sets of 40 corresponding to the successive trials of the various series of words, then in successive sets of 200, each corresponding to the 200 responses for the five trials of one series, and finally by successive sets of 400. First, each record is inspected to detect any tendencies to reverse favoritism in any two consecutive trials. No such were found.

Secondly, each record is inspected to detect any systematic shifts in favoritism (such as a steady change from favoring 1 and 2 much to favoring them little, or from favoring 2, 3, 4 and 5 much to favoring them little or vice versa). There were few such shifts.

Thirdly, each record is inspected to detect any clear cases of short-lived changes in favoritism. It is, of course, hard to draw the line between such and chance variations in choices.

If there is no evidence of systematic shifts, or of genuine short-lived tendencies, the average influence of favoritism operating at any one time is estimated as follows: $a^2 + b^2 + c^2 + d^2 + e^2 + f^2 / n^2$ is computed for each successive 400 (or for so many 400's as we have) and the average of the determinations is taken. This permits undetected genuine short-lived tendencies to favoritism to count somewhat, but still does not interpret chance variations in choice as genuine favoritism. If there are any special shifts, the 400's are so chosen as not to swamp the influence of the favoritism, and are checked by using sets of 200 each.

As a result of much labor expended in the ways stated, a probability of repetition of the same number in the responses to the same word in two successive trials has been estimated for each of the 24 subjects. They range from 0.170 to 0.220, twenty being between 0.174 and 0.205. These are shown in Table 1 together with the excess frequencies of repetition for punished occurrences at various degrees of remoteness from any rewarded connection.

Even at a remoteness of five or more steps from any rewarded connection the frequency of repetition in the next trial for one punished occurrence of a connection is clearly in excess of what would be expected by chance plus number favoritism. It is + in 19 cases out of 24, and the median (16 permilles) is about three times its probable error. A punished connection gains more strength by occurring once than it loses by being punished once.

TABLE 1

The strengthening due to one (first) occurrence of a punished connection.
Experiment Q

EXCESS OVER THE EXPECTED FREQUENCY FOR THE ACTUAL FREQUENCIES
OF REPETITION IN THE FOLLOWING TRIAL FOR FIRST OCCURRENCES
OF PUNISHED CONNECTIONS. PERMILLES

SUBJECT	PROBABILITY OF REPETITION BY CHANCE PLUS NUMBER FAVORITISM	ALL PUNISHED CONNECTIONS	BETWEEN TWO REWARDED CONNECTIONS	NEXT TO ONE REWARDED CONNECTION	TWO STEPS REMOVED FROM EACH OF TWO REWARDED CONNECTIONS	TWO STEPS REMOVED FROM ONE REWARDED CONNECTION	THREE OR FOUR STEPS REMOVED FROM ONE OR TWO REWARDED CONNECTIONS	FIVE OR MORE STEPS REMOVED FROM ANY REWARDED CONNECTION
1	200	109	145	107	157	107	119	091
2	174	033	008	038	063	053	039	026
3	170	027	071	057	008	009	024	002
4	189	—003	071	005	081	—051	—011	005
5	185	010	041	017	093	019	011	003
6	196	007	057	013	035	025	—023	024
7	210	030	167	036	—130	026	030	—017
8	199	031	126	023	—045	025	017	050
9	175	064	075	075	044	081	082	019
10	185	071	081	073	194	090	070	077
11	174	020	072	050	039	—006	—031	—036
12	208	035	109	045	023	049	026	—009
13	180	039	146	044	106	—005	027	030
14	180	025	107	035	120	037	023	002
15	180	050	060	039	—013	046	040	069
16	174	045	022	081	159	023	038	042
17	177	004	058	055	109	—001	—027	—020
18	182	042	032	079	100	012	057	004
19	205	014	032	022	045	007	028	—019
20	189	111	061	094	144	078	144	107
21	183	048	117	075	140	039	035	011
22	190	052	174	081	041	013	038	042
23	220	033	018	014	165	049	044	042
24	180	008	111	000	062	—004	—008	013
Median	184	032	071.5	044.5	072	025	029	016
Average	188	038	082	048	073	030	033	023

[The next six pages of the original article report the results from treating the facts of five other experiments in a similar manner. After allowance for number favoritism, the median amounts of strengthening due to one punished occurrence five or more steps removed from any reward were (in permilles): 084, 098, 046, 048, and 073 in Experiments H, J, L, M and P, respectively. The average amounts were somewhat higher.]

In the case of Experiment F (in which the choice was of a number from 1 to 10) the individual records of actual repetitions of punished connections remote from a reward were from too few cases to deserve computation. The totals for the group of twenty subjects were: 605 first occurrences five or more steps removed from any reward, of which 74 or 12.2 per cent were repeated in the following trial. [Number favoritism may be adequate to account for the excess above chance in this experiment.]

[The most probable explanation of the facts found in these seven experiments is that the mere occurrence of a connection strengthens it. Three other possibilities may, however, be considered, namely]:

(*a*) spread or scatter beyond four steps, (*b*) the possible persistent suggestion of a particular response (here a number, a part of a diagram or a position in a line) by the situation, and (*c*) a possible occasional confirming reaction due to the satisfyingness of making any choice and response.

Observation and experiment can, with enough labor, learn what allowances, if any, are needed for (*a*) and (*b*). We have evidence already that there is no spread or scatter of the confirming influence of a reward beyond four steps in many of the seventeen revelant experiments in which there is certainly a large excess over chance, and almost certainly an excess over chance plus number favoritism. There is also evidence that some persons who are entirely unaware of any persistent suggestions of particular responses of the sort described in (*b*) show large excesses over chance plus number favoritism. Though doubtless a real cause, (*b*) does not seem likely to be an adequate one.

I have not found it possible, within such multiple-choice experiments as these, to distinguish between a confirming reaction due to the satisfyingness of making *any* choice and response and a strengthening influence due to the mere use of a connection.

The former is conceivable; it would permit the explanation of all strengthening of connections by one physiological function or mechanism; it would explain the phylogenetic development of learning by one variation, the appearance of a confirming reaction, rather than by two; it would avoid the difficulty of explaining why the mere use of some connections does strengthen them whereas the mere use of others does not. But there is no direct evidence for it in the experiments. The subjects feel no observable satisfaction at saying *any* number or marking *any* part of a diagram. Their satisfaction seems to them limited to the connections that are rewarded (or that, in later stages of an experiment, they know will be rewarded, even before they make them). And, in general, the evidence here seems to be against it, as in the experiments of Chapter IV of the *Fundamentals of Learning*, and as in the formation of conditional reflexes by Cason ['22], by Hudgins ['33] and by others who have used techniques in which the subjects gain nothing by the formation of such connections.

There is still another possibility allied to (*c*). The mere occurrence of a connection may strengthen it and yet do so indirectly and occasionally by arousing the confirming reaction, not directly and uniformly by the action of the connection itself. I have elsewhere suggested, as a working hypothesis to explain the "spread" or "scatter" phenomenon, that the confirming reaction, being a physiological rather than a logical influence, occasionally misses the connection which the reward follows and belongs to, and influences by mistake a punished connection coming a little earlier or later. In a somewhat similar way the confirming reaction itself, which is in such experiments probably in a state of extreme excitability or sensitiveness or readiness to act, may occasionally be set off, not by its normally adequate stimulus, a state of affairs satisfying to the mental set or purpose or controlling powers, but by mistake by stimuli that normally would be inadequate. This hypothesis would have the merits noted above for (*c*) and would perhaps be consistent with the facts of other experiments. But discussion of all these possibilities may well be deferred until further experiments bearing upon them have been made.

[In the fifteen years since this was written little has been done that bears on the problem of whether the strengthening of connections has two distinct sorts of causation or only one. It seems to me likely that the confirming reaction should operate occasionally spontaneously (i.e. for no externally manifested reason). But I can think of no direct evidence that it does so. Perhaps such may be found by an investigation of cases where certain items in a series of occurrences are remembered for no observable reason.]

REFERENCES

CASON, H., "Conditioned Pupillary Reactions," *J. Exp. Psych.*, 5, (1922), 108–146.

HUDGINS, C. V., "Conditioning and the Voluntary Control of the Pupillary Light Reflexes," *J. Gen. Psychol.*, 8, (1933), 3–51.

LORGE, I., "The Efficacy of Intensified Reward and of Intensified Punishment," *J. Exp. Psych.*, 16, (1933), 177–207.

LORGE, I., and THORNDIKE, E. L., "The Comparative Strengthening of a Connection by One or More Occurrences of It in Cases Where the Connection Was Punished and Was neither Rewarded nor Punished," *J. Exp. Psych.*, 16, (1933), 374–382.

THORNDIKE, E. L., and the Staff of the Division of Psychology, of the Institute of Educational Research, *The Fundamentals of Learning* (1932).

THORNDIKE, E. L., "An Experimental Study of Rewards," Teachers College, Columbia University Contributions to Education, No. 580 (1933).

CHAPTER V

The Influence of Mental Systems *

I. THE COMPLEXITY OF MENTAL CONNECTIONS

THE connections which we have investigated so far [in *The Fundamentals of Learning*] have been simple links between an external situation and an overt response or, less often, between the first and second terms of a simple pair, such as a word heard and a number heard or thought of. Each has also been, as a rule, a rather independent unit by itself easily isolated from the rest of the person's behavior and learning.

Such uniformity, simplicity, and independence are desirable in experiments on the fundamental questions with which we have been concerned, but it would be unfortunate if either we or our readers got the impression that they are characteristic of the actual connections which are formed in the world's learning. On the contrary these are usually varied, complicated, and influenced by their contexts.

Connections lead from states of affairs within the brain as well as from external situations. They often occur in long series wherein the response to one situation becomes the situation producing the next response and so on. They may be from parts or elements or features of a situation as well as from the situation as a whole. They may be largely determined by events preceding their immediate stimuli or by more or less of the accompanying attitude or set of the person, even conceivably by his entire make-up and equipment. They lead to responses of readiness and unreadiness, awareness, attention, interest, welcoming and rejecting, emphasizing and restraining, differentiating and relating, directing and coördinating.

* *The Fundamentals of Learning*, pp. 353–382, in part.

The things connected may be subtle relations or elusive attitudes and intentions.[1]

In some cases the part or aspect is much more important than the gross total. This is rather the rule with seen words, for example, in which the pattern is the essential. Whether the word is black or blue or red or gray, whether the print is large or small, whether it is sensed by cones in the right or the left side of the fovea, does not matter. In hundreds of varying gross total sense impressions the same pattern is used to connect with the main response. The color of the word or its size or its position in the line is responded to as an accessory of the pattern. Something of the same sort is true of heard words, musical phrases, geometrical forms, and common objects in which a pattern dominates.

Connection and selection coöperate in intimate ways. A very common type of connection is one in which the situation evokes as its response whatever acts attain a certain result. The situation being, for example, the sight of a letter to be signed, the response is to do whatever particular movements get it signed. The particular movements may vary according to whether pen or pencil is at hand, and where the letter lies. The connection is in the nature of an order to do what seems suitable until the goal of getting said letter signed is attained. Such *order*——>*fill it* connections may lead to much selection of ways and means. If the selection is important and obvious, we call them problems and solutions rather than situations and responses. But there is no fundamental distinction between *Letter to be signed*——>*signing it* and *Square root of 729638 to be computed*——>*computing it*.

As a result of the variety of responses, piecemeal activity (that is, connections from and to elements or aspects), differential potency, coöperative action, the mixture of selective procedures with associative, and the determination of connections by mental trends and sets, the connections of a human mind are complicated almost beyond description. Almost

[1] Each sentence in this paragraph could well be made the subject of a chapter. . . .

every prophecy which we make about a man's behavior has to be prefaced by "other things being equal." The thinking and learning of a single ten-year-old for a single day would present a picture hardly recognizable as a collection or system of S——→R connections of the simple type studied here. Many psychologists would indeed deny that any system of connections was adequate to explain his behavior, and would invoke powers of analysis, insight, purpose, and the like to supplement or replace the simple process of connection-forming by repetition and reward.

In this chapter we shall deal particularly with the frequent and important action of certain mental systems which seem, at least on the surface, to compete with the laws of habits and be inexplicable by them.

II. MENTAL SYSTEMS APPARENTLY UNEXPLAINED BY ORDINARY CONNECTIONS

. . . Such mental systems might be of four (and perhaps more) sorts. First, there might be sensory systems whereby a stimulus which belonged in one sense-field, say hearing, would tend to evoke responses in sense-field, beyond what repetition and reward could account for. Second, there might be instinct-systems whereby a stimulus which had a place in some original or early established tendency, such as *being thwarted in movement*——→*struggle, weariness*——→*states of rest, anger* ——→*blows*, or *courtship*——→*mating behavior*, to evoke responses constituting that original tendency beyond what repetition and reward could account for. Third, there might be (and surely are) customary systems like the alphabet, the number series, the family or the schoolroom, whereby stimuli which were parts of these systems would evoke other parts thereof. Such customary systems would themselves have been built up by the ordinary action of repetition and reward, but once established might exercise a dominion of their own. Finally, there might be what I shall call transcendent systems, not referable to any organization of the brain to fit either its systems of receptors, or its systems of connections subserving eating, defense, sex behavior, or the like, and certainly not created by experience, exercise, and effect. There might conceivably be, for example, a tendency inherent in mind for the thought of any quality to arouse the thought of the opposite of that quality, or a tendency for the thought of any whole to arouse thoughts of its parts, regardless of what particular connections had been formed in the mind in question.

Experiment 87

Experiment 87 was planned to secure facts about the influence of systems in directing the course of thought and, in particular, to ascertain the probability that the original organization of the brain or mind directs thought otherwise than by the formation of connections by exercise and effect, that is, by repetition, reward, and punishment.

The form of the experiment was the well-known free-association test, used by Kent and Rosanoff, the stimulus words being chosen to give opportunity for sense-fields, instinct systems, customary systems, and what we have labelled transcendental systems to operate. . . .

Among the stimulus words are:

(1) *loud, music, patter, rumble,* and *thunder;*
(2) *hard, rough, soft,* and *smooth;*
(3) *bitter, bread, butter, cake, cheese, cabbage, eating, fruit, gravy, mutton, pie, salt, soup, sour, sweet, tobacco,* and *whiskey;* and
(4) *black, blue, dark, green, moon, red, white,* and *yellow.*

Do the responses to these show any evidence of greater frequency of response within the sense-field of the stimulus than can be accounted for by the laws of exercise and effect?

Among the stimulus words are *hungry, thirsty, afraid, anger, joy, man, woman, boy,* and *girl.* Do the responses to them show evidence of the direction of response by organization around certain fields or strands of original interests and aversions?

The influence of certain customary systems, due to circumstances and habit, will be studied in the responses to such groups of stimulus words as *add, decimal, multiply, fraction, 4, 6, 7,* and *8; oui, merci, garçon,* and *maison; t, b,* and *u; doctor, health,* and *sickness; coat, collar, hat,* and *shoe.*

The influence of what we have termed transcendental systems may be studied in the responses to *ball, cone, crooked, square,* and *triangle; always, future, later,* and *now; Boston, Chicago, Italy,* and *Paris.* If the brain of man is so organized as to have its actions directed by shape, time or locality as abstract forms of thought imposed upon the organization due to ordinary instincts and habits, the fact may be revealed by the responses to these stimuli. Also evidence of a subtler character may be sought in ways to be described later.

III. SENSORY SYSTEMS

The number of responses to *loud, music,* etc., *hard, rough,* etc., *bitter, bread,* etc., *blue, green,* etc., which are suggestive of hearing, touch, taste, and color vision, respectively, is very large. Whether there are more than would be expected by frequency and fitness is, however, very doubtful. The lists in summary form are given below. There are a few responses, the appearance of which is easy to explain by attraction toward one sense-field, and hard to explain by frequency and fitness. These are as follows: *loud ear,* 1; *patter thump,* 1; *soft sand,* 1; *smooth touch,* 1; *smooth soft,* 16; *smooth brittle,* 1; *smooth hard,* 5; *cheese lemon,* 1; *cheese sour,* 1; *cheese vinegar,* 1; *salt soda,* 1; *cabbage syrup,* 1; *soup syrup,* 1; *blue orange,* 2; *blue pink,* 4; *green pink,* 1; *red indigo,* 1; *red pink,* 6; *red tan,* 1; *yellow gray,* 1.

Summary Lists [of Responses Suggestive of Sensory Systems. The total number of responses in each list is shown in parentheses.]

Hearing
(162) *loud:* soft, 39, noise, 56; noisy, 6; bang, clap, cornet, crash, drum, ear, quiet, radio, sound, still, talk, voice, yell, 27.
(162) *music:* piano, 12; song, 19; band, concert, drum, fiddle, melody, noise, opera, orchestra, organ, saxophone, sound, tone, trombone, violin, 37.

(192) *patter:* chatter, clatter, noise, sound, talk, thump, 19.

(192) *rumble:* noise, 35; hear, mumble, patter, rattle, roar, sound, still, talk, thunder, 31.

(162) *thunder:* crash, loud, noise, roll, 16.

Touch

(192) *hard:* soft, 95; glass, iron, nail, rock, stone, 26.

(162) *soft:* hard, 62; bed, candy, chair, collar, cushion, down, feathers, etc., making a long list of things which feel soft, summing to 48; also feel and felt, 3; mushy, 2; pressure, 1.

(162) *smooth:* rough, 55; soft, 16; brittle, cloth, even, floor, hard, lead, satin, sheet, silk, skin, velvet, 28.

(162) *rough:* smooth, 49; board, cloth, hard, material, paper, sandpaper, touch, 9.

Taste

From the many words in our lists, I select *cheese, eating, salt,* and *bitter* for summary.[2]

(192) *cheese:* bread, butter, cake, crackers, eat, lemon, milk, pie, salad, sandwich, sour, vinegar, 61; cream, Roquefort and other names of varieties of cheese, 35.

(162) *eating:* food, 30; dinner, lunch, supper, 8; bread, cake, candy, chicken, corn, dumplings, eggs, fish, meat, pie, steak, 22; bitter, salt, sour, and sweet never appear.

(192) *salt:* pepper, 20; sugar, 22; almonds, bread, food, meat, savor, soda, soup, taste, tasty, 28; bitter, 8; sour, 8; sweet, 6.

(162) *bitter:* sweet, 99; salt, 6; sour, 6; taste, 6; acid, almond, aloes, chocolate, drink, fruit, lemon, lemonade, medicine, persimmon, quinine, sweets, tang, 27.

Color

(192) *blue:* all but 11 are of visual objects or qualities, including black, 10; gray, 3; green, 6; orange, 2; pink, 4; red, 19; white, 6; yellow, 6.

(162) *green:* all but 8 are visual, including black, 2; blue, 16; gold, 1; pink, 1; red, 22; white, 3; yellow, 11.

(162) *red:* all but 6 are visual, including black, 5; blue, 32; carmine, 1; crimson, 1; green, 19; indigo, 1; orange, 2; pink, 6; scarlet, 1; tan, 1; white, 9; yellow, 5.

(192) *yellow:* all but 8 are visual, including black, 3; blue, 9; gold, 2; gray, 1; green, 15; orange, 7; pink, 5; red, 9; white, 7.

On the whole, there is some, but far from conclusive, evidence that the impressions received from any one system of receptors are somewhat affiliated and that their affiliations

[2] The entire list has been searched for responses hard to explain by frequency and fitness, and these are typical of all that were found.

produce affiliations between the ideas which develop from these impressions, with the result that an idea which has been equally often and profitably connected with two ideas, one inside that sensory field and one outside it, will have a somewhat stronger tendency to evoke the former. Further experiments, and experiments of a more crucial character, are necessary to settle the question. One thing is sure from even our rough survey. The power of attraction within a sensory field, if it exists, is not great. If it were, we should find words like *shrill, squeaky, cry, laugh,* and *sing* occurring oftener as irrelevant (except as being sound words) responses to *loud, music, patter, rumble,* and *thunder.* Similarly, *tickle, scratchy, wet, slimy,* and *itch* should occur oftener as responses to *hard, soft, smooth,* and *rough. Sweet, sour, salt, bitter, fruity,* and *oily* should occur oftener as responses to *cheese, eating,* and the like. They are very rare as responses to *bread, fruit, gravy, mutton, pie, soup, tobacco,* and *whiskey,* the total for *sweet, sour, salt,* and *bitter* being 7, or about one response out of two hundred.

IV. INSTINCT SYSTEMS

I have inspected the responses to *hungry, thirsty, afraid, anger, joy, man, woman, boy,* and *girl* for any indications of tendencies for thought to be organized by the instinctive activities of food-getting, fear, anger, sex, and family life. There are very few such, but this may well be because these words are not very well adapted to elicit them, and because some of them may have been repressed. I will present the details in the case of *anger,* which is typical.

The commonest original provocatives of anger are thwarted impulses or expectations and pain. Among its common original expressions are a hot feeling, struggling, yelling, and blows. Among 124 responses to *anger,* the only ones suggesting any of these original provocatives and expressions are fight, 1; heat, 1; hot, 2.

V. CUSTOMARY SYSTEMS

Of the existence and potency of these there is no doubt. *4, 6, 7,* or *8* evokes some other number in about 40 per cent of the cases, and the word *number* in about 15 per cent. *Add, decimal, multiply,* and *fractions* evoke *arithmetic, number,* or *figure* in about 35 per cent of the cases and the name of some other arithmetical operation in about 25 per cent. *Oui, merci, garçon,* and *maison* evoke their English meanings in about half the cases. The letters *t, b,* and *u* evoke the word *letter* in about a fifth of the cases and some individual letter in about a third of them. *Coat, collar, hat,* and *shoe* have frequent sartorial sequents due to the systems built up when we dress ourselves, buy our clothes, and the like. They have other local sequents due to the systems built up as we dress ourselves or look at other persons. So out of 192 responses to *hat* we find *cane, cap, chapeau, cloak, clothes, clothing, coat, dress, hook, rack, sleeve, scarf, shoe* occurring 81 times, and *head* occurring 32 times.

These systems are created by the laws of exercise and effect, things being kept together in the mind which have gone together often and with resulting satisfaction. They are not different in their fundamental causation from the tendencies which make us respond to $2 \times 7 = ?$ by *14* or to *Say the alphabet* by *a, b, c, d,* etc., or to *Columbus discovered* by *America.* They are elaborate groups of connections and interconnections just like the simple pairs which we have experimented with. . . .

VI. TRANSCENDENT SYSTEMS

We shall take first the form of relation which makes the strongest case for the transcendent systems, namely, opposition or contrariety. If the tendency of ideas and words to evoke their opposites can be explained as a consequence of repetition and reward, we need not go further. If it seems to transcend these simple facts, we can proceed to examine the weaker cases in turn.

RESPONSES BY OPPOSITES [3]

The tendency to respond to certain words by their opposites is, especially in intellectual adults, very strong. We find the following percentages: *Add——→substract, 33; multiply ——→divide, 30; crooked——→straight, 36; square——→round, 19; pro——→con, 43; hot——→cold, 43; future——→past, 19; now ——→then, 27; sour——→sweet, 32; sweet——→sour, 28.* These percentages average 32½.

But these facts are not evidence that oppositeness in and of itself has a general potency. That is disproved by the following facts. First, the words which often evoke their opposites also, though less often, evoke their synonyms. We have, for example, percentages as follows: *hot——→warm, 3; now——→present, 11; always——→never, 28,* and *always——→ ever* (or *forever*), *27; beautiful——→ugly, 12,* and *beautiful ——→fine* (or *pretty* or *lovely*), *9; late——→early, 38, late——→ tardy, 9.*

Second, the foreign words almost never evoke their opposites. *Oui——→non* (or *no*); *garçon——→fille* (or *mademoiselle* or *girl*), and *nein——→ja* (or *yes*) occur in only 5 per cent of the cases, though *yes——→no, boy——→girl,* and *no——→yes* would appear in about 60 per cent.

Third, *4, 6, 7,* and *8* never evoke *—4, —6 —7, —8, 1/4, 1/6, 1/7,* or *1/8;* though the opposite is especially definite and complete in these cases. The per cents are 0, 0, 0, and 0.

Fourth, the forms with *dis, in,* and *un* as prefixes, or phrases with *not* are evoked very rarely. If the factor at work was oppositeness in and of itself, it should, one would suppose, express itself rather often by these clear and easily available signs. *Comfort——→discomfort, justice——→injustice, religion*

---

[3] The source of much of the evidence presented in the following pages is Table 128, which occupies pages 383–391 of *The Fundamentals of Learning,* but is omitted here.

——>*irreligion*, and *afraid*——>*unafraid*, comprise less than 1 per cent of the responses to these four words. Of the *not-x* phrases given as responses to 60 words taken at random from our list, not one was given as a negative of the stimulus word.

Fifth, the cases of pseudo-opposites (like *man*——>*woman*, *boy*——>*girl*, and *hand*——>*foot*) where there is no real contrariety, but rather a great resemblance with a contrast in one or more particulars, show percentages comparable to the cases where the two words represent different directions from a zero point or opposite extremes of a scale of amount of something, or acts each of which undoes the result of the other. The percentages for *man*——>*woman*, *woman*——>*man*, *boy*——>*girl*, *girl*——>*boy*, *hand*——>*foot*, *foot*——>*hand*, *command*——>*obey*, and *king*——>*queen* are 50, 52, 62, 54, 18, 14, 15, and 36, averaging 37. . . .

[I omit several pages presenting further lines of evidence that any power of contrariety transcending the powers of repetition and reward (that is, of the occurrence of connections and their after-effects) is unsuited to cause the opposites found in experiment 87 or in other word association tests. I turn to facts showing that certain connections formed in reading and hearing are the real causes.]

VII. REPETITION AND REWARD VERSUS TRANSCENDENT SYSTEMS

We may now turn to examine the forces of repetition and reward, the adequacy of which seemed questionable in the light of the relative frequencies of *yours*——>*mine* and *yours* ——>*truly*, *no*——>*yes*, and *no*——>*sir*, *good*——>*bad*, *good*——> *morning*, and the like.

The discrepancy is, I think, largely due to the failure so far to consider certain very important connections which are formed with words in the course of hearing and reading. The most frequent and most satisfying connection which a word makes is, as a rule, that with its meaning. When we see or hear *afraid* or *bread* or *cold* or *dear* or *in* or *long*, the usual *sine qua non* for successful progress in our activity is that the word should evoke its meaning. If we read *She was afraid of having no bread and meat,* or *It is a cold day, my dear child, so come in the house,* the connection *afraid——>of* is of trivial importance compared with the connection *afraid——>meaning of afraid;* the connections *bread——>and* and *cold——>day* are of trivial importance compared with the connections *bread——>meaning of bread* and *cold——>meaning of cold.* In well over nine-tenths of its occurrences in hearing and reading, namely, in all except those in which the word loses its identity in some idiom, or is heard as nonsense, it evokes its meaning. The mental stuff in which the meaning comes we need not now describe. It varies greatly in different individuals for different words.

The history of the experience whereby words get meanings attached to them is what we need to consider first. It is clear. The meaning a word has comes either (A) from the things, qualities, acts, events, and relations with which it has been connected, or (B) from the verbal statements, synonyms, definitions, and the like with which it has been connected. Pictures, diagrams, and other non-verbal representations may for our present purpose be classified under A. Algebraic, numerical, chemical symbols, and the like may be classified under B. Thus the meaning of *bread* is learned partly by its being connected with loaves seen in the kitchen and slices seen and eaten at the table, and partly by hearing *Bread is made of flour. Bread is good for you. Bread is a food. We eat bread. The baker makes bread.*

Without such connections *bread* is a nonsense syllable.

When a person hears or sees a word and has its meaning, he may have it only sufficiently to enable him to fulfill his purpose of the time being. He need not, for example, on hearing *bread* have any image of loaf or slice or taste, or, say, a clear idea *Bread is a food.* He does, however, know somehow, what *bread* means, probably by reduced or incipient associative tendencies which originated in the experiences described above and which would, if allowed to act fully, lead him on to representations of *bread* and its qualities, or verbal judgments about it.

The nature of the mental stuff in which these associative tendencies exist or by which their presence is indicated, in ordinary hearing and reading, is of much less importance to our inquiry than the fact that such associative tendencies do exist.

The meaning of a word is derived originally from its connections with realities and with other words, and is fully realized at any time by permitting these connections to operate. In one form or another, and in greater or less degree, these connections remain attached to the word, especially as heard or seen.[4]

If a word is seen or heard and a person's mind is set toward reporting the first word "that it suggests" or "that comes to mind," these connections constitutive of meaning will be likely to operate. If one or more of them do operate, the person will think of some thing, quality, act, event, or relation which has frequently and fitly gone with the word or of some verbal expression which gives it meaning. If the former occurs, the person may write the name of the real thing, quality, act, event, or relation as his response, or may proceed further to some associated idea and its name. If the latter occurs, the person may think of a synonym and write it, or of the name of some feature or property that gives meaning, or of the name of the class to which the fact belongs, or the like. In some cases, and this is important, the connections which give a word meaning may lead to the word's opposite. *Long, what does it mean, cold, what does it mean, sweet, what does it mean*—these situations may call up representations, realities, but these can only be named *long, cold,* and *sweet,* and the subject hesitates to name them thus. So the connections leading to *not short, not hot, not sour* and *not bitter,* may determine his response. . . .

How else can one define *long* than by thinking of length

[4] With it spoken or written such connections are weaker, the connections with sequent words being then relatively stronger.

and its extremities? Only by connections leading to cases of long things, no one of which alone has much strength.

Many of the responses which are reported and which are hardest to explain as habitual sequences in speech or reading or writing are explainable as products of such word-meaning connections. The records for *cold* from 162 educated adults may serve as an illustrative evidence of this. I have arranged them tentatively in groups as shown below. There may well be differences of opinion about the particular assignments of some of the responses, but there can be little doubt that all save the *heat, hot, warm,* and nine others are explainable as the products of either habitual sequences or word-meaning connections. If our explanation of the opposites is valid, the data of the free-association experiment may be regarded as a very strong support to connectionism in general.

Caused by word-meaning connections due to real experiences, or to verbal representations of, or references to, real experiences.
br-r-r-r
catarrh
cough
frost
frozen
ice (16)
ice-cream
like ice
sick (2)
sneeze
snow (7)
winter (20)

Caused by word-meaning connections due to verbal statements and the like.
Alaska
Canada
chilly
disagreeable
discomfort
frigid
icy

Probably caused by word-meaning connections.
heat (3)
hot (46)
warm (25)

Caused by habitual sequences in speech or writing.
air
cream

day
head (3)
meat
shoulder
shower
sweat (2)
water (5)
weather (3)

Caused by phonetic connections.
hold
mold

Caused by connections not known.
fine
hard (2)
H_2O
pain
wet
[no response]

Evidence in support of our hypothesis that the responses which are not due to habitual sequences are due largely to connections between words and their meanings may also be found in the differences between the responses of children and those of adults.

A comparison of the frequencies for one thousand children reported by Woodrow and Lowell ['16, pp. 33–71] with the average of the Kent-Rosanoff and O'Connor results shows the following for the first six words (in alphabetical order) and for the next six which show many opposites in the adult responses.

		Adults	Children
1 afraid	fear	241	14
	dark	82	151
	scared	176½	290
	brave	29	4
	night	11½	51
2 anger	mad	175½	471
	temper	100½	8
	wrath	82½	0
	cross	28½	56
	fight	14	57
3 baby	child	281	172
	infant	135½	20
	small	53	90
	cry	38	119

4 bath	clean	134½	192
	cleanliness	85	1
	wash	107½	143
	water	319	295
5 beautiful	pretty	179	280
	handsome	77½	13
	nice	51	169
	ugly	84½	0
	homely	58½	4
6 bed	sleep	429½	453
	rest	97	17
	soft	40	39
	night	11½	106
7 black	color	96	104
	dark	176½	315
	white	422	27
	dress	16½	63
	dirty	less than 10	42
8 boy	child	65½	45
	girl	414	32
	man	108	61
	male	50½	9
	ball	5½	55
	cap	less than 10	53
	pants	"	63
	play	21	84
9 cold	hot	238	12
	ice	82½	84
	warm	181	25
	winter	105½	103
	snow	38	62
	freeze and freezing	not over 28	108
10 dark	light	526½	68
	black	80½	90
	night	191½	416
	afraid	less than 10	49
11 deep	shallow	238	11
	water	123½	154
	sea	90½	21
	down	21½	45
	hole	26	251
	well	47½	154
12 girl	boy	399½	40
	female	73½	22
	woman	80½	8
	dress	21	240
	hair	less than 10	38

The responses by opposites are less than one-tenth as frequent for the children. Responses by the abstract quality which gives or helps to give the word's meaning occur much less often. In place of these the children report what the thing meant by the word does (as in *baby*——→*cry, anger*——→*fight, boy*——→*play, cold*——→*freeze*), or when and where it is found (as in *bed*——→*night, black*——→*dress, dark*——→*night, dark* ——→*afraid, deep*——→*hole, deep*——→*well*), or what concrete earmarks or characteristics it has.

This is just what we should expect if the word-meaning connections were potent influences in both adults and children. In an adult's mind *boy*——→*meaning of boy* would naturally lead on to *man, male*, (not a) *girl*. In a child's mind *boy*——→*meaning of boy* would by the same token lead on to *ball, cap, pants, play*.

When word-meaning connections lead on to verbal synonyms we would expect these to differ with maturity just as they do in fact differ. As we pass from adults' responses to children's responses, *afraid*——→*scared* rises from 176½ to 290; *baby*——→*infant* drops from 135½ to 20; *anger*——→*mad* rises from 175½ to 471; *anger*—*temper* drops from 100½ to 8, and *anger*——→*wrath* from 82½ to 0; *beautiful*——→*pretty* rises from 179 to 280, and *beautiful*——→*nice* from 51 to 169, while *beautiful*——→*handsome* drops from 77½ to 13, and *beautiful*——→ (not) *ugly* drops from 84½ to 0.

The Woodrow-Lowell records permit us to make a test of the hypothesis that the responses by opposites in the free-association test are due partly to connections of habitual concatenations and sequences in speech and writing, but chiefly to the word-meaning connections of hearing and reading. If it is correct, the following should hold good: Let all the responses to eight or ten words amongst adult records, except the opposites, be assigned to (A) habitual concatenations and sequences, (B) word-meaning connections or their outcomes, and (C) other special influences.

Let the responses of children to these same words be assigned similarly. Then, using *a, b,* and c with the meanings for the children's records which A, B, and C have for the adult's records, and using D and d for the per cent of opposites, $a + b + d$ should equal $A + B + D$, though D is very much larger than d, the excess of D being made up in children by word-meaning connections leading to childish synonyms, concrete features, and symptoms, objects in which the quality in question inheres, and the like.

We have made this test with the first ten words of the Kent-Rosanoff list which have an opposite as response in 25 per cent or more of the cases, and occur also in the Woodrow-Lowell list. These are *black, boy, cold, dark, girl, hard, heavy, high, king,* and *light*. We use our records for adults because they are complete. The details of our assignments, which we have sought to make entirely impartial, are on file at Teachers College.

The results appear in Table 127. The sum of $A + B + D$ is very nearly that of $a + b + d$, though A is larger than a and D is nearly ten times as large as d. The reader should note that, if our allotments are valid, nearly 95 per cent of the responses are explainable by connections formed by repe-

TABLE 127

Frequencies (per mille) of various sorts of connections according to our classification of the responses in the free-association test

	Children					Educated Adults				
	Rhymes	Common Expressions	Meanings (except Opposites)	Opposites	Not Allocated	Rhymes	Common Expressions	Meanings (except Opposites)	Opposites	Not Allocated
black	2	81	827	27	63	6	136	315	469	74
boy	5	105	806	34	50	0	92	255	632	21
cold	6	160	761	39	33	12	117	370	457	43
dark	2	63	780	122	33	6	124	352	481	37
girl	0	165	771	42	22	12	162	175	576	75
hard	5	239	635	67	54	0	281	141	526	52
heavy	1	35	886	54	24	0	193	349	380	78
high	4	69	844	43	40	5	117	292	555	31
king	2	86	796	50	66	5	245	292	388	70
light	5	194	604	116	81	11	198	236	412	43

tition and reward in the course of hearing and seeing and using words.

If we take any other transcendental system, such as a linking by likeness, or by membership in a class or genus, we find the same result from the association-test material. At first thought, certain connections seem to have strength beyond what frequency and fitness could have created, and in agreement with what the transcendental potency or tendency would produce. But more thorough consideration shows that the transcendent potency would not produce what we find, and that frequency and fitness would produce a great deal of it.

CHAPTER VI

The Influence of the Impressiveness of the First Member of a Related Pair

[The reader will benefit most from what follows if he will first do the following experiment on himself:

Read aloud what is printed on the next three pages at a constant rate (for example, as fast as you can). Then take the test on page 104. In the test some of the first part of a line on pages 100 to 102 will be shown and you will write the rest of the line if you remember what it was, or, if you do not remember, you will write the first word or number that comes to your mind. You need not, however, make any effort to learn any of what is printed on pages 100, 101, and 102. You may be as relaxed and inattentive as you like. Or you may try as hard as you like, provided you try equally hard on all three pages. The most comfortable procedure is to read pages 100, 101, and 102 aloud ás fast as you can with no more attention than is required to be sure that you skip no line.]

* This chapter is a modification of Chapter V of *The Fundamentals of Learning*.

dumb 57
border 98
mitten 42
crude 31
logic 19
dinner 26
marble marble marble 61
remove 87 87 87
spiral 24
insane 84
pavement 48 48 48
293 chart chart chart
vacation 52
427 427 427 bald
borax 32
elm elm elm 46
vomit 21
logic 19
remove 87 87 87
denote denote denote 18
dinner 26
neutral 65 65 65
427 427 427 bald
collect 91
293 chart chart chart
marble marble marble 61
vacation 52
vomit 21
spiral 24
borax 32
596 596 596 hook
pavement 48 48 48
denote denote denote 18
528 nasal nasal nasal
logic 19
insane 84
elm elm elm 46
neutral 65 65 65

collect   91
dinner   26
remove   87   87   87
596   596   596   hook
293   chart   chart   chart
borax   32
pavement   48   48   48
vomit   21
spiral   24
marble   marble   marble   61
insane   84
vacation   52
528   nasal   nasal   nasal
borax   32
neutral   65   65   65
vacation   52
denote   denote   denote   18
vomit   21
marble   marble   marble   61
logic   19
427   427   427   bald
collect   91
dinner   26
spiral   24
elm   elm   elm   46
528   nasal   nasal   nasal
remove   87   87   87
insane   84
neutral   65   65   65
vomit   21
pavement   48   48   48
596   596   596   hook
borax   32
528   nasal   nasal   nasal
293   chart   chart   chart
remove   87   87   87
spiral   24
dinner   26

427   427   427   bald
elm   elm   elm   46
neutral   65   65   65
logic   19
pavement   48   48   48
collect   91
vacation   52
denote   denote   denote   18
spiral   24
marble   marble   marble   61
borax   32
remove   87   87   87
596   596   596   hook
293   chart   chart   chart
vomit   21
collect   91
427   427   427   bald
denote   denote   denote   18
596   596   596   hook
dinner   26
insane   84
elm   elm   elm   46
528   nasal   nasal   nasal
293   chart   chart   chart
denote   denote   denote   18
528   nasal   nasal   nasal
insane   84
neutral   65   65   65
pavement   48   48   48
596   596   596   hook
logic   19
collect   91
427   427   427   bald
elm   elm   elm   46
vacation   52
marble   marble   marble   61
crude   31
dumb   57
mitten   42
border   98

Test

Write after each of these words the number that followed it. If you do not remember that number, write the first number that comes to your mind.

borax

collect

dinner

insane

logic

spiral

vacation

vomit

denote

elm

marble

neutral

pavement

remove

Write after each of these numbers the word that came after it. If you do not remember that word, write the first word that comes to your mind.

293

427

528

596

[If a dozen or more persons do this experiment and pool the results they will probably find that the connections of *dinner, insane, vacation,* and *vomit* with 26, 84, 52 and 21 are stronger than those of *borax, collect, logic,* and *spiral* with 32, 91, 19, and 24. Psychologists would have expected that the more impressive words themselves would be better remembered than the less impressive, but no psychologist had argued that the impressiveness of a word would strengthen its connection with an irrelevant sequent number. That it does so is proved by many extensive experiments described in detail in *The Fundamentals of Learning,* pp. 80–87 and 131–146. It does so even when the impressiveness does not come from interest, but from mere repetition of the first number of a pair, as in *denote denote denote* 18 or *elm elm elm* 46. Why it does is a puzzle.

If enough pairs are used it will also be found that *denote denote denote* 18 and the like gain more strength per occurrence than *pavement* 48 48 48, and the like. This is even more puzzling. Psychologists would have expected the contrary, because *pavement* can be kept in mind while 48 48 48 is being seen or heard. Since the second member is what has to be recalled, it would seem more profitable to have it be impressive than to have the first member be impressive.

When the results of the main experiments described in *The Fundamentals of Learning* are combined, we have the following comparable numbers of correct responses]:

Pairs with impressive words as first members (like *cigar, vacation, devil, insane*) versus pairs with ordinary words as first members, 765 and 330.
Pairs with these impressive words as second members versus pairs with ordinary words as second members, 83 and 66.
Pairs with first members repeated three times versus pairs with slightly more impressive first terms unrepeated: When word is first, 324 and 206. When number is first, 257 and 35.
Pairs with first members repeated three times versus pairs

with second members repeated three times: When word is first, 503 and 308. When number is first, 257 and 50.

I did not solve either puzzle but made some progress, as stated in what follows.

One explanation might be that the impressiveness of the first term caused a general receptivity and alertness which faded out gradually. Another might be that it caused some condition limited to the connection between it and its first sequent.]

. . . As a means of differentiating between them we devised the following experiment: a series of pairs (the *force* series) is made in which a certain neutral pair always follows a pair whose first term is exciting or interesting. If the effect described above is due to a continuance of a general receptivity and alertness, the following pair should benefit somewhat therefrom. If, on the other hand, the effect is due wholly to the tendency of an energetic neural action to connect energetically with its belonging sequent, the following pair should not benefit, since neither of its members "belongs to" the interesting first member.

Experiment 39

. . . The instructions were as follows: "I shall read a long series of pairs of words and numbers like *bread 46, sing 92, ducat 58*. You need not try to remember them, but simply listen with a moderate degree of attention to them. The numbers will all be two-figure numbers, i. e., from 10 to 99."

The pairs were read monotonously at the rate of about 1½ seconds per pair.

[The series, called the *force* series, included 15 pairs occurring from 18 to 30 times and 16 occurring 6 times each used to compare scattered occurrences with sequences; also 12 pairs in which the number was repeated three times; also certain other pairs. But these features of it do not now concern us. What does concern us now is that it included 15 pairs with impressive first terms occurring from 3 to 12 times each and 20 pairs in two sets of 10 chosen for equality in percentage correct in previous experiments, occurring from 6 to 21 times each.]

The *force* series contained ten pairs directly following: *love 47, kiss 63, vomit 21, candy 52, vacation 52, greasy 51, cancer 54, dandruff 86, dinner 26, insane 85, turkey 46, dirty 24, devil 96, blond 68, and beauty 39* in the one case, and ten other pairs directly following: *paste 75, crude 31, neglect 64, plot 54, stand 74,* and other pairs found to be weak or neutral in previous experiments. The pairs so placed were two groups chosen for equality in percentage correct in previous experiments. Thus, *leafy 23,* which had 35 correct in a certain experiment as a result of 21 occurrences, is put after impressive word pairs, and *album 41* which had 36 correct under the same conditions is put after weak word pairs. *Group 53* and *bag 32,* with 18½ and 20 correct in a previous experiment, are the next choices, and so on for twenty word-number pairs, ten being used after impressive word pairs and ten, of equal previous per cents correct, after weak word-pairs.

The potency of an impressive word like *kiss, love, cancer,* or *insane* does not extend beyond the number which follows it and belongs to it.

. . . [Combining the results from this and other experiments, pairs following pairs with impressive first members gave 335 correct responses and pairs following pairs with weak or ordinary first members gave 365 correct responses. These facts rule out one false solution, but the essential puzzle remains as a very important fact for theory and practice.]

CHAPTER VII

Analytic and Selective Processes *

The Partial or Piecemeal Activity of a Situation—One of the commonest ways in which conditions within the man determine variations in his responses to one same external situation is by letting one or another element of the situation be prepotent in [its] effect. Such *partial* or *piecemeal* activity on the part of a situation is, in human learning, the rule. Only rarely does man form connections, as the lower animals so often do, with a situation as a gross total—unanalyzed, undefined, and, as it were, without relief. He does so occasionally, as when a baby, to show off his little trick, requires the same room, the same persons present, the same tone of voice and the like. Save in early infancy and amongst the feeble-minded, however, any situation will most probably act unevenly. Some of its elements will produce only the response of neglect; others will be bound to only a mild awareness of them; others will connect with some energetic response of thought, feeling or action, and become positive determiners of the man's future.

The elements which can thus shake off the rest of a situation and push themselves to the front may be in man far subtler and less conspicuously separate to sense than is the case in animals. Perhaps a majority of man's intellectual habits are bonds leading from objects which a dog or cat would never isolate from the total fields of vision or hearing in which they appear. Very many of his intellectual habits lead from words and word-series, from qualities of shape, number, color, intent, use and the like, and from relations of space, time, like-

---

* From *The Psychology of Learning*, (1913), pp. 27–53, in part.

ness, causation, subordination and the like—elements and relations which would move the lower animals only as the component sounds and relations of a symphony might move a six-year-old destitute of musical capacity and training.

Such prepotent determination of the response by some element or aspect or feature of a gross total situation is both an aid to, and a result of, analytic thinking; it is a main factor in man's success with novel situations; the progress of knowledge is far less a matter of acquaintance with more and more gross situations in the world than it is a matter of insight into the constitution and relations of long familiar ones.

Man's habits of response to the subtler hidden elements, especially the relations which are imbedded or held in solution in gross situations, lead to consequences so different from habits of response to gross total situations or easily abstracted elements of them, that the essential continuity from the latter to the former has been neglected or even denied. Selective thinking, the management of abstractions and responsiveness to relations are thus contrasted too sharply with memory, habit, and association by contiguity. As has been suggested, and as I shall try to prove later, the former also are matters of habit, due to the laws of readiness, exercise and effect, acting under the conditions of human capacity and training, the bonds being in the main with elements or aspects of facts and with symbols therefor.

Assimilation or Response by Analogy—The laws of instinct, exercise, and effect account for man's responses to new as well as to previously experienced situations. To any new situation man responds as he would to some situation like it, or like some element of it. In default of any bonds with it itself, bonds that he has acquired with situations resembling it, act.

To one accustomed to the older restricted view of habits, as a set of hard and fast bonds each between one of a number of events happening to a man and some response peculiar to that event, it may seem especially perverse to treat the connections formed with new experiences under the same principle as is used to explain those very often repeated, very sure, and very invariable bonds, which alone he prefers to call habits. The same matter-of-fact point of view, however, which finds the laws of exercise and effect acting always, though with this or that conditioning set or attitude in the man, and with this or that element only of the total external situation influential, finds them acting also whether the situation has been experienced often, rarely, or never.

If any learned response is made to the situation—if anything is done over and above what man's original nature provides—it is due to the action of use, disuse, satisfaction and discomfort. There is no arbitrary *hocus pocus* whereby man's nature acts in an unpredictable spasm when he is confronted with a new situation. His habits do not then retire to some convenient distance while some new and mysterious entities direct his behavior. On the contrary, nowhere are the bonds acquired with old situations more surely revealed in action than when a new situation appears. The child in the presence of a new object, the savage with a new implement, manufacturers making steam coaches or motor cars, the school boy beginning algebra, the foreigner pronouncing English—in all such cases old acquisitions are, together with original tendencies, the obvious determiners of response, exemplifying the law stated above.

Were the situation so utterly new as to be in no respect like anything responded to before, and also so foreign to man's equipment as neither to arouse an original tendency to response nor to be like anything else that could do so, response by analogy would fail. For all response would fail. Man's nature would simply be forever blind and deaf to the situation in question. With such novel experiences as concern human learning, however, man's responses follow the law that a new situation, *abcdefghij*, is responded to as *abcdelmnop* (or *abcdeqrstu*, or *fghiabyd*, or the like) which has an original or learned response fitted to it, would be.

The law of response by analogy is left somewhat vague by the vagueness of the word "like." "For situation A to *be like* situation B" must be taken to mean, in this case, "for A to arouse in part the same action in the man's neurones as B would." This may or may not be such a likeness as would lead the man to affirm likeness in the course of a logical or scientific consideration of A and B. For example, diamonds and coal-dust are much alike to the scientific consideration of a chemist, but it is unlikely that a person who had never seen a diamond would call it coal-dust as a result of the law of analogy. Science, as we know, is often a struggle to educate the neurones which compose man's brain to act similarly toward objects to which, by instinct and the ordinary training of life, they would respond quite differently, and to act diversely to objects which original nature and everyday experience assimilate.

One obvious set of habits remains to be noted, which often substitute for or alternate with, or combine with, response by analogy. Children acquire early, and we all to some extent maintain, the habits of response to certain novelties in situations by staring in a futile way, saying "I don't know," feeling perplexed and lost, and the like. That is, man responds to the *difference* as well as to the likeness in a situation. By original nature differences of certain sorts provoke staring, curious examination, consternation, and the like; by training differences provoke "I don't know," "What's that?" and the like. The action of any situation, as was noted in the previous volume, is the combined action of its elements. Whatever in it has been bound to certain responses acts, by the laws of habit, to produce the phenomena of assimilation or response by analogy. Its quality or feature of foreignness, bafflingness, true novelty, acts by instinct or habit to produce wonder, confessions of inability, and such questions as have in the past brought satisfying results in similar cases. We might indeed say that these apparent exceptions to response by analogy really illustrate it, the new novelty being treated as was the old novelty like it.

. . . All man's learning, and indeed all his behavior, is *se-lective*. Man does not, in any useful sense of the words, ever absorb, or re-present, or mirror, or copy, a situation uniformly. He never acts like a *tabula rasa* on which external situations write each its entire contribution, or a sensitive plate which duplicates indiscriminately whatever it is exposed to, or a galvanometer which is deflected equally by each and every item of electrical force. Even when he seems most subservient to the external situation—most compelled to take all that it offers and do all that it suggests—it appears that his sense organs have shut off important features of the situation from influencing him in any way comparable to that open to certain others, and that his original or acquired tendencies to neglect and attend have allotted only trivial power to some, and greatly magnified that of others.

All behavior is selective, but certain features of it are so emphatically so that it has been customary to contrast them sharply with the associative behavior which the last chapter described. A notable case is the acceptance of some one very subtle element of an outside event or an inner train of thought to determine further thought and action. In habit-formation, memory, and association by contiguity, the psychologist has declared, the situation determines the responses with little interference from the man, the bond leads from some one concrete thing or event as it is, and the laws of habit explain the process. In the deliberate choice of one or another feature of the present thought to determine thought's future course, on the other hand, the man directs the energy of the situation, the response which the situation itself would be expected to provoke does not come, and new faculties or powers of inference or reasoning have to be invoked.

Such a contrast is almost necessary for a first rough description of learning, and the distinction of such highly selective thinking from the concrete association of totals is useful throughout. We shall see, however, that learning by inference is not opposed to, or independent of, the laws of habit, but really is their necessary result under the conditions imposed by man's nature and training. A closer examination of selective thinking will show that no principles beyond the laws of readiness, exercise, and effect are needed to explain it; that it is only an extreme case of what goes on in associative learning as described under the "piecemeal" activity of situations; and that attributing certain features of learning to mysterious faculties of abstraction or reasoning gives no real help toward understanding or controlling them.

It is true that man's behavior in meeting novel problems goes beyond, or even against, the habits represented by bonds leading from gross total situations and customarily abstracted elements thereof. One of the two reasons therefor, however, is simply that the finer, subtle, preferential bonds with subtler and less often abstracted elements go beyond, and at times against, the grosser and more usual ones. One set is as much due to exercise and effect as the other. The other reason is that in meeting novel problems the mental set or attitude is likely to be one which rejects one after another response as their unfitness to satisfy a certain desideratum appears. What remains as the apparent course of thought includes only a few of the many bonds which did operate, but which, for the most part, were unsatisfying to the ruling attitude or adjustment.

THE SUBTLER FORMS OF ANALYSIS

Stock cases of learning by the separation of a subtle element from the total situations in which it inheres and the acquisition of some constant element of response to it, regardless of its context, are: learning so to handle the number aspect of a collection, the shape of an object, the "place-value" of a figure in integral numbers, the "negativeness" of negative numbers, the pitch of sounds, or the "amount of heat" in an object. The process involved is most easily understood by considering the significance of the means employed to facilitate it.

The first of these is having the learner respond to the total situations containing the element in question with the attitude of piecemeal examination, and with attentiveness to one element after another, especially to so near an approximation to the element in question as he can already select for attentive examination. This attentiveness to one element after another serves to emphasize whatever appropriate minor bonds from the element in question the learner already possesses. Thus, in teaching children to respond to the "fiveness" of various collections, we show five boys or five girls or five pencils, and say, "See how many boys are standing up. Is Jack the only boy that is standing here? Are there more than two boys standing? Name the boys while I point at them and count them. (Jack) is one, and (Fred) is one more, and (Henry) is one more. Jack and Fred make (two) boys. Jack and Fred and Henry make (three) boys." (And so on with the attentive counting.) The mental set or attitude is directed toward favoring the partial and predominant activity of "how-many-ness" as far as may be; and the useful bonds that the "fiveness," the "one and one and one and one and one-ness" already have, are emphasized as far as may be.

The second of the means used to facilitate analysis is having the learner respond to many situations each containing the element in question (call it A), but with varying concomitants (call these V.C.) his response being so directed as, so far as may be, to separate each total response into an element bound to the A and an element bound to the V.C.

Thus the child is led to associate the responses—"Five boys," "Five girls," "Five pencils," "Five inches," "Five feet," "Five books," "He walked five steps," "I hit my desk five times," and the like—each with its appropriate situation. The "Five" element of the response is thus bound over and over again to the "fiveness" element of the situation, the mental set being "How many?," but is bound only once to any one of the concomitants. These concomitants are also such as have preferred minor bonds of their own (the sight of a row of boys *per se* tends strongly to call up the "Boys" element of the response). The other elements of the responses (boys, girls, pencils, and so on) have each only a slight connection with the "fiveness" element of the situations. These slight connections also in large part [1] counteract each other, leaving the field clear for whatever uninhibited bond the "fiveness" has.

The third means used to facilitate analysis is having the learner respond to situations which, pair by pair, present the element in a certain context and present that same context with *the opposite of the element in question,* or with something at least very unlike the element. Thus, a child who is being taught to respond to "one fifth" is not only led to respond to "one fifth of a cake," "one fifth of a pie," "one fifth of an apple," "one fifth of ten inches," "one fifth of an army of twenty soldiers," and the like; he is also led to respond to each of these *in contrast with* "five cakes," "five pies," "five apples," "five times ten inches," "five armies of twenty soldiers." Similarly the "place values" of tenths, hundredths, and the rest are taught by contrast with the tens, hundreds, and thousands.

These means utilize the laws of connection-forming to disengage a response-element from gross total responses and attach it to some situation-element. The forces of use, disuse, satisfaction and discomfort are so manoeuvred that an element which never exists by itself in nature can influence man almost as if it did so exist, bonds being formed with it that act almost or quite irrespective of the gross total situation in which it inheres. What happens can be most conveniently put in a general statement by using symbols.

Denote by a b, a g, a l, a q, a v, and a β certain situations alike in the element a and different in all else. Suppose that, by original nature or training, a child responds to these situations respectively by $r_1 r_2$, $r_1 r_7$, $r_1 r_{12}$, $r_1 r_{17}$, $r_1 r_{22}$, and $r_1 r_{27}$. Suppose that man's neurones are capable of such action that $r_1, r_2, r_7, r_{12}, r_{17}, r_{22}$ and r_{27}, can each be made singly.

If now the situations, a b, a g, a l, etc., are responded to (each once), the result by the law of exercise will be to strengthen bonds as shown in Scheme A, the situation-elements noted in the top line of the table being bound to each of the

---

[1] They may, of course, also result in a fusion or an alternation of the responses, but only rarely.

response-elements noted at the left side of the table as noted by the numbers entered in the body of the table.

SCHEME A

	a	b	g	l	q	v	β
r_1	6						
r_2	1	1					
r_7	1		1				
r_{12}	1			1			
r_{17}	1				1		
r_{22}	1					1	
r_{27}	1						1

The bond from a to r_1, has had six times as much exercise as the bond from a to r_2, or from a to r_7, and so on. In any new gross situation, a θ, a will be more predominant in determining response than it would otherwise have been; and r_1 will be more likely to be made than r_2, r_7, r_{12}, and so on, the other previous associates in the response to a situation containing a.

Suppose further that g is opposite to, or notably unlike, b; that q is opposite to or notably unlike l; and that β is notably unlike v. Let "opposite to" and "unlike" have the meaning that the response elements r_2 and r_7, r_{12} and r_{17}, r_{22} and r_{27} are, in the case of each pair, *in no respect identical, and in large measure incapable of being made by the same organism at the same time.* Express this fact by replacing r_7 by r_{not2} r_{17} by r_{not12}, and r_{27} by r_{not22}. Then, if the situations, a b, a g, a l, a q, and so on, are responded to each once, the result by the law of exercise will be to strengthen bonds as shown in Scheme B below, whose plan is the same as that of Scheme A.

The bond from a to r_1 has again had six times as much exercise as the bond from a to r_2, or from a to r_7, and so on. The bonds from a to r_2 and to r_{not2} tend to counterbalance each

SCHEME B

	a	b	g(opp. of b)	1	q(opp of 1)	v	β(opp. of v)
r_1	6						
r_{not1}							
r_2	1	1					
r_{not2}	1		1				
r_{12}	1			1			
r_{not12}	1				1		
r_{22}	1					1	
r_{not22}	1						1

other in the sense that the tendency is for neither r_2 nor r_{not2} to occur,[2] the field being left free for whatever unimpeded tendency the element a possesses. Similarly for the effect of the a-r_{12} and a-r_{not12} bonds.

Denote by "opp. of a" an element which is the opposite of, or at least very unlike, a. Let "opposite to" and "unlike" have as before the meaning that the original or acquired responses to "opp. of a" have few or no elements in common with the responses to a, and in large measure cannot be made by the same organism at the same time as the response to a. Then, if the situations, a b, (opp. of a) b, a g, (opp. of a) g, a l, (opp. of a) l, etc., are responded to each once, the result by the law of exercise will be to strengthen bonds as shown in Scheme C.

The element a is thus made to connect six times with r_1 and once with each element of the counteracting pairs, r_2 and r_{not2}, r_{12} and r_{not12}, r_{22} and r_{not22}. The element opp. of a is made to connect with r_{not1} six times, and with r_2, r_{not2}, etc. each once. b, g, l, q, v and β are made to connect with the counteracting

---

[2] They can not occur together. They may occasionally appear in alternation; or the one of them which by casual physiological happenings has an advantage may appear. But the effect of the exercise of the bonds leading from the situations, a b, a g, etc., is to make a call up neither r_2 nor r_7, neither r_{12} nor r_{17}, since another unimpeded bond and response is at hand.

Scheme C

	a	(opp. of a)	b	g(opp. of b)	l	q(opp. of l)	v	β (opp. of v)
r_1	6		1	1	1	1	1	1
r_{not1}		6	1	1	1	1	1	1
r_2	1	1	2					
r_{not2}	1	1		2				
r_{12}	1	1			2			
r_{not12}	1	1				2		
r_{22}	1	1					2	
r_{not22}	1	1						2

r_1 and r_{not1}, each equally often. Thus, by the law of exercise, r_1 is being connected with a; the bonds from a to anything else are being counteracted; and the slight connections from b, g, l, etc. to r_1 are being counteracted. The element a becomes predominant in situations containing it; and its bond toward r_1 becomes relatively enormously strengthened and freed from competition. . . .

The process of learning to respond to the difference of pitch of tones from whatever instrument, to the "square-root-ness" of whatever number, to triangularity in whatever size or combination of lines, to equality of whatever pairs, or to honesty in whatever person and instance, is thus a consequence of associative learning, requiring no other forces than those of use, disuse, satisfaction, and discomfort. What happens in such cases is that the response, by being connected with many situations alike in the presence of the element in question and different in other respects, is bound firmly to that element and loosely to each of its concomitants. Conversely any element is bound firmly to any one response that is made to all situations containing it and very, very loosely to each of those responses that are made to only a few of the situations containing it. The element of triangularity, for example, is bound firmly to the response of saying or thinking "triangle" but only very loosely to the response of saying or thinking white, red, blue, large, small, iron, steel, wood, paper and the like. A situation thus acquires bonds not only with some response to it as a gross total, but also with responses to each of its elements that has appeared in any other gross totals. Appropriate response to an element regardless of its concomitants is a necessary consequence of the laws of exercise and effect if an animal learns to make that response to the gross total situations that contain the element and not to make it to those that do not. Such prepotent determination of the response by one or another element of the situation is no transcendental mystery, but, given the circumstances, a general rule of all learning. . . .

Learning by analysis does not often proceed in the carefully organized way represented by the most ingenious marshalling of comparing and contrasting activities. The associations with gross totals, whereby in the end an element is elevated to independent power to determine response, may come in a haphazard order over a long interval of time. Thus a gifted three-year-old boy will have the response element of "saying or thinking *two*," bound to the "two-ness" element of very many situations in connection with the "how-many" mental set; and he will have made this analysis without any formal, systematic training. An imperfect and inadequate analysis already made is indeed usually the starting point for whatever systematic abstraction the schools direct. Thus, the kindergarten exercises in analyzing out number, color, size and shape commonly assume that "one-ness" *versus* "more-than-one-ness," black and white, big and little, round and not round are, at least vaguely, active as elements responded to in some independence of their contexts. Moreover, the tests of actual trial and success in further undirected exercises usually coöperate to confirm and extend and refine what the systematic drills have given. Thus the ordinary child in school is left by the drills on decimal notation with only imperfect power of response to the "place-values." He continues to learn to respond properly to them by finding that $4 \times 40 = 160$, $4 \times 400 = 1600$, $800 - 80 = 720$, $800 - 8 = 792$, $800 - 800$

$= 0, 42 \times 48 = 2116, 24 \times 48 = 1152$, and the like, are satisfying; while $4 \times 40 = 16, 24 \times 48 = 832, 800 - 8 = 0$, and the like, are not. The process of analysis is the same in such casual, unsystematized formation of connections with elements as in the deliberately managed, piecemeal inspection, comparison and contrast described above.

THE HIGHER FORMS OF SELECTION

In human thought and action a situation often provokes responses which have not been bound to it by original tendencies, use or satisfaction. Such behavior, apparently in advance of, or even in opposition to, instinct and habit, appears in adaptive responses to novel data, in association by similarity, and in the determination of behavior by its aim rather than its antecedents which is commonly held to distinguish purposive thinking and action from "mere association and habit."

Successful responses to novel data, association by similarity and purposive behavior are, however, in only apparent opposition to the fundamental laws of associative learning. Really they are beautiful examples of it.

Man's successful responses to novel data—as when he argues that the diagonal on a right triangle of 796.278 mm. base and 137.294 mm. altitude will be 808.022 mm., or that Mary Jones, born this morning, will sometime die—are due to habits, notably the habits of response to certain elements or features, under the laws of piecemeal activity and assimilation.

Nothing looks less like the mysterious operations of a faculty of reasoning transcending the laws of connection-forming, than the behavior of men in response to novel situations. Let children who have hitherto confronted only such arithmetical tasks, in addition and subtraction with one- and two-place numbers and multiplication with one-place numbers, as those exemplified in the first line below, be told to do the examples shown in the second line.

Add	Add	Add	Subt.	Subt.	Multiply	Multiply	Multiply
8	37	35	8	37	8	9	6
5	24	68	5	24	5	7	3
—	—	23	—	—	—	—	—
		19					
		—					

Multiply	Multiply	Multiply
32	43	34
23	22	26
—	—	—

They will add them, or subtract the lower from the upper number, or multiply 3×2 and 2×3, etc., getting 66, 86, and 624, or respond to the element of "Multiply" attached to the two-place numbers by "I can't" or "I don't know what to do," or the like, for the reasons stated on page 110; or, if one is a child of great ability, he may consider the "Multiply" element and the bigness of the numbers, be reminded by these two aspects of the situation of the fact that "$\frac{9}{9}$ multiply" gave only 81, and that "$\frac{10}{10}$ multiply" gave only 100, or the like; and so may report an intelligent and justified "I can't," or reject the plan of 3×2 and 2×3, with 66, 86 and 624 for answers, as unsatisfactory. What the children will do will, in every case, be a product of the elements in the situation that are potent with them, the responses which these evoke, and the further associates which these responses in turn evoke. If the child were one of sufficient genius, he might infer the procedure to be followed as a result of his knowledge of the principles of decimal notation and the meaning of "Multiply," responding correctly to the "place-value" element of each digit and adding his 6 tens and 9 tens, 20 twos and 3 thirties; but if he did thus invent the shorthand addition of a collection of twenty-three collections, each of 32 units, he would still do it by the operation of bonds, subtle but real.

It has long been apparent that man's *erroneous* inferences —his *unsuccessful* responses to novel situations—are due to the action of misleading connections and analogies to which he is led by the laws of habit. It is also the fact, though this is not so apparent, that his *successful* responses are due to fruitful connections and analogies to which he is led by the same laws. It is not a difference in the laws at work, but in the nature of the habits that produce the variations and select from them for the further guidance of thought. The insights of a gifted thinker seem marvellous to us because the subtle elements which are prepotent for his thought elude us; but in the same way our insights into the operations of new machines, new chemical compounds, or new electrical apparatus would seem marvellous to a savage to whom levers, screws, reducing gears, oxygen, hydrogen, electrical energy and electric potential were elements utterly concealed in the gross complexes before him. We should succeed with these novel situations as the savage could not, because we should accentuate different elements, and these elements would have bound to them different associates.

Association by similarity is, as James showed long ago, simply the tendency of an element to provoke the responses which have been bound to it. *Abcde* leads to *awxyz* because *a* has been bound to *wxyz* by original nature, exercise or effect. . . .

Purposive behavior is the most important case of the influence of the attitude or set or adjustment of an organism in determining (1) which bonds shall act, and (2) which results shall satisfy.

James early described the former fact, showing that the mechanism of habit can give the directedness or purposefulness in thought's products, provided that mechanism includes something paralleling the problem, the aim, or need, in question. The nature of this something he indicated in the terms common to the brain physiology of his time of writing. . . .

The second fact, that the set or attitude of the man helps to determine which bonds shall satisfy, and which shall annoy, has commonly been somewhat obscured by vague assertions that the selection and retention is of what is "in point," or is "the right one," or is "appropriate," or the like. It is thus asserted, or at least hinted, that "the will," "the voluntary attention," "the consciousness of the problem" and other such entities are endowed with magic power to decide what is the "right" or "useful" bond and to kill off the others.

The facts are that in purposive thinking and action, as everywhere else, bonds are selected and retained by the satisfyingness . . . which they produce; and that the potency of the man's set or attitude to make this satisfy and that annoy . . . is in every way as important as its potency to set certain conduction-units in actual operation. Whatever else it be, purposive thought or action is a series of varied reactions or "multiple response." Point by point in the series, that response is selected for survival and predominant determination of future response which relieves annoyances or satisfies cravings which rule the thinker. In intellectual matters, and in the activities of man that are only indirectly connected with the common instinctive wants, these annoyances and satisfactions and their effect on learning may be, and indeed usually have been, overlooked because they lack intensity of effect and uniformity of attachment. But they should not be. The power that moves the man of science to solve problems correctly is the same as moves him to eat, sleep, rest, and play. The efficient thinker is not only more fertile in ideas and more often productive of the "right" ideas than the incompetent is; he also is more satisfied by them when he gets them, and more rebellious against the futile and misleading ones. "We trust to the laws of cerebral nature to present us spontaneously with the appropriate idea," and also *to prefer that idea to others.*

CHAPTER VIII

The Psychology of Thinking in the Case of Reading *

IF a person is presented with a paragraph to read and questions about it, his responses provide useful material for studying some of the facts and laws of thinking. Consider, for example, the following task and the following responses made to the first question by pupils of grades 5 and 6:

I

Read this and then write the answers to 1, 2, 3, 4, and 5. Read it again as often as you need to.

Nearly fifteen thousand of the city's workers joined in the parade on September seventh, and passed before two hundred thousand cheering spectators. There were workers of both sexes in the parade, though the men far out-numbered the women.

1. What is said about the number of persons who marched in the parade?

. . . .

2. Which sex was in the majority?

. . . .

3. What did the people who looked at the parade do when it passed by?

. . . .

4. How many people saw the parade?

. . . .

5. On what date did the event described in the paragraph occur?

. . . .

Two hundred people	Ninety thousand
Three thousand	Twenty-five thousand
Thousand	About thirty-five thousand
Eighteen thousand	Nearly twenty thousand
Two thousand	More than ten thousand
Five thousand	There were about 25000

* From *The Psychological Review*, Vol. 24, (May, 1917), pp. 220–234.

200,000
It was 200,000
A lot of people
Congregation
There were a great lot of men
The men outnumbered the women
The men were more than the women
There were more men
About two thousand
Maybe No. 12
About 2700
Two hundred thousand spectators workers in the parade
Two hundred thousand spectators
Two hundred cheering
Nearly sixteen thousand
Nearly 115,000 on Sept. of people
Hundred thousand spectators
It is said about the number or group of people
It is said that they are great
A very great deal
They passed nearly 5000
Passed before two hundred spectators
They marched before cheering spectators
Three thousand cheering them
People of both sexes cheering them
They are cheered
They outnumber the women
There the par on number the
The men were far ahead of the women
Men and women
Citizens
They were workers
There were workers of both sexes
Workmen in the parade
Of all the working men

That the city workers joined the parade
Workers joined the parade
That they rejoin in the parade
They were joined
A number of workers joined the parade
Joined the parade
Workers join
They joined
They pass two hundred spectators
Before the spectators
Passed before two hundred thousand spectators
They two hundred thousand cheering spectators
Passed before 200000 and 15000
Parade before two hundred spectators
Parade spectators
They marched nice
They marched very nice
They kept in step
They marched very straight
They did good or bad
They look so nice
They clap their hands when they see the American flag
They keep their step and many others
There character
Honorable and good
The people said the parade large
Most of them were old
They are soldiers and marched
They say halt
The captain says march
There was a lot of floats
The people are killed by the war
The meddles
September seventh
Irish

The variety of responses to this one fairly unambiguous question is a challenge. There is a challenge also in the relative frequency of the different responses.

I shall report here some general facts which are displayed

by some hundreds of responses to each of a dozen or more sets of questions upon a paragraph which I have examined. The first is that:

When a question on a paragraph is answered, any one word may be over-potent in determining the response. As a limit we have the case where a word produces a response due to that word alone irrespective of all else in the situation. Or, more generally, any element in a situation may be over-potent to any degree.

The evidence supporting this claim is the existence of answers or elements in answers which could come as probable results of over-potent action of single words, but whose occurrence otherwise is highly improbable. For example, in the case of the words of the paragraph such influence is seen of:

thousand, in this answer to 3: "The people cheered thousands."
city, in this answer to 2: "City workers."
workers, in these answers to 2: "Workers," "Workers of sex";
    and in this answer to 3: "There were workers."

In what follows a number in parentheses preceding a response designates the question as an answer to which the response was given.

joined, in (1) "They joined," (1) "They were joined," (3) "They joined in," (3) "They were joined in the parade," (3) "They cheered then joined in."
parade, in (2) "In the parade," (2) "Both in parade," (2) "Sexes in the parade."
September, in (2) "There were workers of the September."
seventh, in (2) "Seventh," (3) "September seventh," (3) "Seventh Avenue."

Lest the bizarre nature of some of these errors lead the reader to fancy that they are fragments, or answers misplaced a line too high or too low, I may note here that every quotation that has been or will be given in this article is, unless specially noted at the time, a complete answer, as given by some pupils, and undoubtedly intended for the question whose number it bears. Quotations are exact except that the first word is capitalized whether or not this was done by the pupil.

passed, in (3) "Two hundred thousand cheering spectators passed."
spectators, in (1) "Parade spectators," (1) "Cheering spectators," (1) "Two hundred thousand spectators workers in the parade," (2) "Spectators and working," (3) "The people who looked cheered the spectators," (3) "The people looked and cheered the spectators," (2) "The sex spectators."
cheering, in (2) "Cheering."
both, in (2) "There were both workers," (3) "There were workers in both spectators."
sexes, in (3) "Six in the parade," (3) "Sixes," (3) "Cheered the sex in the parade."
though, in (2) "Though the men marched in the parade," (2) "Though the men far outjoined parade."
men, in (3) "They cheered the men in the parade."
far, in (2) "Far out women."
out, in (3) They counted out how many women."
numbered, in (3) "The men numbered women," (3) "Numbered the women," (3) "They numbered the people."
out-numbered, in (2) "Sex out numbered of women," (2) "Outnumbered."
women, in (2) "Sexes of women," (2) "Men and women," (3) "The women."

Any phrase or other part of a sentence tends in a similar manner to produce a response due to that phrase *per se.*

Thus, *fifteen thousand* appears as an answer to questions 2, 3 and 4 and (in "Passed before 200,000 and 15,000") as an answer to question 1. The following are responses probably explainable by the independent action of phrases or other groups of words:

the city's workers, (2) "City workers."
joined the parade, (1) "Joined the parade," and (2) "They joined the parade."
September seventh, (1) "September seventh."
passed before two hundred, (3) "Passed before two hundred."
two hundred, (1) "Passed before 200 spectators," (2) "Two hundred spectators," and (4) "Two hundred."
hundred thousand, (4) "About a hundred thousand."
two thousand, (1) "Two thousand," and (4) "Two Thousand."
two hundred thousand, (1) "Two hundred thousand," (2) "Two hundred thousand," and (3) "Two hundred thousand."
There were workers, (2) "There were workers."
of both sexes, (1) "People of both sexes cheering them," and (5) "Sept. 7th both sexes."
There were workers of both sexes, (1) "There were workers of both sexes," and (3) "There were workers of both sexes in the parade."

though the men, (3) "Though the men far out joined parade," and (5) "Thought the man fat out."

outnumbered the men, (1) "They outnumbered the women," and (2) "Sex outnumbered of women." . . .

In the illustrations given so far the action of the element has been accompanied usually by some vague action of the situation as a whole, but cases may be found where this reduces to about as near zero as is possible, provided the pupil writes any answer whatever.

Consider, for example, the following responses to questions 1, 2, and 5 on paragraph I.

Question 1

"Most of them were old," which shows almost no effect of anything save the *persons.*

"There were a lot of floats," which shows almost no influence save of *parade.*

"Irish," which could fit any paragraph or any question provided *parade* or *persons* or both occurred therein, almost as well as it fits this.

Question 2

"The chief commander of all" and "Captain and lieutenant" seem to show no influence save the *major* of majority plus a faint effect of *parade.*

Question 5

"1492" and "1776" seems the products of *date* in total neglect of all else in the question and paragraph.

[One of the paragraphs that was used in my experiments read:

You need a coal range in winter for kitchen warmth and for continuous hot water supply, but in summer when you want a cool kitchen and less hot water, a gas range is better. The XYZ ovens are safe. In the end ovens there is an extra set of burners for broiling.

The XYZ was used instead of the maker's name to avoid propaganda for any private business. I predict that no matter what question is asked about this paragraph some pupil in grade 5 or 6 will be misled by over-potency of even this queer triad of letters. Among a few hundred such children I got the following to four of my six questions:

1. *What two varieties of stoves does the paragraph mention?*
   "XYZ," "Gas range and XYZ," "XYZ ovens and end ovens."
2. *What is needed to provide a supply of hot water all day long?*
   "The XYZ ovens are safe."
3. *For what purpose is the extra set of burners?*
   "The XYZ ovens."
4. *In what part of the stove are they situated?*
   "The XYZ oven side."]

Some of the cases above, if taken alone, are perhaps as explainable by other causes as by the tendency of each word to act irrespective of the total of which it is an element, but no one, I think, will assume that the collection [as a whole] can be well explained save by supposing that the single words do have that tendency. We must then think of the pupil who examines the paragraph and the questions as beset by a tendency to answer each question by each word in the paragraph and have each word in the questions evoke a response that is bound to it alone. Most of these tendencies are of so nearly zero strength that they almost never compete successfully with other tendencies: and most of the resulting thoughts are so absurd that if they come to mind they are promptly dismissed. But a sound theory must accept their existence. . . .

Just as any element of the situation may be, relatively to others, far too potent in determining the response, so also it may be not nearly potent enough. Calling Pa the potency of element a and Pb the potency of element b, Pa/Pb may vary between 0 and ∞ as limits.

The following are some cases of under-potency in the case of paragraph I, [which I repeat here for the reader's convenience]:

Nearly fifteen thousand of the city's workers joined in the parade on September seventh, and passed before two hundred thousand cheering spectators. There were workers of both sexes in the parade, though the men far outnumbered the women.

Question 1. [What is said about the number of persons who marched in the parade?]

nearly—(Failure to include this in the response to 1 is of course very, very common.)

fifteen—"Thousand"

what is said about the—"Honorable and good," "They march very nice," "They marched very straight," "They did good or bad," and many similar responses.

number of persons—"They were workers," "Men and women," "That they rejoin in the parade," "Passed before cheering spectators."

who marched in the parade—The many responses of "200000," "They cheered them," and so on.

All of question 1 except *parade* is under-potent—"There were a lot of floats."

Question 2. [Which sex was in the majority?]

the "out" of outnumbered—"A number of women."

which—"Both sexes was in the parade." "There were both sexes there," "Workers of both sexes," "Men and Women," "Two Sexes," "Two of them."

sex—"City workers," "City workers of N.Y.," "The chief commander of all," "Working," "The front ones," "Spectators," "Cheering," "Fifteen thousand."

in the majority—"Women," "Sex outnumbered of women."

which . . . was in the majority—"The sex spectators," "Sexes," "In the parade," "Sexes in the parade," "There were men of other sex in the parade."

Question 3. [What did the people who looked at the parade do when it passed by?]

what did the . . . do—"They were cheered by the people," "Two hundred."

people—"Tip his hat."

people who looked at—"Passed before two hundred," "Passed before a number of cheering spectators."

when it passed by—"Two hundred thousand cheering spectators passed."

it—"They saluted them," "They cheered them."

cheering—"Inspected the parade," "They were glad to see it," "They talked about it" (and many others).

All save *parade* underpotent—"September seventh," "Seventh Avenue."

Question 4. [How many people saw the parade?]

saw the parade—"The men outnumbered the women," "Far outnumbered."

two—"About 100000," "One hundred thousand," "Three hundred thousand."

hundred—"Two thousand."

thousand—"Two hundred."

two hundred (thousand)—"Fifteen thousand," "Nearly fifteen thousand," "Over 25000," "Over five hundred," "About 10000," "About 5000," "About 1000."

> *Question* 5. [On what date did the event
> described in the paragraph occur?]

what date—"There were workers of both sexes in the parade," "Thought the man fat out," "Described," "Sexes of the parade," "The parade," "And outnumbered women."

event described in paragraph—"March 4, 1915," "March 17," "April 23, 1903," "November 4," "December 4," "On Friday," "March 17," "March 18," "St. Patrick's day," "On the twenty-second of February," "St. Pattac," "1492," "1776," "1820." . . .

Elements may act in substantially correct potency but out of their proper relations. Responses to arithmetical problems will illustrate this richly. In reading we have such cases as "A cool kitchen is used for a gas range," in response to *What effect has the use of a gas range instead of a coal range upon the temperature of the kitchen?*

The connections leading from any element or group of elements may be wrong whether the element is under-potent, of correct potency, or over-potent. They may be *wrong in toto* in the sense of leading to unserviceable responses to that element for any purpose, or *wrong for any defined set of purposes,* or *wrong for the test's purpose* in the sense of leading to responses unserviceable for the particular need or problem. . . .

To the question, on paragraph *T*, *What do you think "heaven's azure" means?* we find the following answers from college freshmen, in whom right bonds leading from *azure* are either absent or so weak as to be suppressed by the wrong (for the purpose) bonds leading from *heaven* or from the general sense of glorified moralizing which the passage establishes. Only about one college freshman in three thinks of so plain a thing as *the blue sky!*

T.

But it is to you, ye Workers, who do already work, and are as grown men, noble and honorable in a sort, that the whole world calls for new work and nobleness. Subdue mutiny, discord, widespread despair, by manfulness, justice, mercy and wisdom. Chaos is dark, deep as Hell; let light be, and there is instead a green flowery world. Oh, it is great, and there is no other greatness. To make some nook of God's creation a little fruitfuller, better, more worthy of God; to make some human hearts a little wiser, manfuller, happier, more blessed, less accursed! It is work for a God. Sooty Hell of mutiny and savagery and despair can, by man's energy, be made a kind of Heaven; cleared of its soot, of its mutiny, of its need to mutiny; the everlasting arch of Heaven's azure overspanning it too, and its cunning mechanisms and tall chimney-steeples, as a birth of Heaven; God and all men looking on it well pleased.

"The everlasting rainbow,"
"Peace,"
"Peace, universal,"
"Peace progress and justice one to another,"
"Peace and the world purged of strife,"
"Peace and happiness love and manliness,"
"The peace and love of man's fellow men,"
"The peacefulness one sees in a God-fearing community,"
"Harmony in life,"
"The millenium,"
"Appreciation of the beauty of nature,"
"Wisdom mercy,"
"Happiness,"
"God's love,"
"God's influence,"
"God's approval of work,"
"God's creation,"
"A world in which +," (+here and later means that more was contained in the response; but nothing correct),
"A place where men +,"
"The light of the world,"
"The light of a new method—of freedom and happiness,"
"Man's outlook on life,"
"High ideal +,"
"The clearing of mutiny,"
"Perfect condition of things with every one happy and working for the best,"
"The work that man has accomplished,"
"Eternity,"
"Enjoyment,"
"The happiness and contentment that comes + "
"Eternal life,"
"Eternal blessing,"
"Love your neighbor as yourself + "
"God is love. Do unto others as ye would have others do unto you."

We must then think of a pupil who answers the questions concerning a paragraph as beset by tendencies of each word and word group in the question to assume undue potency, to become dislocated from its proper relations, and to call up its past accompaniments and sequents. For him to answer rightly means that an elaborate hierarchy of bonds is active and that an intricate set of forces maintains a balance of power. One may become directly aware of at least a part of this complex coördination and subordination of tendencies if he will note just what it implies to respond correctly to this question on paragraph *T: What does the author refer to as a "Sooty Hell of mutiny and savagery and despair"?* One may infer it less directly but more adequately by surveying the hundreds of different tendencies to respond which a paragraph and question evokes in a thousand pupils and realizing that almost or quite all of the tendencies were present as truly in any one successful pupil, but were prevented from determining final response by some organization within themselves or by some guiding tendencies from without.

Sometimes the correct balance or organization reduces to the simple case of letting one element be as potent as it may and reducing the potency of all other elements to negligible amounts. We then have the case of reasoning of which James has given the classic description. But the task of thought is, it seems, not usually to choose only one element in the situation for potency, or to accept one only of the facts evoked by that element. Usually there are many elements to be let work together and many evoked facts to be used for the purpose at hand. In our illustration, the "workers," "sooty," "mechanisms," and "tall chimney" all need to be given potency to secure the response of "a region of factories," "a manufacturing community," "a factory town disturbed by labor troubles," or the like, and the "God," "chaos," "Hell" and "Heaven" of Carlyle's grandiloquence all need to be somewhat tempered in their tendencies to call up the world, human nature, or other things of vast scope and great moral importance.

Elaborate as are the compositions of forces which give thought its final motion and direction, the forces themselves are of simple nature, being elements in situations and connections leading from these elements to responses which use and (in my opinion) satisfying accompaniments have yoked to each element.

Three simple mechanisms—under-potency and over-potency of elements, dislocation or disrelation of elements, and wrongness or inadequacy of connections—seem to be all that are needed to explain errors in thinking. Conversely, proper balance and organization of elements and right bonds therewith seem to explain correct thinking, no matter how elaborate or subtle. Thinking and reasoning do not seem to be in any useful sense opposites of automatism, custom, or habit, but simply the action of habits in cases where the elements of the situation compete and coöperate notably.

It is of course the case that, along with the balanced action of elements, there goes an inspection and validation of them and the ideas or acts they evoke, whereby each succeeding situation is often amended by increasing or reducing the potency of certain of its elements, and whereby certain futile ideas may be cast away entirely. These welcomings and rejectings, retainings and letting go, are however themselves nothing more than situation-response bonds, where the response is attending to or turning from, cherishing, repeating, saying *no* or *yes* to, or the like. It is also the case that the "set" or adjustment of the organism plays a more striking rôle in reasoning than it does in mere day-dreaming or routine habit-action, but not a different sort of a rôle.

I conclude therefore that the general laws of human behavior which explain why a pupil puts his clothes on or off and eats or leaves uneaten his breakfast explain why he succeeds or fails in making geometrical demonstrations or scientific researches, and that there exists no fundamental physiological contrast between fixed habits and reasoning.

CHAPTER IX

Ideo-Motor Action *

THE theory of ideo-motor action has been for a generation one of the stock "laws" of orthodox psychology. It is taught as almost axiomatic in standard treatises—is made the explanatory principle for phenomena of suggestion, hypnotism, obsessions and the like—and is used as the basis for recommended practices in education, psychiatry, religion—even in salesmanship and advertising.

In spite of contrary evidence brought forward by Kirkpatrick, Woodworth, Burnett, and others, probably nine out of ten of the members of this association believe, or think that they believe, in one or another form of this doctrine that an idea tends to produce the act which it represents or resembles or is "an idea of," or "has as its object."

Against this most respectable doctrine I early rebelled, and I somewhat greedily seize this occasion,[1] which requires that in courtesy you listen to me for an hour, to justify this apostasy and convert you also, if I can, to the view that the idea of a movement, or of any other response whatsoever, is, in and of itself, utterly impotent to produce it.

The course of the argument will be plainer if I state first what potency I do attach to ideas of movements, or of the resident and remote sensations produced by movements, or of other results of movements; or to any image or other inner state of awareness which represents, or means, or is like, or has as its object, a movement or act or, for that matter, anything else. Any such mental state has, in my opinion, no

* *Psychological Review*, Vol. 20, (March, 1913), pp. 91–105.
[1] Presidential address before the American Psychological Association.

dynamic potency save that its physiological parallel will evoke whatever response is bound to it or to some part of it by inherited connections, or by the law of habit—including in the latter the power of satisfying states of affairs to strengthen whatever connections they accompany or closely follow. I admit a slight tendency for a mental state which is produced immediately before and along with a movement—in one pulse of cerebral activity, as it were—to reinstate the movement by reinstating that total pulse of activity. The connections formed by the laws of habit work mainly forward, but slightly sidewise and even, indirectly, backward. The gist of my contention is that any idea or other situation tends to produce the response which heredity has connected with it or which has gone with it or some part of it with a satisfying or indifferent resulting state of affairs. An idea has no power to produce an act save the power of physiological connections born in man, or bred in him as the consequence of use, disuse, satisfaction and discomfort.

The doctrine of ideo-motor action, however stated, means that certain ideas or images have some further power than this—that between them and the responses which they represent, or have as their objects, or are "ideas of," or are similar to, some effective bond creates itself beyond what the connections made in the person's past can explain. Its classic statement by James reads, as you all know, "We may then lay it down for certain that every representation of a movement awakens in some degree the actual movement which is its object; and awakens it in maximum degree whenever it is not kept from so doing by an antagonistic representation present simultaneously to the mind."

Wundt asserts that the mere apperception of an image of a movement is followed by the movement unless some contrary force acts, and that in children and primitive men the presence of a vivid idea of a movement of their own bodies does therefore cause the movement to take place.

William McDougall writes to the same effect that: "In the special case in which the object to which we direct our attention by a volitional effort is a bodily movement, the movement follows immediately upon the idea, in virtue of that mysterious connection between them of which we know almost nothing beyond the fact that it obtains," and elsewhere, "the representation of a movement of one's own body . . . like all motor representations tends to realize itself immediately in movement."

Two intelligible meanings can be attached to the phrases —"the representation of a certain movement by an idea," an idea having a certain movement "as its object," an idea being "of a certain movement," "motor representation," and the like. The first is that the idea in question *is like* the movement— is to some extent a copy or correspondent of it in much the same way that the mental image of a square inch of red is like a square inch of red. The second is that the idea *means* the movement in much the same way that the thought of the words "square inch of red" means such a square. For the sake of clearness I shall in general restrict argument to the first of these meanings of the doctrine, it being an easy task to disprove it in the second sense once it has been disproved in the first.

That the kind of an idea which is supposed by the ideo-motor theory to be able by some "mysterious connection" to produce a movement is the idea which *is like* the movement appears more clearly in Miss Washburn's statement: "A movement idea is the revival, through central excitation, of the sensations, visual, tactile, kinesthetic, originally produced by the performance of the movement itself. And when such an idea is attended to, when, in popular language, we think hard enough of how the movement would 'feel' and look if it were performed, then, so close is the connection between sensory and motor processes, the movement is instituted afresh. This is the familiar doctrine expounded by James."

Professor Calkins still more explicitly states that in voluntary action we arouse a certain response by getting in mind an idea that is *like* the response.

An "outer" volition being a volition to act in a certain way and an "inner" volition being a volition to think in a certain way, "the volition is the image of an action or of a result of action which is normally *similar* . . . to this same action or result. My volition to sign a letter is either an image of my hand moving a pen or an image of my signature written, and my volition to purchase something is an image of myself in the act of handing out money or an image of my completed purchase—golf stick or Barbédienne bronze." "Inner volitions," she adds, "do not so closely resemble their results. The volitional image of an act may be, in detail, like the act as performed"; but the volitional image of a thought is followed by only a "partially similar" thought.

The issue is now clear. Does an idea tend to produce only the movements which it or some element of it *has* produced (or accompanied in one total response), or does it tend also to produce the movement by which the sensory stuff of which it is the image *was* produced, and which it resembles?

I shall try to prove that an idea of a movement has, apart from connections made by use and satisfying results, no stronger tendency to produce the movement which it resembles, than to produce any other movement whatsoever,— no stronger tendency to produce what it represents or has as its object than an idea of an event outside man's body has— that, apart from connections made by use and satisfying results, the idea of throwing a spear or of pinching one's ear, or of saying "yes" tends to produce the act in question no more than the idea of a ten-dollar bill or of an earthquake tends to produce that object or event.

Why should it? Why should the likeness between John Smith's mental image and some event in nature have any greater potency when that event is in the muscles of John Smith than when it is in the sky above or the earth beneath him? Why should McDougall's "mysterious connection" be allowed to "obtain" just here and not elsewhere?

The reasons why it should not are an attractive theme, but the evidence that it *does* not is our present concern.

First of all, an idea or image certainly *need* not arouse the movement which it represents, or "is of." Let each one of you now summon the most lively and faithful representation that he can of sneezing, then, after five seconds, of hiccoughing. Free your mind of any contradictory ideas, giving yourselves wholeheartedly to thinking hard of the "visual, tactile and kinesthetic sensations of sneezing." We hear no universal chorus of nasal outburst or diaphragmic spasm. Either ninety-nine out of a hundred of you cannot get such representations of these movements as the theory requires or the theory is at fault. But if the theory requires a representation which not one person in a hundred can get of so definite and frequent and interesting a movement as a sneeze, the theory seems very dubious. As a matter of fact a large percentage of you would report that you could get as vivid and faithful an image of a sneeze as of the movements of your hand in signing your name or in handing out money.

To retort that sneezing and hiccoughing are not subject to voluntary control is futile. By the ideo-motor theory they *should be*. The retort witnesses rather to the fact that for a movement to be subject to voluntary control means not "to be capable of representation in thought," but "to be connected as response by the laws of habit to some situation which one can summon at will."

In the second place, in at least a majority of the cases quoted to support the ideo-motor theory—cases where an idea of a movement does have the movement as its sequent,—the connection can be shown to have been built up by habit—by use and satisfying results. When one has the idea of going to bed and goes, or of writing the word "cat" and writes it, the explanation is found in the previous training that has connected the idea of going to bed with situations, such as being sleepy, to which the act is the original or accustomed sequent, or has otherwise connected the act of going to bed as response to the situation of thinking of so doing. The stock case most often quoted from James is that of a man getting out of bed—"The idea flashes across me, 'Hollo! I must lie here no longer'—an idea which at that lucky instant awakens no contradicting or paralyzing suggestions, and consequently produces immediately its appropriate motor effects." Here the idea is patently not a representation of the movement at all. The "*Hollo*" and "*I must*" show clearly that it is in words,[2] not in images of leg, trunk and arm movements. Its motor effects are appropriate, not in the sense of being in the least like it or represented by it, but in the sense of being the effects which that idea, when uncontested, had, by exercise and effect, come to produce in that man. The "Hollo! I must" is a lineal descendant of the sensory admonitions from others received during life and connected each with its response by use, satisfaction, and the discomforting punishment attached to opposite courses.

In the third place, the supposedly crucial cases in favor of the ideo-motor theory really show the person *making the movement in order to get the idea of it*. Some of you have doubtless instructed your students as follows: "Try to feel as if you were crooking your finger, whilst keeping it straight. In a minute it will fairly tingle with the imaginary change of position; yet it will not sensibly move because *its not really moving* is also a part of what you have in mind. Drop *this* idea, think of the movement purely and simply, with all brakes off; and, presto! it takes place with no effort at all" (James's "Principles," II., p. 527). Now the essential fact here is that when anybody is told to try to feel as if he were crooking his finger, he tends, in the case of many subjects, to respond by taking an obvious way to get that feeling, namely, by actually crooking his finger. He responds to the request, regardless of any ideas beyond his understanding of the words, by a strong readiness to crook his finger. Being forbidden, he restrains the impulse. The "tingling" is not from the *imaginary change* of the finger's position but from the *real restraint from* changing its position. The tingling occurs with individuals who cannot image the finger's movement. Far from showing that the imagined movement is adequate in and of itself to cause the

---

[2] If by any sophistry it could be twisted into a representation of leg and trunk movements, it would be only the representation of lying still plus the idea of negation.

movement, such cases show that it is unsafe to infer that the image comes first in cases where deliberately evoked images of movements are accompanied by the movements or parts thereof. If, in the experiment with ideas of sneezing, a stray individual does sneeze, it is ten to one that he has the rare power to make himself sneeze and has done so, intentionally or unintentionally, in order to get a more adequate idea of how it feels to sneeze.

These facts have long seemed to me adequate evidence that an idea can produce only what it, in whole or in part, has produced in the past, not what it is like or what it means. And I venture to hope that, by realizing just what the somewhat cryptic terms—to represent, to have as object, to be an idea of—mean and by noting just what happens in even the most favored cases for the production of a movement by an idea's likeness to it, you are made somewhat suspicious of the "mysterious" and "so close" bond by which every "motor representation tends to realize itself immediately in movement."

I shall now attack the doctrine from within, showing first that its own apostles think more highly of it the less clearly and emphatically it is stated, and even believe that the power of an idea's likeness to a movement to produce that movement is in inverse ratio to the amount of likeness—that the power of an idea to arouse the movement it is like grows greater, the less alike they are!

Last spring many of the members of this association kindly ranked in order of truth from four to ten statements concerning the general power of ideas to produce the acts which they resemble, or the power of some particular idea to produce some particular act. I take this occasion to thank them for their coöperation. These rankings, to which reference will be made repeatedly in what follows, represent a collection of judgments that are expert and, so far as my argument is concerned, impartial. Whatever errors of carelessness in reading, writing and the like affect them are such as have no prejudicial effect upon any of the conclusions which will be drawn from them.

From them we can measure the relative acceptability of

each of a series ranging from clear and emphatic to obscure and mild statements of the power of motor representations to realize themselves in movement.

Consider, for example, these four statements:

30. A movement idea is the revival, through central excitation, of the sensations, visual, tactile, kinesthetic, originally produced by the performance of the movement itself. And when such an idea is attended to, when, in popular language, we think hard enough of how the movement would "feel" and look if it were performed, then, so close is the connection between sensory and motor processes, the movement is instituted afresh.

32. In the special case in which the object to which we direct our attention by a volitional effort is a bodily movement, the movement follows immediately upon the idea.

31. We may then lay it down for certain that every representation of a movement awakens in some degree the actual movement which is its object.

33. If a child or a primitive man has a vivid idea of a movement of his own body, that movement is thereby made unless it is prevented by some contrary idea.

The first two are obviously more emphatic statements of the doctrine of ideo-motor action than the last two, but they are less acceptable to a random picking from this association. Respect for the genius of James perhaps accounts for part of this, but other features of the returns show that the belief in ideo-motor action thrives on qualifications—turns gladly to "a child" or a "primitive man," "a vivid idea," "unless it is prevented," and the like.

Consider next what should be the effect of attention to an idea upon the strength of its tendency to arouse the movement which it represents, supposing it to have such a tendency. Should we not, on all general principles, expect with Miss Washburn that "when such an idea is attended to, when we think hard enough of how the movement would feel and look," its power would be increased? Such seems the inevitable inference from consistent use of the ideo-motor theory. But, as will be seen still more clearly later, there is in the adherents to the theory a struggle between its principles and their sense of actual concrete facts; and the result here is that, in their concrete judgments, they deny the implication of the theory and insist that attention to the idea *weakens* its tendency to arouse the movement which it represents.

For example, the second of the two statements which I shall presently read differs from the first by supposing the movement-idea to be attended to (and also by supposing the idea to be one which resembles the movement a little more closely). The first statement is:

6. To make your spear fly straight and pierce the breast of your enemy it is useful to call to mind the sensations you had when, on other occasions, you saw your spear hurtling through the air straight at an enemy and striking him full in the breast.

The second is:

9. To make your spear fly straight and pierce the breast of your enemy, it is useful to think hard of the visual sensations, originally produced by the performance of the movement itself.

This association would vote over three to one that the second statement was the less true or more false.

The same point can be tested by two other statements from those rated. These are:

8. To make your spear fly straight and pierce the breast of your enemy, it is useful to imagine the sensations you had when, on other occasions, you felt the spear leave your hand, saw it fly through the air straight at an enemy and strike him full in the breast.

11. To make your spear fly straight and pierce the breast of your enemy, it is useful to think hard of the visual, tactile and kinesthetic sensations originally produced by the performance of the movement itself.

As before, the second statement adds the element of attentiveness (and also makes the idea in question a closer representative of the movement and emphasizes the kinesthetic element). This association would vote over two to one that the second statement was less true or more false than the first.

Still more damaging to the theory that ideas tend to evoke the movements which they resemble is the fact that, within certain limitations, the more closely they resemble them the less likely they are, according to your own judgments, to evoke them.

Among the forty statements rated were eight forming a series beginning with:

4. "To make your spear fly straight and pierce the breast of your enemy, it is useful to imagine the spear striking him full in the breast,"

in which, as you see, the idea is of a very remote result of the movement, not at all clearly like it or representative of it more than of many other movements. From this the series proceeded by graduated differences, through cases of closer and closer resemblance to the movement, to number 11, which was an almost verbatim adaptation of Miss Washburn's general statement to this particular case, namely:

11. To make your spear fly straight and pierce the breast of your enemy, it is useful to think hard of the visual, tactile and kinesthetic sensations originally produced by the performance of the movement itself.

The ratings show that although nine out of ten members of this association assert the truth of one or another form of the ideo-motor theory, their sagacious sense of fact compels them to go dead against it by assigning an order of truth to these eight statements, directly opposite to that which the theory requires. You vote overwhelmingly that a mere picture of the spear striking the enemy is more likely to produce the proper cast of the spear than a full and exact representation of the movement itself. You vote that "any idea tends to produce that act which it resembles," but you vote that the more it resembles it the less it tends to produce it! The first vote you cast under pressure from the "steam-roller" of traditional orthodoxy; the second is the result of the "direct primary" permitted by my questionnaire and reveals you as true progressives at heart.

If we let distance along a horizontal line FT stand for differences in truth, as judged by you, one foot equalling such a difference between two statements as seventy-five out of a hundred expert psychologists will distinguish correctly, No. 11, the statement concerning the close representative of the movement, is put nearly three feet *falser* than No. 4.

Some of you may suspect that my earlier phrase "within certain limitations" conceals facts favorable to the ideo-motor theory. On the contrary, if time permitted, these limitations could be shown to be those expected by the habit-theory. The rule is that mere likeness does nothing; when, as here, an increase in likeness goes with a decrease in the strength of habit's bonds, likeness has the appearance of diminishing an idea's potency to arouse its act; when greater likeness of an idea to an act implies greater frequency of the idea as *situation leading to the act* in past behavior, then greater likeness has the appearance of increasing the tendency of the idea to arouse the act. Nor is the series quoted above a solitary or exceptional one. If one were free to get forty statements rated by each of you instead of four, one could report a dozen similar cases.

In general the ratings witness to a conflict in the minds of psychologists between adherence to the speculative doctrine that the conscious representation of a movement is, in and of itself, potent to produce it and a sense for concrete facts which insists that it is thus potent only when it has for some reason been in the past the situation leading to it. The theory claims that an idea produces what is like it; observation teaches that an idea produces what has followed it.

Why, then, one naturally asks, did the theory ever gain credence, and why is it still cherished? The answers to these questions which I shall try to justify furnish my last and perhaps strongest reason why it should be cherished no longer. My answers are that the ideo-motor theory originated some fifty thousand years ago in the form of the primitive doctrine of imitative magic, and is still cherished because psychology is still, here and there, enthralled by cravings for magical teleological power in ideas beyond what the physiological· mechanisms of instinct and habit allow.

Shocking as it may seem, it can be shown that the orthodox belief of modern psychologists that an idea of a movement tends to produce the movement which is like it, is a true child of primitive man's belief that if you sprinkle water in a proper way your mimicry tends to produce rain, that if you first drag a friend into camp as if he were a dead deer you will be more successful in the day's hunt, or that if you make a wax image of your enemy and stab it he will tend to sicken and die.

Evidence that the accepted doctrine of ideo-motor action is homologous to, and a lineal descendant or vestigial trace of, the crassest forms of imitative magic may be sought along two lines—the comparative and the historical or, as the biologists would say, the palæontological. In comparative anatomy two forms of an individual or of an organ testify to a common ancestry—are rightly suspected of being homologous—in proportion as they are linked by intermediate forms and differ only, as we say, in degree. After a somewhat similar fashion I shall try to prove that the difference in falsity (or truth) between the absurdest magical superstition and the most approved form of the ideo-motor theory is one of degree only, and that the latter is linked to the former by a chain of intermediate forms.

As magical superstitions we may take the following:

1. "To make your spear fly straight and pierce the breast of your enemy it is useful to make a wax image of your enemy with a spear stuck through his breast."

24. "If a man draws secretly a picture of you with the words 'Yes, I will!' coming out of your mouth and then asks you 'Will you give me your coat?' you are more likely to answer 'Yes, I will!' than you would have been if he had not drawn the picture."

As what is in fact the most approved of the stock statements of the ideo-motor theory we may take James's familiar statement:

31. "We may then lay it down for certain that every representation of a movement awakens in some degree the actual movement which is its object."

Either of the two assertions of magical potency would be voted false by the association with practical unanimity. James's statement would be voted true by a comfortable majority. We regard the doctrine of imitative magic as sheer nonsense and the doctrine of ideo-motor action as substantially true. But our own judgments indicate that the latter is close kin to the former, when we treat them as we treat any set of judgments of difference in measuring the discriminability of objects.

Indeed only two intermediate links are required to show and measure the kinship. Recall Professor Washburn's statement:

30. "A movement idea is the revival, through central excitation, of the sensations, visual, tactile, kinesthetic, originally produced by the performance of the movement itself. And when such an idea is attended to, when, in popular language, we think hard enough of how the movement would 'feel' and look if it were performed, then, so close is the connection between sensory and motor processes, the movement is instituted afresh."

And consider also this vague statement, that:

5. "To make your spear fly straight and pierce the breast of your enemy, it is useful to imagine the spear hurtling through the air straight at him and striking him full in the breast."

These five statements, James's, Miss Washburn's, the one about an image of a hurtling and striking spear, the one about contemplating a wax image, and the one about writing in secret the words you wish a man to speak, differ, in respect to truth, only in degree. For people are able to compare them as to truth nearly or quite as readily and confidently as they can compare in respect to truth any five dubious statements chosen at random from psychological treatises. And when they so compare them the results are as follows:

Let the line *FT* represent a scale for truth. Let the point marked 1 Magic represent the location on the scale of the truth (or falsity) of the statement (No. 1) about the potency of the wax image. Let each inch on the scale represent the amount of difference in truth necessary in order that seventy-five per cent of this association shall judge the difference correctly, one out of every four being in error. Then statements 5, 30 and 31 are located as shown in Fig. 1. For the

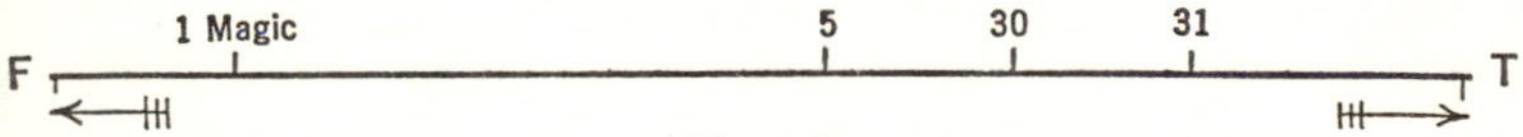

Fig. 1.

difference in truth between statement 1 and statement 5 is 1.64. It is measured by the fact that of 37 psychologists who compared them, 28 judged that 5 was truer or less false, 5 rated them as equally true or false, and 4 judged 1 to be truer than 5. The difference between statement 5 and statement 30 is .53. It is measured by the fact that of 24 psychologists who compared them 14 judged that 30 was truer or less false, 2 that they were equally true, and 8 that 5 was truer than 30. The difference between statement 30 and statement 31 is .5. It is measured by the fact that of 17 psychologists who compared them 9 judged that 31 was truer or less false, 3 that it was equally true and 5 that 30 was truer than 31.

Thus the truth of statement No. 1—of the potency of fabricating a wax image of your enemy is about 1⅔ below the truth of statement No. 5—of the potency of vague thoughts about the spear striking him, 2¼ *below the truth of Miss Washburn's statement* and 2¾ *below the truth of James's statement*. The links are truly intermediate. The most approved statements of the ideo-motor theory are by their own advocates confessed to be only a little more truthful or less false than the rankest magical nonsense. . . .

Some of you may be skeptical concerning this method of measuring differences of credibility in the minds of a given class of thinkers, harboring the suspicion that the individual reports were invalidated as measures of the individuals' opinions by the incommensurability of the statements. Some of you, indeed, refused to rate the statements. But, as a matter of fact, the main difficulty experienced with the various sets out of the forty-two statements which were issued was not that they were incommensurate as to truth, but that the differences were too small to be distinguished with any feeling of surety. I regret that the poll of this association is not complete, owing to the fact that some individuals refused, justly enough, to spend their time in grinding my axe, and that some canny ones refused to be drawn into any testifying that might conceivably be held against them later. It seems certain, however, that the membership of this association experienced—or would have experienced, had they tried to make the comparisons—no greater sense of incommensurability than they would have experienced in grading advertisements for "appeal," drawings for skill, or poems for beauty. Reports of such difficulties were very rare.

Whatever validity attaches to your belief that you know what you are about and mean something real when you judge that James's familiar statement is less false than the assertion about the potency of secretly writing "Yes, I will" as a persuasive fetich, or that about the potency of wax constructions of one's enemy in warfare, attaches to all the comparisons that I have used. But had I asked for only this one comparison every member of the association would have made it with no sense of incommensurability or trickery, but only with a sad surprise that I should ask so foolish, because so easy, a question. This method of measuring differences in credibility in the minds of a defined group is in fact sound, and, I may add, is useful in the case of very many problems in the mental sciences.

In the present case it teaches us that our belief that an idea tends to produce the act which it is like, or represents, or "is an idea of" or "has as its object," is kith and kin with our forebears' belief that dressing to look like a bear will give you his strength or that burning an effigy of the foe will make him die, and with the modern charlatan's belief that thinking one can walk will mend a broken bone. . . .

[Ideo-motor action as a universal principle of behavior is untenable, but certain phenomena of suggestion and hypnotism seem to most psychologists and psychiatrists to require some power of some ideas to produce some acts by virtue of likeness or congruity. For example, if a youth of eighteen, hypnotized and told "You are a feeble old man, shaking with palsy," forthwith enacts that rôle passably, his behavior seems to go beyond what past occurrences and rewards could have caused. If a shy youth, told that he is a great mixer and lady-killer, goes about the room slapping the men on the back and saluting the women with compliments and kisses, we seem compelled to accept some influence over and above his past history (or to make drafts upon tendencies hitherto hidden in his unconscious!).

An exhaustive investigation of the phenomena of suggestion may show that the apparent exceptions to a simon-pure connectionism are really consistent with it. Hull's admirable study [3] points that way. Years ago when suggestion was being popularized as a therapeutic agency I found nothing that did not seem better explainable by repetition and reward than by a power of ideas to create the acts or states that they were ideas of. For example, at that time Coué was one of the most successful employers of suggestion in psychotherapy. The essence of his treatment was having patients repeat the slogan, "Every day in every way I am getting better and better." So vague an assertion could hardly do anything by ideo-motor action. But by the laws of exercise and effect it would lead away from misery and fear toward calmness and optimism, and so give a chance to the *vis medicatrix naturae.*]

[3] *Hypnosis and Suggestibility, An Experimental Approach,* (New York, Appleton-Century-Crofts, Inc., 1933), pp. xi and 416.

CHAPTER X

The Influence of Primacy *

IT HAS been a common, not to say orthodox, doctrine that other things being equal, the response which is made to a situation by an individual the first time that he encounters it becomes connected with that situation more strongly by that one experience than does any response made to any single later occurrence of the situation by that one experience.

Thus Seashore writes: "In experimental psychology a more specific formulation of laws in terms of force of the association has gained recognition. The chief of these are: (1) *primacy:* other things being equal the association first formed will prevail." [1] Pillsbury writes: ". . . We find the factors that determine the strength of the connection between one element and those that have been associated with it. These have been shown to be the *frequency* with which the two elements have appeared together, the *recency* of their association, . . . and the *primacy* of the association. Professor Calkins has shown that the earlier one element enters into an association with another, the more likely it is to be recalled with that than with any other with which it has been associated at a later period." [2]

We have subjected this doctrine to rather extensive experimental tests, the net result of which is to prove that primacy in and of itself has zero potency. We shall show, for example, that, other things being equal, an individual's second or third response to a situation is as prophetic of, and similar to, his later responses to it as his first response, and that in a series of *n* recurrences of a situation, the last response is as indicative of, and similar to, responses 2 to $n - 1$ as the first response is, if other things than temporal position are kept equal. . . .

* *The Journal of Experimental Psychology*, Vol. 10, (1927), pp. 18–29.
[1] C. E. Seashore, *Introduction to Psychology*, (1923), 158.
[2] W. B. Pillsbury, *The Fundamentals of Psychology*, (1922), 285 f.

[Seven experiments agreed in showing no influence of primacy. I quote the facts for Experiment 5 as a sample.]

Experiment 5

In Experiment 5 the external situations presented were the sound of *a* (as in late), *ee* (as in week), *ou* (house), *o* (home), *aw* (saw), *k* (kind), *f* (fence) and *s* (so). The response was, in each case, to represent the sound by a letter or letters. The sounds appeared in three-syllable nonsense words [spoken by the experimenter] which the subjects spelled. For each sound for each of 105 subjects, we have a record of the first twelve spellings in order.

We compare the occurrences, in responses III to X, of the spellings which were given the first time that a sound occurred, the second time, the eleventh time and the twelfth time respectively. The totals are 3,398, 3,485, 3,626 and 3,627. The first response thus has no advantage over the second or twelfth or thirteenth; but, on the contrary, is less potent in determining what the eight responses from the third to the tenth are to be. The lack of special potency of the first experience is seen even more closely when we eliminate the many cases where the second (or eleventh, or twelfth) spelling, as the case may be, was the same as the first. The frequencies in III to X of spellings I and II, when these are different, are 902 and 991. Those of I and XI, when these are different, are 1,016 and 1,237. Those of I and XII, when these are different, are 898 and 1,136. . . .

We have not been able to find any clear evidence in the literature of association in support of the doctrine that the first connection made with a situation has, by being first, any advantage. The experiments of Calkins referred to by Pillsbury do not, as we interpret them, necessarily show that "the earlier one element enters into association with another, the more likely it is to be recalled with that than with any other with which it has been associated at a later period"; but rather that being first in a series of twelve paired-association tasks has an advantage over being in the middle of such a series. It seems probable that the advantage is not due to primacy in and of itself, but to the factors which make both the beginning and the end of a series better remembered than the middle.

It seems probable that the facts, to explain which the doctrine of primacy was fabricated, are better explained by two corollaries of the general laws of learning. The first is that, other things being equal, the stronger a connection is, the oftener, and so the earlier, it will show itself. Being first does not make a connection stronger, but being strong makes a connection likely to be first. Let $S_1 \rightarrow R_1$, $S_1 \rightarrow R_2$, $S_1 \rightarrow R_3$, $S_1 \rightarrow R_4$ have strengths of 5, 2, 2 and 1, respectively. Then when S_1 occurs R_1 will be the first response five times as often as R_4 will, and also it will later occur five times as often.

The second is that when responses are connected with situations to which there are no pre-existing connections of more than infinitesimal strength (as in some cases of learning the names of strangers, the English equivalents of foreign words, and the like), the first experience raises the frequency from approximately 0 to 1, the second experience of the same connection raises it from 1 to 2, and so on. The *relative* strength of the connection with its competing infinitesimals is raised to 1–to–0 by the first experience, and only to 2–to–0 by the second experience. This is an effect of frequency caused by position and is allied to the facts of diminishing returns and overlearning. It is different from the alleged primacy effect. If, in such a case, we have two different responses, one in first position and the other in second position of occurrence, each will be raised to a relative strength of 1–to–0 compared with the infinitesimals; and the one in first place will be at no advantage over the one in second place.

These two simple facts, plus certain influences of novelty on attention, seem likely to be adequate to account for all that is true in the popular doctrine that first impressions are strongest.

The advantage for attention or memory of the first event

of a series over later events in the series is, of course, a matter with which primacy, as defined here, has nothing to do.

We conclude, therefore, that the . . . general theory of connection-forming may be relieved from the incubus of the special theory that the response made by an individual to a situation the first time that he encounters it becomes, by virtue of that one experience, more strongly connected with that situation—other things being equal—than does any response made to any single later occurrence of the situation by virtue of a like single experience.

CHAPTER XI

Mental Abilities *

Most of us use freely such terms as musical ability, mathematical ability, a good memory, a superior faculty of imagination, inventiveness, inability to control one's temper, inability to concentrate, poor judgment, lack of reasoning power, inferior intelligence, and lack of mental balance. We have more or less definite notions of what we mean by these terms and could point out persons who exemplified them. We could grade a hundred persons whom we knew intimately on a scale from low to high, or little or much, or weak to strong, for any of these abilities, though with some doubt and questioning. Popular notions of these mental abilities are, however, extremely vague and variable in comparison with popular notions of length, area, volume, weight, density, temperature, and many other physical facts.

Psychology has advanced beyond popular knowledge by constructing means of measuring these abilities, or, more accurately, means of measuring various behaviors which are symptomatic of these abilities. These mental meters, commonly called tests, began with such simple matters as the speed and accuracy of finding and canceling the A's on a page of mixed capital letters, or the number of digits that a person can remember correctly from a single hearing. The former was called a test of attention, and the latter a test of memory span.

At first psychology accepted the popular view that attention, memory, imagination, reasoning and the like were funda-

* *Proceedings of The American Philosophical Society*, Vol. 84, (June, 1941), pp. 503–513.

mental and unitary faculties or powers of the mind. If you had a notably superior memory it would be equally superior for words, numbers, faces, localities, and so forth. If your faculty of attention was weak, you would be unable to concentrate well on lessons, stories, games and all else. Consequently, it was expected that a dozen or score of rather simple tests would reveal the fundamental abilities of a person and measure them, at least, roughly.

Two lines of experimentation, begun about forty years ago, caused the abandonment of this expectation. The first studied the training of abilities and found such facts as the following: If a person practices finding and checking A's, he gains notably in speed and accuracy, but his ability to find and check B's shows much less improvement, and his ability to find and check words containing two given letters, such as e and s, or n and o, or i and p, shows little or none. If a person is trained at memorizing series of digits or series of nonsense syllables, he may improve notably in the amount that he remembers from, say, ten minutes of study, but when he transfers his efforts to memorizing shapes, or poems, or passages of music, he shows very little improvement over the ability he had before the training. What has been improved by the training is not a general power of attention, or a general faculty of memory that operates regardless of what is to be memorized.

The second line of experimentation studied the correlations or covariances of different manifestations of an ability and found such facts as the following: If a thousand twelve-year-old boys are tested in respect of the ability to add integers, the ability to add fractions, the ability to divide integers by integers, and the ability to divide fractions by fractions, the correlations or covariances of these sub-abilities are far from perfect. The boy who is ablest in adding integers will not be the ablest in the other three sub-abilities. A boy's rank among the thousand will not be the same in all four, but will vary rather widely. Mathematical ability is not one thing, but a complex of many.

If the thousand boys take a number of tests chosen to measure intelligence, their scores on the tests that concern words will not correlate perfectly with their scores in the tests that concern pictures, or space relations, or numbers. Intelligence is not a unitary ability that operates regardless of the data on which it operates.

Mental abilities are not an orderly retinue of a few easily defined and unitary faculties or powers, somewhat like the chemical elements, for each of which a mental meter or test can be found by sufficient labor and ingenuity. A mental ability is a probability that certain situations will evoke certain responses, that certain tasks can be achieved, that certain mental products can be produced by the possessor of the ability. It is defined by the situations, responses, products, and tasks, not by some inner essence.

Except for certain powers which depend upon definite features of the eyes, ears, or other sense organs, intelligence is one of the most definite and unitary abilities that have been studied; and certain plausible hypotheses have been set up concerning a simple biological causation of it. But even it is regarded by prudent psychologists as a probability that certain mental achievements will be achieved, and is defined by these achievements.

Hence we find the most expert measurers of intelligence stating that an intelligence-test score measures only the ability in that test and whatever correlates perfectly with that score. Hence we find that an intelligence meter that is perhaps the most dependable yet devised is not called a test of intelligence, but only a test of intelligence CAVD, that is of sentence-completion, arithmetical problems, vocabulary, and the comprehension of directions or paragraphs. These facts seem like confessions of weakness in the science of psychology, but are really signs of health and strength.

Three or four hours testing of a person with suitable intelligence tests or meters gives a score which is highly indicative of how well he will do in school, how likely he is to escape confinement in an institution for the feeble-minded, and how well he will understand the sermons he hears, the policies for

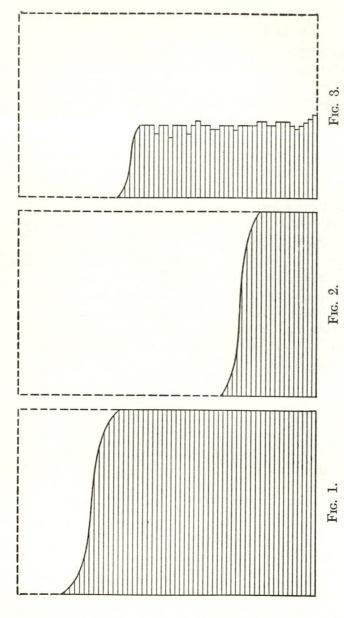

FIG. 1.　　　　FIG. 2.

FIG. 3.

The entire area of the rectangle represents, in each case, a sampling of n tasks at each of 64 levels of difficulty for the ability in question, from a very easy task at the bottom to very hard tasks at the top of the rectangle. The shaded area represents tasks accomplished successfully. The white area represents the tasks on which the person failed. Fig. 1 represents a person with a high ability, Fig. 2, a person with low ability, Fig. 3 represents a person who had about the same number of successes as the person of Fig. 2, but who succeeded with much harder tasks, failing on many easy tasks.

158

which he votes, and the like. It is usefully indicative of his fitness to make wise decisions as a parent, neighbor, and citizen. Such a score obtained at age eight to eighteen is probably equal in value to a careful physical examination at that age by an expert physician. It is a valuable supplement to the ratings by parents, teachers and others who have long and intimate acquaintance with the person.

It should, however, be noted that the ability measured by such tests is perhaps better named abstract intelligence, or intelligence operating with symbols. Intelligence operating with actual individual things—machines, storms, traffic jams, stoves, cakes, pies, etc., etc.—may differ considerably from the intelligence that determines scores in Stanford-Binet or CAVD tests. So also may intelligence operating with actual people,—as in the managing, persuading and comforting of a politician, foreman, salesman, or nurse.

Our best present definitions and measurements of mental abilities are inventories of a person's actual or possible responses to certain tasks. The single score he obtains is some sort of an expression of the quantity and quality of his responses. It is customary to select or arrange the tasks so that each response will be completely right or completely wrong. The inventory can then be fully expressed by listing the tasks according to their difficulty and stating the percentage of successes at each level of difficulty. This concept of difficulty is of so great importance that I shall ask you to note a few illustrations of it. To give the opposite of *unless* is the same sort of task as to give the opposite of *up*, but is more difficult intellectually in the sense that fewer persons can do it and that those who can will average higher in intelligence by any reasonable measure of it. Similarly for supplying words to complete these sentences: A dog has four . . . ; The relation between a number and its reciprocal is . . . Similarly for answering these questions: What number is the sum of six and fourteen? What number is as much greater than half of six dozen as it is less than three-fifths of twenty dozen. In the case of musical ability it is more difficult to play a Beethoven symphony than to play chopsticks or Yankee Doodle, in the sense that fewer persons can do it and that those who can will average higher in musical ability by any reasonable measure of it.

Measurements of a person having much and a person having little of a mental ability which is an ability to do tasks alike in nature but differing in difficulty, are presented in Fig. 1 and Fig. 2.

The height of an ability, that is, the difficulty of the tasks the person can master, is more important than its width, because greater width can be obtained from more work by the person or from using more persons, but nothing can substitute for deficiency in height.

The scientific study of mental abilities early discovered that correlation, not compensation, was the rule. Nature does not balance superior reasoning power by inferior imagination, or superiority in learning by inferiority in remembering, or genius in music by idiocy in business. And this fact of the positive affiliations of estimable abilities has been confirmed again and again by later researches. This fact has very important consequences for man's life and work, mostly beneficent. But as far as concerns the exact description and measurement of abilities it is a nuisance. Psychology wishes to know each ability pure and undefiled, and to measure all of it and nothing but it. For example, it wishes three tests or meters of ability to appreciate color, rhythm and musical harmony. But it finds that in spite of its utmost ingenuity and effort, each test measures all three to some extent and also various potencies of the sense-organs, and also the person's general intelligence, so-called. Each score is contaminated, so to speak, by including more or less influence from other abilities. Each ability, as we actually measure it, is a mixture of abilities. We do not attain purity.

For various reasons psychologists would like to be able to replace a set of such impure abilities with positive intercorrelations by a set of abilities that are pure and unitary or independent in the sense of having zero correlations one with another. And some psychologists cherish the hope that such pure abilities would prove to be more fundamental and more revealing of the mind's structure and of its physiological bases than the abilities found by direct observation and tests.

The methods of factorial analysis developed by Kelley, Hotelling, Thurstone and others succeed in discovering components or factors which would correlate zero one with another if we could get measurements of them in real people, and which are defined to a certain extent by their relations to measurable abilities. Work along this line has been carried on vigorously during the past five years, especially by Thurstone and his pupils. Few psychologists have mastered and used the methods of factor analysis, and those who have vary widely in their opinions of the results. Some expect that the factors discovered will inaugurate great advances in knowledge about, and control of, human abilities; some think that these factors are unrealizable abstractions, like an animal defined as 40 per cent man, 30 per cent turtle, 20 per cent shark and 10 per cent earthworm. The tests of the work will come when it progresses to the measurement of these components or factors, to using them for explanation and prediction, and to relating them to biological facts about the brain. This third test, however, is yet to be met not only by factor analysis but by the great bulk of psychological work on abilities as well.

It is fitting to note at this point that the important work of Spearman and his pupils, begun in 1904, was a stimulus to the recent work of factor analysis, though Spearman's main interest was in arguing that a group of abilities could, in the case of certain important groups, be represented by one factor common to all and many specific factors none of which was present in more than one of the abilities of the group.

Mental abilities are functions of the neurones or nerve cells that constitute the brain, sense organs and other parts of the nervous system, and psychology will not be satisfied until it succeeds in relating mental abilities to their neural causes, bases, parallels, or counterparts. Not much is known at pres-

ent, and almost all of that concerns sensory abilities. The ability to see starts with specialized cells in the retina, the rods
and cones. The cones give sensations of color; the rods do not.
The ability to see in bright light is different from the ability to
see in dim light, and the rods play an important role in the latter. The two right-hand halves of the two eyes are put into
intimate relation within the brain (and similarly for the two
left-hand halves). Beginning with such simple facts as these
and continuing to Dr. Selig Hecht's recent discoveries concerning the sensitivity of the visual purple, a great deal is
known about the ability to see. But very little is known about
the neural basis of the ability to draw or paint, or even the
ability to have lively visual images, pictures before the mind's
eye. Much is known also about the ability to hear, and psychologists are proud of Dr. Wever's share in this. But very little
is known about the neural bases of the ability to understand
language or to play the violin.

Relatively little is known, compared to what we would like
to know, about the billions of neurones that compose the
brain. We know that neurones conduct and a good deal about
how they conduct. We have recently learned that neurones
may act as glands secreting substances which may activate
neurones which the secretion reaches. We know that the
topography of the brain is influential on its action, certain
functions being localized in certain systems of neurones. We
know that the neurones in idiots' brains are relatively simple
and coarse in structure. But if we had the brains of Newton,
Beethoven, Darwin, Shakespeare and Bismarck all sectioned
for examination, our best neurologists probably could not tell
which had great mathematical ability, which had great musical ability, and so on, or which knew English and which knew
German. We are not even sure that we know where to look, or
what to look for, in the search for the neural bases of such
mental abilities.

The neurologists of two generations ago thought that they
did know. They assumed that the brain consisted of "centers"
each of which was of prime importance for some ability or

abilities, and "pathways" from sense organ to center, center to center, and center to muscles and glands. A well developed "center" implied a high degree of the ability and was something like a combination of a factory and a storehouse. The so-called cell-body, that is, the thickened part of a neurone containing its nucleus, was supposed to be the main agent of neurones in causing abilities.

We now know that a brain is not much like a system of factories and storehouses interconnected by railroad tracks. It is more like a telephone and telegraph system with the added feature of more or less permanent modification by all the connections made and messages sent. It may include an elaborate system of resonators. What corresponds to an ability is more like a system of connections and modifications involving all army or navy activities than like a regiment of cell-bodies. The cell bodies indeed may only nourish and care for the conducting parts of the neurones. What the pattern of the neurones' actions is may often be more important than which particular neurones they are.

Localization of abilities in "centers" had been discarded a generation ago, and replaced by localization in groups of conductors and synapses with diffusion to other groups and convergence to common final paths. The localization was fairly complex for even such simple abilities as to scratch an itching spot, or clench the hand, or close the eyes, at will; and was increasingly complex for broader abilities. This doctrine of localization was attacked as too inflexible by a psychologist, Franz, who showed that the work done by one system of neurones could, to an unexpected degree, be taken over by another; and another psychologist, Lashley, has continued and greatly widened the attack in a brilliant series of experiments in which various parts of the brain of the white rat are extirpated and the resulting changes in the rat's abilities are observed and measured.

I lack time to describe Lashley's facts and inferences, and lack both time and ability to appraise them. But I think a consensus of competent students of the brain and mind would still hold that localization has real and great influence and that what an ability is depends in part upon which neurones are acting, but would admit that the localization within the cerebrum is far more complex and more indeterminate than had been supposed, and that it may be supplemented by selective sensitivities or resonances. Lashley's startling doctrine that the amount of cerebrum that is cut out rather than which part is cut out is often decisive for a rat's ability to learn may not be true for man, but it can reinforce a useful lesson—that in man every ability normally operates under an overhead control by his past development and present status and purposes. The man himself coöperates in most of his abilities.

I hope that my account of mental abilities has satisfied you. It will not satisfy my psychological colleagues. They will protest "Why did you omit all reference to the theories of the neural basis of intelligence that have been set forth by psychologists, including your own? Why did you say nothing about the differences between the sexes and between races, and the great differences between individuals? Why did you not evaluate the contributions of heredity and environment to various representative abilities? Why did you not trace the course of mental abilities from birth to maturity and on to old age? Why did you not report the careful work that has been done on certain special abilities, such as the ability to read and the ability to learn to sing?" Psychology has been active in all these fields and my only excuse for not including them is that if I had, this report would have been over twice as long.

CHAPTER XII

The Constitution of Arithmetical Abilities

IT WOULD be a useful work for someone to try to analyze arithmetical learning into the unitary abilities which compose it, showing just what, in detail, the mind has to do in order to be prepared to pass a thorough test on the whole of arithmetic. These unitary abilities would make a very long list. Examination of a well-planned textbook will show that such an ability as multiplication is treated as a composite of the following: knowledge of the multiplications up to 9×9; ability to multiply two (or more)-place numbers by 2, 3, and 4 when "carrying" is not required and no zeros occur in the multiplicand; ability to multiply by 2, 3, ... 9, with carrying; the ability to handle zeros in the multiplicand; the ability to multiply with two-place numbers not ending in zero; the ability to handle zero in the multiplier as last number; the ability to multiply with three (or more)-place numbers not including a zero; the ability to multiply with three- and four-place numbers with zero in second or third, or second and third, as well as in last place; the ability to save time by annexing zeros; and so on and on through a long list of further abilities required to multiply with United States money, decimal fractions, common fractions, mixed numbers, and denominate numbers.

The units or "steps" thus recognized by careful teaching would make a long list, but it is probable that a still more careful study of arithmetical ability as a hierarchy of mental habits or connections would greatly increase the list. Consider, for example, ordinary column addition. The majority

* From *The Psychology of Arithmetic*, (1922), pp. 51–74, *passim*.

of teachers probably treat this as a simple application of the knowledge of the additions to 9 + 9, plus understanding of "carrying." On the contrary there are at least seven processes or minor functions involved in two-place column addition, each of which is psychologically distinct and requires distinct educational treatment.

These are:

A. Learning to keep one's place in the column as one adds.
B. Learning to keep in mind the result of each addition until the next number is added to it.
C. Learning to add a seen to a thought-of number.
D. Learning to neglect an empty space in the columns.
E. Learning to neglect 0s in the columns.
F. Learning the application of the combinations to higher decades may for the less gifted pupils involve as much time and labor as learning all the original addition tables. And even for the most gifted child the formation of the connection "8 and 7 = 15" probably never quite insures the presence of the connections "38 and 7 = 45" and "18 + 7 = 25."
G. Learning to write the figure signifying units rather than the total sum of a column. In particular, learning to write 0 in the cases where the sum of the column is 10, 20, etc. Learning to "carry" also involves in itself at least two distinct processes, by whatever way it is taught.

We find evidence of such specialization of functions in the results with such tests as Woody's. For example, $2 + 5 + 1 = \ldots$ surely involves abilities in part different

$$\frac{2}{4}$$

from 3 because only 77 per cent of children in grade 3 do the former correctly, whereas 95 per cent of children in that grade do the latter correctly. In grade 2 the difference

is even more marked. In the case of subtraction $\underline{4}$ involves abilities different from those involved in $\underline{3}$, being much less

often solved correctly in grades 2 and 4. $\underline{0}$ is much harder than either of the above.

43
1   21
2   33
13 is much harder than 35.

It may be said that these differences in difficulty are due to different amounts of practice. This is probably not true, but if it were, it would not change the argument; if the two abilities were identical, the practice of one would improve the other equally.

I shall not undertake here this task of listing and describing the elementary functions which constitute arithmetical learning, partly because what they are is not fully known, partly because in many cases a final ability may be constituted in several different ways whose descriptions become necessarily tedious, and partly because an adequate statement of what is known would far outrun the space limits of this chapter. Instead, I shall illustrate the results by some samples.

KNOWLEDGE OF THE MEANING OF A FRACTION

As a first sample, consider knowledge of the meaning of a fraction. Is the ability in question simply to understand that a fraction is a statement of the number of parts, each of a certain size, the upper number or numerator telling how many parts are taken and the lower number or denominator telling what fraction of unity each part is? And is the educational treatment required simply to describe and illustrate such a statement and have the pupils apply it to the recognition of fractions and the interpretation of each of them? And is the learning process (1) the formation of the notions of part, size of part, number of part, (2) relating the last two to the numbers in a fraction, and, as a necessary consequence, (3) applying these notions adequately whenever one encounters a fraction in operation?

Precisely this was the notion a few generations ago. The

nature of fractions was taught as one principle, in one step, and the habits of dealing with fractions were supposed to be deduced from the general law of a fraction's nature. As a result the subject of fractions had to be long delayed, was studied at great cost of time and effort, and, even so, remained a mystery to all save gifted pupils. These gifted pupils probably of their own accord built up the ability piecemeal out of constituent insights and habits.

At at all events, scientific teaching now does build up the total ability as a fusion or organization of lesser abilities. What these are will be seen best by examining the means taken to get them. (1) First comes the association of ½ of a pie, ½ of a cake, ½ of an apple, and such like with their concrete meanings so that a pupil can properly name a clearly designated half of an obvious unit like an orange, pear, or piece of chalk. The same degree of understanding of ¼, ⅛, ⅓, ⅙, and ⅕ is secured. The pupil is taught that 1 pie = 2 ½s, 3 ⅓s, 4 ¼s, 5 ⅕s, 6 ⅙s, and 8 ⅛s; similarly for 1 cake, 1 apple, and the like.

So far he understands $\frac{1}{x}$ of y in the sense of certain simple parts of obviously unitary ys.

(2) Next comes the association with ½ of an inch, ½ of a foot, ½ of a glassful and other cases where y is not so obviously a unitary object whose pieces still show their derivation from it. Similarly for ¼, ⅓, and so on.

(3) Next comes the association with ½ of a collection of eight pieces of candy, ⅓ of a dozen eggs, ⅕ of a squad of ten soldiers, etc., until ½, ⅓, ¼, ⅕, ⅙, and ⅛ are understood as names of certain parts of a collection of objects.

(4) Next comes the similar association when the nature of the collection is left undefined, the pupil responding to ½ of 6 is . . . . ,   ¼ of 8 is . . . . ,   2 is ⅕ of . . . . , ⅓ of 6 is . . . . ,   ⅓ of 9 is . . . . ,   2 is ⅓ of . . . . , and the like.

Each of these abilities is justified in teaching by its intrinsic merits, irrespective of its later service in helping to constitute the general understanding of the meaning of a fraction. The habits thus formed in grades 3 or 4 are of constant service then and thereafter in and out of school.

(5) With these comes the use of $\frac{1}{5}$ of 10, 15, 20, etc., $\frac{1}{6}$ of 12, 18, 42, and so on, as a useful variety of drill on the division tables, valuable in itself, and a means of making the notion of a unit fraction more general by adding $\frac{1}{7}$ and $\frac{1}{9}$ to the scheme.

(6) Next comes the connection of $\frac{3}{4}$, $\frac{2}{5}$, $\frac{3}{5}$, $\frac{4}{5}$, $\frac{2}{3}$, $\frac{1}{6}$, $\frac{5}{6}$, $\frac{3}{8}$, $\frac{5}{8}$, $\frac{7}{8}$, $\frac{3}{10}$, $\frac{7}{10}$, and $\frac{9}{10}$, each with its meaning as a certain part of some conveniently divisible unit, and, (7) and (8), connections between these fractions and their meanings as parts of certain magnitudes (7) and collections (8) of convenient size, and (9) connections between these fractions and their meanings when the nature of the magnitude or collection is unstated, as in $\frac{4}{5}$ of 15 = . . ., $\frac{5}{8}$ of 32 = . . .

(10) That the relation is general is shown by using it with numbers requiring written division and multiplication, such as $\frac{7}{8}$ of 1736 = . . ., and with United States money.

Elements (6) to (10), like elements (1) to (5), are useful even if the pupil never goes farther in arithmetic. One of the commonest uses of fractions is in calculating the cost of fractions of yards of cloth, and fractions of pounds of meat, cheese, etc.

The next step (11) is to understand to some extent the principle that the value of any of these fractions is unaltered by multiplying or dividing the numerator and denominator by the same number. The drills in expressing fractions in lower and higher terms which accomplish this are paralleled by (12) and (13) simple exercises in adding and subtracting fractions to show that fractions are quantities that can be operated on like any quantities, and by (14) simple work with mixed numbers (addition and subtraction and reductions), and (15) improper fractions. . . . As hitherto, the work of (11) to (15) is useful in and of itself. (16) Definitions are given of the following type:—

Numbers like 2, 3, 4, 7, 11, 20, 36, 140, 921 are called whole numbers.

Numbers like $\frac{7}{8}$, $\frac{1}{5}$, $\frac{2}{3}$, $\frac{3}{4}$, $1\frac{1}{8}$, $\frac{7}{6}$, $\frac{1}{3}$, $\frac{4}{3}$, $\frac{1}{8}$, $\frac{1}{6}$ are called fractions.

Numbers like $5\frac{1}{4}$, $7\frac{3}{8}$, $9\frac{1}{2}$, $16\frac{4}{5}$, $315\frac{7}{8}$, $1\frac{1}{3}$, $1\frac{2}{3}$ are called mixed numbers.

(17) The terms numerator and denominator are connected with the upper and lower numbers composing a fraction.

Building this somewhat elaborate series of minor abilities seems to be a very roundabout way of getting knowledge of the meaning of a fraction, and is, if we take no account of what is got along with this knowledge. Taking account of the intrinsically useful habits that are built up, one might retort that the pupil gets his knowledge of the meaning of a fraction at zero cost. . . .

LEARNING THE PROCESSES OF COMPUTATION

As another instructive topic in the constitution of arithmetical abilities, we may take the case of the reasoning involved in understanding the manipulations of figures in two (or more)-place addition and subtraction, multiplication and division involving a two (or more)-place number, and the manipulations of decimals in all four operations. The psychology of these is of special interest and importance. For there are two opposite explanations possible here, leading to two opposite theories of teaching.

The common explanation is that these methods of manipulation, if understood at all, are understood as deductions from the properties of our system of decimal notation. The other is that they are understood partly as inductions from the experience that they always give the right answer. The first explanation leads to the common preliminary deductive explanations of the textbooks. The other leads to explanations by verification; e. g., of addition by counting, of subtraction by addition, of multiplication by addition, of division by multiplication. . . .

Crucial experiments are lacking, but there are several lines of well-attested evidence. First of all, there can be no doubt that the great majority of pupils learn these manipulations at the start from the placing of units under units, tens under tens, and so forth, in adding, to the placing of the decimal point in division with decimals, by imitation and blind following of specific instructions, and that a very large proportion of the pupils do not to the end, that is to the fifth school-year, understand them as necessary deductions from decimal notation. It also seems probable that this proportion would not be much reduced no matter how ingeniously and carefully the deductions were explained by textbooks and teachers. Evidence of this fact will appear abundantly to any one who will observe schoolroom life. It also appears in the fact that after the properties of the decimal notation have been thus used again and again; e. g., for deducing "carrying" in addition, "borrowing" in subtraction, "carrying" in multiplication, the value of the digits in the partial product, the value of each remainder in short division, the value of the quotient figures in division, the addition, subtraction, multiplication, and division of United States money, and the placing of the decimal point in multiplication, no competent teacher dares to rely upon the pupil, even though he now has four or more years' experience with decimal notation, to deduce the placing of the decimal point in division with decimals. It may be an illusion, but one seems to sense in the better textbooks a recognition of the futility of the attempt to secure deductive derivations of those manipulations. I refer to the brevity of the explanations and their insertion in such a form that they will influence the pupils' thinking as little as possible. At any rate the fact is sure that most pupils do not learn the manipulations by deductive reasoning, or understand them as necessary consequences of abstract principles.

It is a common opinion that the only alternative is knowing them by rote. This, of course, is one common alternative, but the other explanation suggests that understanding the manipulations by inductive reasoning from their results is another and an important alternative. The manipulations of "long" multiplication, for instance, learned by imitation or mechanical drill, are found to give for $25 \times A$ a result about twice as large as for $13 \times A$, for 38 or $39 \times A$ a result about three times as large; for $115 \times A$ a result about ten times as large as for $11 \times A$. With even the very dull pupils the procedure is verified at least to the extent that it gives a result which the scientific expert in the case—the teacher—calls right. With even the very bright pupils, who can appreciate the relation of the procedure to decimal notation, this relation may be used not as the sole deduction of the procedure beforehand, but as one partial means of verifying it afterward. Or there may be the condition of half-appreciation of the relation in which the pupil uses knowledge of the decimal notation to convince himself that the procedure *does,* but not that it *must* give the right answer, the answer being "right" because the teacher, the answer-list, and collateral evidence assure him of it. . . .

I conclude, therefore, that school children may and do reason about and understand the manipulations of numbers in this inductive, verifying way without being able to, or at least without, under present conditions, finding it profitable to derive them deductively. I believe, in fact, that pure arithmetic *as it is learned and known* is largely an *inductive science.* At one extreme is a minority to whom it is a series of deductions from principles; at the other extreme is a minority to whom it is a series of blind habits; between the two is the great majority, representing every gradation but centering about the type of the inductive thinker. . . .

THE IMPORTANCE OF HABIT-FORMATION

The importance of habit-formation or connection-making has been grossly underestimated by the majority of teachers and writers of textbooks. For, in the first place, mastery by deductive reasoning of such matters as "carrying" in addition, "borrowing" in subtraction, the value of the digits in the partial products in multiplication, the manipulation of the figures in division, the placing of the decimal point after multiplication or division with decimals, or the manipulation of the figures in the multiplication and division of fractions, is impossible or extremely unlikely in the case of children of the ages and experience in question. They do not as a rule deduce the method of manipulation from their knowledge of decimal notation. Rather they learn about decimal notation by carrying, borrowing, writing the last figure of each partial product under the multiplier which gives that product, etc. They learn the method of manipulating numbers by seeing them employed, and by more or less blindly acquiring them as associative habits.

In the second place, we, who have already formed and long used the right habits and are thereby protected against the casual misleadings of unfortunate mental connections, can hardly realize the force of mere association. When a

$$\begin{array}{r} 15 \\ 19 \\ 16 \\ \underline{18} \end{array}$$

child writes sixteen as 61, or finds 428 as the sum of 18 or gives 642 as an answer to 27×36, or says that 4 divided by $\frac{1}{4} = 1$, we are tempted to consider him mentally perverse, forgetting or perhaps never having understood that he goes wrong for exactly the same general reason that we go right; namely, the general law of habit-formation. If we study the cases of 61 for 16, we shall find them occurring in the work of pupils who after having been drilled in writing 26, 36, 46, 62, 63, and so on, in which the order of the six in writing is the same as it is in speech, return to writing the 'teen numbers. If our language said onety-one for eleven and onety-six for sixteen, we should probably never find such errors except as "lapses" or as the results of misperception or lack of memory. They would then be more frequent *before* the 20s, 30s, and so on, were learned.

If pupils are given much drill on written single column addition involving the higher decades (each time writing the two-figure sum), they are forming a habit of writing 28 after the sum of 8, 6, 9, and 5 is reached; and it should not surprise us if the pupil still occasionally writes the two-figure sum for the first column though a second column is to be added also. On the contrary, unless some counter force influences him, he is absolutely sure to make this mistake.

The last mistake quoted $(4 \div \frac{1}{4} = 1)$ is interesting because here we have possibly one of the cases where deduction from psychology alone can give constructive aid to teaching. Multiplication and division by fractions have been notorious for their difficulty. The former is now alleviated by using *of* instead of $\times$ until the new habit is fixed. The latter is still aproached with elaborate caution and with various means of showing why one must "invert and multiply" or "multiply by the reciprocal."

But in the author's opinion it seems clear that the difficulty in multiplying and dividing by a fraction was not that children felt any logical objections to canceling or inverting. I fancy that the majority of them would cheerfully invert any fraction three times over or cancel numbers at random in a column if they were shown how to do so. But if you are a youngster inexperienced in numerical abstractions and if you have had *divide* connected with "make smaller" three thousand times and never once connected with "make bigger," you are sure to be somewhat impelled to make the number smaller the three thousand and first time you are asked to divide it. Some of my readers will probably confess that even now they feel a slight irritation or doubt in saying or writing that $16\frac{6}{1} \div \frac{1}{8} = 128$.

The habits that have been confirmed by every multiplication and division by integers are, in this particular of *"the ratio of result to number operated upon,"* directly opposed to the formation of the habits required with fractions. And that is, I believe, the main cause of the difficulty. Its treatment then becomes easy. . . .

Lest the last few paragraphs be misunderstood, I hasten to add that the psychologists of to-day do not wish to make the learning of arithmetic a mere matter of acquiring thousands of disconnected habits, nor to decrease by one jot the pupil's genuine comprehension of its general truths. They wish him to reason not less than he has in the past, but more. They find, however, that you do not secure reasoning in a pupil by demanding it, and that his learning of a general truth without the proper development of organized habits back of it is likely to be, not a rational learning of that general truth, but only a mechanical memorizing of a verbal statement of it. They have come to know that reasoning is not a magic force working in independence of ordinary habits of thought, but an organization and coöperation of those very habits on a higher level.

CHAPTER XIII

Heredity and Environment

[Knowledge of what heredity and environment can and do do in making *homo sapiens* of 1950 differ as he does from other species of mammals is of great practical importance. The original nature of man resides in his chromosomes and is changed by selective breeding. Additions to it and subtractions from it are made by foods, drugs, customs, schools, books, and so on. The former is like changing the nature of seeds; the latter is like enriching or cultivating the soils the plants grow in. If selective breeding takes a gene out from human chromosomes or puts a new gene in, the effect is lasting because self-perpetuating. The work of foods, drugs, customs, schools, and so on usually has to be done anew for each generation; few customs can be guaranteed to be self-perpetuating. Other things being equal, improvements of the human species by improving the genes are more dependable and much more economical than improvements of it by improving its environment.

The other things are not equal. We can easily add to science and put the additions in books, models, and apparatus, but to add to human genes the knowledge that water is made of hydrogen and oxygen would be impossible without millions of millions of experimental births and lives (and probably even with them).

In view of the great importance for human engineering of knowing what to attempt via the genes and what to attempt via their nurture before and after birth, it is regrettable that this knowledge has been clouded by ignorance and prejudice. Certain writers discuss at great length the fact that inherited nature always has to have the coöperation of a certain environment, and use it as an argument against the potency of heredity. The real workers in the field take this for granted. To say that fishes have by heredity the ability to swim is not to say they would swim without water to swim in. To say that the genes of man have a certain influence upon intellect and character means that they will do so and so when nurtured in human wombs and in human families or some substitute therefor. Certain writers who should know better put forth claims which require the transmission to offspring of traits acquired by the parents. Freud and Jung seem to me to do this. Certain writers have regarded the activities of the ants, bees, and wasps as significant forerunners of the social activities of man!

What nature and nurture can and do do in making one human individual or group differ from another individual or group is also of great practical importance. Ova from the same mother fertilized by the same father are by no means identical, but the variation among such is reduced from the variation of all human fertilized ova. The collection of genes carried by one person need not be identical with the collection carried by another, and commonly is not. Education will presumably be more successful if it takes account of original differences in abilities and proclivities than if it denies or neglects them.

As selections relevant to the original inherited nature of *homo sapiens* I use a contribution to a symposium of 1942 and a few typical extracts from *The Original Nature of Man.*]

HUMAN INSTINCTS AND DOCTRINES ABOUT THEM *

The Old Use of the Term "Instinct"

THE older treatment of instincts was one feature of a faculty psychology that was satisfied to explain events by naming their unknown causes. Up till about 1900 the words *instinct*

* *The British Journal of Educational Psychology*, Vol. 12, Part II, (June, 1942), pp. 85–87.

and *instincts* were used by students of psychology and education as names for propensities or mixtures of propensities and abilities much as sensation, attention, imagination, memory and reasoning were used as names for abilities. The mind was endowed with mysterious powers to respond to certain vibrations by sensations of green, and to respond to the judgment that "All men are mortal" and that "Socrates is a man," by the inference that Socrates is mortal, and similarly with mysterious propensities to respond to certain situations by anger and attack and to others by love and caresses.

A factual psychology that described mental events by the situations, the states of the organism, and the responses concerned, and sought the causation in biological events in man's nervous system, abandoned instincts in the older sense, but retained the word as a name for certain unlearned connections between situation and response or unlearned elements in such connections. But the older usage persisted. Freud's theories are full of it. Business psychology adopts it. It is what sociologists who minimize the importance of instincts have in mind.

Genes as the Causes of Behaviour

There are no such magical instincts. There are only certain probabilities, ranging up to near certainties, that certain situations will evoke certain responses as a consequence of features of the fertilized human ovum, and especially of its genes. A man's behaviour is the product of his genes and the environments which they seek out or to which they are subjected. . . . It has been convenient to call the genes' share by some such names as "instincts and capacities," or "unlearned tendencies," or "original nature." It still is convenient in teaching the science of education because students of education know very little about the genes, and because nobody knows enough to trace any particular piece of [human] behaviour back and attribute its causation to observable forces of the environment and observable features of the genes. But the dynamic realities concerned are the genes and the environments. The division between them is also the great practical division, since the genes can be changed beneficially chiefly by selective breeding, whereas the environments can be improved by direct action, for example, by schools.

We cannot observe the contributions of the genes directly, and do not know them surely except in cases where the environmental events, including "accidental" events within the body, are clearly inadequate to account for a person's behaviour. It is, however, safe to say that there are hundreds, probably thousands, of genes influencing intellect, conduct, skill, and other features of behaviour. In the *Original Nature of Man*, published in 1913, I made a rough inventory of tendencies attributable to the genes. On re-examining it I find some cases of too great generosity to the genes, but more cases where the progress of research has transferred causation from environmental to genetic forces.

For example, scientific observations of infants show that the control of the body (from the wobbly searching movements of the head of the new-born to the erect locomotion and the digital explorations of many months later, and including raising the head, turning over from back to belly, turning from belly to back, reaching, grasping without the thumb, opposing the thumb, sitting up, standing up, squatting, and many scores of different performances), is instigated and directed in large measure by the genes. The old notion was that nature gave only a miscellany of random movements any one of which was as likely to occur in any one situation as in any other situation, and that nurture slowly constructed adaptive movements out of these extensions, flexions, wiggles, waves, and spasms. On the contrary, a child gets these movements from the same source and with much the same regularity that it gets its teeth. They would probably suffice to move him adaptively in the normal environment of *homo sapiens*. They serve as the materials out of which in the main even such "artificial" movements as the machinist's, or acrobat's, or pianist's, are created.

There are scores, if not hundreds, of unlearned connections between situations and these responses of bodily movement and posture.

The genetic contributions to a man's life range from big and important to tiny and specialized. Samples of the former are the arrangements whereby voluptuous sensation occurs and strengthens whatever mental connection arouses it, whereby the state known to psychiatrists as "anxiety" occurs and makes miserable and ineffective the person in whom it occurs, and whereby the miscellaneous movements of the mouth parts producing the prattle of infants from about twelve months to about thirty months occur. Samples of the latter are the arrangements whereby a person in air or water without support grasps at any object within reach, whereby a person falling throws out his arms, and whereby a child will follow after a person walking away from him slowly, but run away from the same person walking toward him fast.

Some of these gene-caused determiners of human behaviour cause a person not to do some one thing in response to a certain situation, but rather do one after another of a number of things *until a certain result is attained.*

Some, perhaps all, of them act with a margin of variation or "imperfection" within an individual. The genes and the brain facts produced by them are neither gods nor atoms but biological facts.

Some of them cause a person to make only the coarser and provisional adjustments to situations, leaving the finer and final adjustments to be determined by the general capacity to maintain and retain tendencies which have satisfying consequences.

They coöperate and interfere in multifarious ways, so that a person's behaviour, even if it were utterly uninfluenced by learning, would show a rich array of combinations and fragments from any list of specific, defined connections between situations and responses that one might draw up.

They are, as is well known, modified by environmental forces, dying from disuse, being forestalled by the early acquisition of contrary habits, being distorted by the rewarding of some of their eccentric manifestations, and shifting from their "natural" stimuli to others associated therewith.[1]

The difficulty of estimating what men would be and do apart from experience is no excuse for failing to make the best estimate possible, much less for reverting to a *tabula rasa* doctrine. We can plan better methods of teaching reading if we know the two gene-caused arrangements for eye-movements out of which the movements used in reading are constituted. We can make better plans for the control of bullying if we can learn more about the gene-caused tendencies to dominance and submission. We could, I venture to assert, manage the difficult business of government better if we had better knowledge of what people want by their original natures as contrasted with what they have been taught to want by custom and indoctrination.

FIGHTING *

Pugnacity and anger are usually coupled together (for example, by James ('93, Vol. 2, p. 409 f.), and by McDougall ('08, p. 59 f.)), as the external and internal aspects of the same response. But the facts of original nature are hardly so simple. Pugnacious behavior or fighting and angry behavior are both complexes, which need to be analyzed and which are by no means proved to be inseparable in man's original equipment. There seem, indeed, to be at least six separable sets of connections in the so-called "fighting instinct." [2] These are:

(1) To the situation, "being interfered with in any bodily movements which the individual is impelled by his own con-

---

[1] The ease of such modifications has, however, been exaggerated by many psychologists and educationists, who have, for example, attached great importance to Watson's experiment, but paid no attention to Bregman's much more extensive work which showed that the attachment of fear to a genetically neutral stimulus by "conditioning" is extremely slow and slight.

* From "The Original Nature of Man," *Educational Psychology,* Vol. I, (1913), pp. 68–73.

[2] There is a still different set or sets for the tendencies most usefully called *instinctive anger.*

stitution to make, the interference consisting in holding the individual," the little child makes instinctively responses of stiffening, writhing, and throwing back the head and shoulders. These are supplemented or replaced by kicking, pushing, slapping, scratching and biting in the older. This tendency, if it exists, may be called the instinct of *escape from restraint*.

(2) To a similar situation, with the difference that the interference is by getting in the way or shoving, the responses are: dodging around, pushing with hands or body, hitting, pulling and (though, I think, much less often) slapping, kicking and biting. This may be called the instinct of *overcoming a moving obstacle*.

(3) To the situation "being seized, slapped, chased or bitten (by any object), the escape-movements having been ineffective or inhibited for any reason," the fighting movements. or the paralysis of terror may be the response. When the former occurs, the total complex may be called the instinct of *counter-attack*.

To the particular situations that arise when attack provokes counter-attack, there are, I believe, particular responses. If *A* clings to *B*, trying to throw him down or bite him, *B* will, by original nature, more often try to push *A* away or throw him down than to hit or bite him. If *A* rushes at *B*, slapping, scratching and kicking, *B* will, by original nature, more often hit and kick at *A* than try to push him away or throw him down. I believe that there is a basis in original nature for the distinction in sport between the fight with fists, which I judge to be a refinement (inappropriate as the word may seem) of the "slap-scratch-poke" fighting, and the wrestling match, which I judge to be a refinement of the "push-pull-throw down-jump upon" fighting. When *A* and *B* are both down, the response is an effort to get on top. When *A* is beaten, it is originally satisfying to *B* to sit on him (or it), to stand exulting beside him (or it), and to remain unsatisfied (if *A* is a human being) until *A* has given signs of general submissiveness. Many other specialized original tendencies, such as to remove things from different parts of the body in different ways, and to duck the head and lift up the arm, bent at the elbow, in response to the situation, "an object coming toward the head rapidly," appear in the course of a fight.

(4) To the situation "sudden pain" the response is attack upon any moving object near at hand. This may be called the instinct of *irrational response to pain*. This fact, common in everyone's experience, may of course be interpreted as an acquired habit of response by analogy, but it seems to the writer that it is a true and beautiful case of nature's very vague, imperfect adaptations, which only on the whole and in a state of nature are useful. When a loving child with indigestion beats its mother who is trying to rock it to sleep (though it would protest still more if not rocked), or when a benevolent master punches the servant who is lifting his gouty foot, the contrary habits seem too strong to be overcome by the force of mere analogy.

(5) To the situation, "an animal of the same species toward whom one has not taken the attitude of submission and who does not take it toward him" the human male responds by threatening movements, shoving the person away, and, if these fail to produce the attitude of submission, by either submission or further attack. The encounter is closed by the submission of either party, which may take place at any point. This tendency may be called the instinct of *combat in rivalry*.

(6) To the situation, "the mere presence of a male of the same species during acts of courtship," the human male tends to respond by threatening or attacking movements until the intruder is driven away or the disturbed one himself flees.

I am less confident of the existence of this than of any of the other specializations of the fighting tendency, but on the whole cannot conquer the suspicion that mere presence without other provocation does arouse resentment in other males engaged in courtship as it would not otherwise, and that the disappearance of the intruder rather than his submission is the satisfying condition in this case much more than in others.

(7) Either as habits of analogy developing from these

specialized tendencies, or as an equally original but vaguer tendency in addition to them, the following behavior occurs:

To the situation—being for some length of time thwarted in any instinctive response by any thing, especially if the thwarting continues after one has done various things to evade it, the response-group of pushing, kicking, hitting, and so on, is made, the attack continuing until the situation is so altered as to produce instinctively other responses, such as fulfilling the original activity, hunting, mangling, triumphing over, or fleeing from, the thwarting thing.

MASTERING AND SUBMISSIVE BEHAVIOR [3]

There is, I believe, an original tendency to respond to "the presence of a human being who notices one, but without approving or submissive behavior" by holding the head up and a little forward, staring at him or not looking at him at all, or alternating staring and ignoring, doing whatever one is doing somewhat more rapidly and energetically and making displays of activity, and by satisfaction if the person looks on without interference or scorn. There is a further tendency to go up to such an unprotesting human being, increasing the erection and projection of the head, looking him in the eye, and perhaps nudging or shoving him. There is also an original tendency to feel satisfaction at the appearance and continuance of submissive behavior on the part of the human beings one meets. These tendencies we may call the instinct of *attempt at mastery*. Such behavior is much commoner in the male than in the female. In her the forward thrust of the head, the approach, displays of strength, nudging and shoving are also commonly replaced by facial expressions and other less gross movements.

If the human being who answers these tendencies assumes a submissive behavior, in essence a lowering of head and shoulders, wavering glance, absence of all preparations for

[3] From "The Original Nature of Man," *Educational Psychology*, Vol. I, (1913), pp. 92–95.

attack, general weakening of muscle tonus, and hesitancy in movement, the movements of attempt at mastery become modified into attempts at the more obvious swagger, strut and glare of triumph. The submissive attitude may also provoke the master to protect the submissive one. If the human being protests by thrusting *his* head up and out, glaring back, and not giving way to advance, the aggressor either becomes submissive or there is more or less of a conflict of looks, gestures, yells, or actual attacks, until, as was described under the fighting instinct, the submission of one or the exhaustion of both.

There is an original tendency to respond to the situation, "the presence of a human being larger than oneself, of angry or mastering aspect," and to blows and restraint, by submissive behavior. When weak from wounds, sickness or fatigue, the tendency is stronger. The man who is bigger, who can out-yell and outstare us, who can hit us without our hitting him, and who can keep us from moving, does originally extort a crestfallen, abashed physique and mind. Women in general are thus by original nature submissive to men in general. Submissive behavior is apparently not annoying when assumed as the instinctive response to its natural stimulus. Indeed, it is perhaps a common satisfier. . . .

The original behavior in mastery and submission, and in approving, disapproving, being approved and being scorned, derided and neglected, becomes very much complicated by differences in the sex of the person who is the situation, and in the sex and maturity of the person who is responding, by an increase in the number of persons who are the situation, and by the presence in the situation of elements provocative of curiosity, fear, anger, repugnance, the hunting instinct, kindliness, sexual attraction and coy behavior. My account of attempt at mastery, for instance, would be only partly true of any cases save those where the situation and the response were the behaviors of two males of about the same degree of physical maturity. Mastery and submission are fit illustrations of the universal fact that the many unit tendencies to respond to characteristic situations combine in elaborately complex totals. This fact makes the original social tendencies of man seem, at first sight, like a hopelessly unpredictable muddle of domineering, subservience, notice, disregard, sex pursuit, aversion, showing off, shyness, fear, confidence, cruelty and kindness. It also makes such unit-tendencies as I have described under approval, scorn, mastery and submission seem abstract and schematic, as indeed they are.

Space is lacking in this book, and knowledge in its author, to trace in the bewildering complexes of human intercourse, the combined effect of the unit-tendencies which I have outlined. We may be confident, however, that, did we know enough, we should find that whether a person will in a given case be shy, or indulge in display, or alternate between the two—whether he will domineer or plead in courtship—whether he will respond toward a given child by approval, domineering, bullying, protection, hunting or fondling—could in every case be prophesied from knowledge of the situation and of him.

Two such problems may be taken as sample tasks. When, we may ask, will mere display or showing off, without further behavior toward mastery, be the response, and when will shyness? Can we do better with these two problems that to note that display is characteristic of the male human being when attracted by a female, and that there is "a certain amount of purely instinctive perturbation and restraint due to the consciousness that we have become objects for other people's eyes?" (James, '93, Vol. 2, p. 432.)

Display—Consider what should happen to mastering behavior in the male if the condition of the one responding, or of the situation to which he responds, possesses elements which inhibit the proud look and threatening approach. Will not the tendency appear in the mutilated form of display alone? Now, to be sexually attracted would, by arousing another form of approach in the responder, inhibit his threats. If the situation were not one human being but many, it would, by arousing readiness to retreat, have a similar effect. Again, if the situation were a much more mature person, one larger and more impressive, but by his encouraging looks not provocative of submissive behavior, the tendency toward mastering behavior would be retained as display alone. The hypothesis that instinctive showing off is what is left of mastering behavior when certain parts of it are kept out seems likely, since it accounts so well for the three main sets of circumstances under which this mild form of self-assertion occurs.

Shyness—In the second problem, we are required to find out what original shyness is, as well as when it occurs. It seems to consist chiefly in hesitancy and restraint of movement (most easily noticed in speech), lowering of eyes, and averted face. I suggest, therefore, that it may be submissive behavior *minus the gross bodily cringing, and the inner acceptance of subserviency,* and that it occurs as what is left of the response of submissive behavior when the condition of the person responding, or of the situation to which he responds, possesses elements which inhibit these. Thus, where a powerful and hostile crowd would provoke submission *in toto,* a *mere* crowd or a fairly friendly crowd provokes shyness, and the speaker simply cannot look at them quite squarely or speak naturally. Similarly, while a sufficiently domineering mistress may provoke submission *in toto,* the ordinary nice girl makes her admirers simply shy. Similarly, the adult whose behavior, if fully masterful, would provoke submission *in toto,* by omitting certain features of his mastering behavior reduces its effect upon others to shyness.

NATURE AND NURTURE AS CAUSES OF INDIVIDUAL DIFFERENCES

[As selections relevant to the influences of nature and nurture in causing difference within the human species, I use parts of six publications. The first is *Measurements of Twins,* No. 1 of the Archives of Philosophy, Psychology, and Scientific Method, pp. vii and 64.

In 1905 when *Measurements of Twins* appeared, the facts concerning the multiple births from a single ovum in the armadillo were unknown and identical twins had been distinguished from others only by bodily appearance, helped out somewhat dubiously by fingerprints. The facts quoted below from pages 7–9 of the monograph are consequently about a mixture of both sorts of twins.]

MEASUREMENTS OF TWINS

4. THE RESEMBLANCES OF YOUNG AND OF OLD TWINS

The older twins show no closer resemblance than the younger twins, and the chances are surely four to one that with an infinite number of twins tested the 12–14 year olds would not show a resemblance .15 greater than the 9–11 year olds. The facts are given in Table 2.

TABLE 2

The resemblances of young and old twins compared

	In Corrected Coefficients		In Raw Coefficients	
	Twins 9–11	Twins 12–14	Twins 9–11	Twins 12–14
1) A test	66	73	58	67
2) Word test	81	62	62	49
3) Misspelled word test	76	74	76	74
4) Addition	90	54	83	46
5) Multiplication	91	69	81	53
6) Opposites	96	88	79	78
Marks in 1), 2) and 3) combined			71	69
Marks in 4), 5) and 6) combined			90	75
Averages	83	70	75	64

5. THE RESEMBLANCES IN TRAITS LITTLE AND IN TRAITS MUCH SUBJECT TO TRAINING

The variations in the closeness of resemblance of the twins in the different traits show little, and possibly no, direct correlation with the amount of opportunity for environmental influences. The traits most subject to training (addition and multiplication) do show closer resemblances than the traits least subject to training (the A test and word test); but on the other hand show less close resemblances than the traits moderately subject to training (the misspelled word test and opposites test). The hypothesis that the true resemblance varies in amount *inversely* with the amount of opportunity for environmental influence would not be irreconcilable with the facts, and the hypothesis that the differences between the different traits are due to chance (including in that term the variable errors of the measurements and the possibility of the unequal inheritance of different traits) is the most probable of all. The difference between the traits most subject and those least subject to training is no greater than the median difference between any one trait of the six and any other. Surely there is no evidence here of any large contribution from similarity of training to similarity of achievement. The facts are given in Table 3.

TABLE 3

The resemblances of twins in traits little and in traits much subject to training

	Coefficients of Correlation	Averages
1) A test	.69	} .70
2) Word test	.71	
3) Misspelled word test	.80 (?) [1]	} .85+
6) Opposites test	.90	
4) Addition	.75	} .795
5) Multiplication	.84	
Marks in 1), 2) and 3) combined	.70 (raw) [2]	
Marks in 4), 5) and 6) combined	.82 (raw) [3]	

[1] The raw coefficient was .754. I have no means of correcting for attenuation except indirectly. The corrected coefficient would be at least .80.

[2] The correction for attenuation would increase this only slightly, since it is derived from seven trials. The true *r* can hardly be above .75.

[3] The case is as noted in 2. The true *r* can hardly be above .85.

6. THE RESEMBLANCES IN MENTAL TRAITS COMPARED WITH THE RESEMBLANCES IN PHYSICAL TRAITS

It is highly probable from the facts given in sections 3–5 that the similarity of twins in ancestry and conditions of conception and birth accounts for almost all of their similarity in mental achievement,—that only a small fraction of it can be attributed to similarity in training. On general principles it is also highly probable that similarity of ancestry and conditions of conception will produce equal similarity in original physical nature and in original mental nature. Certain resemblances in original physical nature are in all probability neither increased nor decreased by such similarities and differences of home training as act upon twins and non-related children, respectively, within a group such as ours; e. g., resemblances in cephalic index, ratio of height sitting to total height, eye color and hair color. Other resemblances in original physical nature are so increased and decreased slightly and perhaps not at all; e. g., circumference of head, length of head, width of head, length of forearm and length of finger joints.

If then the resemblances of twins were almost entirely due to original nature, we should expect them to be only slightly in excess of the resemblances in physical traits. The existence of the latter as a fact may properly be taken as a partial verification of the former as a general hypothesis. The evidence of its existence is given in Table 4.

TABLE 4

The resemblances of twins in mental and in physical traits

In Mental Traits		In Physical Traits	
1. A test	.69	11. Cephalic index	.76
2. Word test	.71	12. Ht. sitting/ht.	.76
3. Misspelled	.80+	13. Height	.78
4. Addition	.75	14. Height sitting	.83
5. Multiplication	.84	15. Circ. of head	.75
6. Opposites	.90	16. Width of head	.86
7. Combined mark in 1–3	.70+	17. Arm length	.72
8. Combined mark in 4–6	.82+	18. Finger length	.71

7, 8 and 12–15 are raw correlations and the correction for attenuation might raise them by .01 or .02.

Median of 1–6	.78	Average of 11–12	.76 (possibly .77)
		" 13–18	.77 (possibly .78 or .79)
Average of 1–6	.78	Median of 13–18	.77 (possibly .78 or .79)
		" 11–18	.76 (possibly .77)
Average of 7–8	.76 (possibly .80)	Average of 11–18	.76 (possibly .77)

[The second selection is from a general account written forty years later.]

HEREDITY AND HOME ENVIRONMENT [4]

The differences of any one person from others in intellect, character, and behavior are due partly to differences in his genes from theirs, and partly to differences in his environment from theirs. It is interesting to argue about what such gene differences can and cannot do in a given environment and about what environmental differences can and cannot do with a given equipment of genes. But it is probably more instructive to observe and measure than to argue. I shall, in fact, limit my comments to measurements, and chiefly to measurements of the influence of genes and environment on abstract intelligence of the sort required to learn facts and principles as in history, science, mathematics, law, medicine, and engineering.

The most famous set of measurements of the relative shares of the genes and home environment are those made by Newman, Freeman, and Holzinger, using twins so closely alike in body that they may be assumed to have developed by the splitting of one egg fertilized by one sperm. Fifty such, brought up each pair in one same home, showed an average difference of 5.4 points I.Q. Nineteen such, brought up each pair in two different homes, showed an average difference of 8.2 points I.Q. Ordinary non-twin siblings brought up in the same home, measured in the same way by Outhit, show an average difference of 12.9 points I.Q.[5] Unrelated children brought up in the same orphanage will differ one from another in such a test by about 19 or 20 points I.Q.

The reductions of (1) ordinary sibs in the same home, (2) identical twins in different homes, and (3) identical twins in the same home from the 19.5 for unrelated children in the same orphanage are, respectively, 6.6, 11.3 and 14.1. The shift from unrelated to sibs, and the shift from sibs to identical

[4] *Eugenical News*, Vol. 29, No. 3–4, (Sept.–Dec., 1944), pp. 39–45.
[5] A Study of the Resemblance of Parents and Children in General Intelligence, *Archives of Psychology*, 1933, No. 149.

twins cause large reductions, (6.6 and 7.5) but the shift from different home to same home makes a relatively small one (2.8).

If the persons concerned in the above measurements were measured a second time independently with some alternative intelligence test, they would differ from themselves, on the average, by about 5 points. So it is desirable to correct the measurements given above which came from records of a single test to what they would probably have been if each person had been measured by a large number of independent tests. When this is done, the reductions that were 6.6, 11.3, and 14.1 become 6.9, 12.3, and 16.8. But the main facts remain the same. The shift from unrelated children in the same orphanage to non-twin sibs in the same home gives a reduction in average difference of 6.9; the shift from non-twin sibs in the same home, to identical twins in the same home gives a reduction of 9.9; the shift from identical twins in different homes to identical twins in the same home gives a reduction of only 4.5. When the uncorrected differences were used the reduction due to the genes of the twins alone was four fifths that due to the genes of the twins plus sameness of home; when the corrected differences are used the former is almost three fourths of the latter.

A similar preponderance of the genes over home environment in causing differences in I.Q. appears in the facts for siblings in the home of birth and in foster homes. Shuttleworth's analysis, which is impartial in the data used and sound in method, finds that 63.9 per cent of the variation in individuals is due to (A) differences in their genes independently of their home environments, 15.4 per cent to (B) differences between their home environments independently of their genes, and 17.8 per cent to (C) differences in something which one's genes and his home environment have in common.[6] I take it this 17.8 per cent is testimony to the fact that intelligent parents, brothers, sisters, grandparents, etc., can

[6] The Nature versus Nurture Problem, *Journal of Educational Psychology*, Vol. 26, (1935), pp. 561–578 and 655–681.

and do produce a family environment that stimulates and augments intelligent behavior. C is then that fraction of the individual's own gene causation of his intelligence score that duplicates gene causation from other members of the family *via* the environment they produce. The 63.9 per cent accounted for by A does not include the influence of all an individual's genes upon intelligence. To compute that we must add the 17.8, making 81.7 for differences in genes and 15.4 per cent for differences in home environments, with 2.9 per cent due to changes in the family environment's influence upon the different children brought up in it.[7]

To say that, with genes as they are and homes as they are in this country today, the differences among individual white children are determined four or five times as much by differences in the former as by differences in the latter is not to say that the genes are everywhere and always four or five times as potent as environments. Insert a hundred persons with very inferior gene equipment and a hundred with very superior gene equipment into the thousand run-of-the-mill homes and the percentage attributable to gene differences will rise. Leave the genes as they were, a random sample of white American children, but let a hundred of the homes be replaced by barren huts, with illiterate and feeble-minded foster parents, in a schoolless community, while another hundred are replaced by America's best, and the percentage attributable to home environment will rise.

School and home environment will presumably have a larger share in determining intelligence scores than home environment alone. Environments taken by random sampling over a space of a thousand years will have a larger share than contemporary environments. The relative shares of genes and environments may also vary greatly with the mental trait in question. If the data had been food preferences instead of intelligence scores, the allotment might perhaps have been

---

[7] I may note that Heerman and Hogben's allotment of only 50 per cent of the causation of differences in IQ to the genes is due to the inexcusable blunder of assuming that the correlation of an Otis Advanced test with another independent test of intelligence will be .97.

15 per cent or less to the genes and 75 per cent or more to the homes.

The differences among human individuals are not explainable by any one rule of allotment to genes and environments. There are millions of different bundles of genes that grow into persons. There are billions of environmental conditions and events that may act upon each person. Consequently, the causation of the thoughts, feelings, and acts of human individuals is infinitely multifarious, and often very complex. But I know of no important trait in which human individuals differ that is immune to scientific inquiry; and I have hopes that knowledge of the causation of many traits will, in the next forty years, advance as rapidly as knowledge of the causation of differences in intelligence has advanced in the last forty.

[The third and fourth selections report measurements of the resemblance of siblings.]

THE RESEMBLANCE OF SIBLINGS IN INTELLIGENCE-TEST SCORES [8]

Most of the investigations of sibling resemblance in intelligence have reported correlation coefficients below .50. But there is now good reason to think that the true resemblance in, say, the native-born white population of the United States is .70 or higher, and that the lowness of many of the coefficients reported in the past was caused by measuring individuals from the mean of some restricted group instead of from the mean of the total population, and by the failure to correct for the inaccuracy of the instrument used to measure intelligence.

I have recently computed the resemblance in 409 pairs of brothers among students in Columbia College. The correlation, using deviations from the mean of the 409 in the test used is .41, but the estimated correlation for brothers in

[8] *The Journal of Genetic Psychology*, 64, (1944), pp. 265–267.

general measured from the mean of the general population is .73.

Fifteen years ago I studied the resemblance of 486 pairs of siblings in a certain city, all being boys or girls who had entered high school and stayed at least two years. The correlation, using deviations from the mean of the group itself, was .435 after correction for attenuation, but the correlation, using deviations from the mean for the general population of that city, was .70. This .70 is, however, subject to the possible selection of an undue proportion of children alike in intelligence because the siblings were found among pupils attending the high school in Grades 9, 10, and 11 in 1922 in Grades 10, 11, and 12 (plus a few pupils held back in Grade 9) in 1923, and also pupils found in Grade 9, September, 1924, and in Grade 10 in June, 1925. In a report made in 1928, I set .60 as the true correlation for the general population. I now think that I then underestimated the influence of the periods of selection in giving too many bright younger sibs and dull older sibs, and overestimated the influence of continuance to high school in giving too many pairs of sibs alike in being brighter than the other children in the family.

At that time I reported without analysis or comment the correlation of .73 for 812 pairs of siblings in high school in another city, deviations being taken from the mean of the general population assuming that to be the same as in the other city. I have re-examined the data from this city and have obtained the following results: The correlation of the 812 pairs, if deviations are taken from the mean of the group itself, is .43 raw and .45 after correction for attenuation. The correlation, using deviations from estimated averages for ages 13 to 18 in the whole population of the city, is, after correction for attenuation, .77. This may be checked by using $\sqrt{1 - r^2} =$ variability of an array/variability of the total population, and assuming that the sib of any child scoring very high in intelligence will, except very rarely, be bright enough to be admitted to high school, so that the variability of the sibs of high arrays of our high-school group will be practically as large as the variability of the sibs of all persons in the general population who scored as high. The standard deviation of an array for the arrays forming the top 13 per cent of the group is 38.8 points of the test score. The standard deviation of the general population may be set as 53.5 for the average of an infinite number of tests such as the two used. Some boys and girls in their teens score 350 and an imbecile would score zero. By this method $r = .69$.

Outhit ('33), measuring father, mother, and children in 51 families, 30 of which had four living children each, and 21 of which had from five to 10 living children, found r for *IQ* of siblings to be .67, uncorrected for attenuation. Since the tests used were Stanford-Binet for those under age 12 and Army Alpha for those older, with only a single trial in both cases, correction for attenuation probably would raise this to .80 or higher. The distribution of the children (mean *IQ* 107.65, *SD* of *IQ* 17.2) is enough like that of the general population to make any correction on that account unimportant.

Outhit gives the *IQ* of each of the 256 siblings so that we can compute the variability within each family from the mean of the sibs of that family. I have done so and the sum of the X^2 is 22899, giving an average intra-family *SD* of 9.5. This is however lower than the *SD* that would be found if the deviations could be taken from the true mean for all conceivable offspring of each pair of parents. That *SD* can be computed indirectly by taking each child's differences from all his sibs, finding the average, dividing by $\sqrt{2}$, and dividing further by .7989. Doing this gives 10.45. The *SD* of the *IQ* from one test with Stanford-Binet or Army Alpha is 17.2 for Outhit's entire population, and that for the entire native white youth of the country is not much different. If it is 17.2, $r = .80$; if it is 18, $r = .81\frac{1}{2}$; if it is 16, $r = .76$.

Raymond Cattell ('38), using the scores of 199 pairs of siblings from a bimodal group with many high-scoring and many low-scoring and few mediocre, but correcting the coefficient for this, computed the resemblance in the general population as .77. He was the first to assert emphatically that estimates of .50 or less for fraternal resemblance in intelligence are far below the truth.

No attempt was made by any of these investigators to measure the relative contributions of heredity and environment in producing the resemblance of siblings, and I will make none here. But it may be noted that the problem takes on a changed aspect if the resemblance is over .70 instead of under .50.

REFERENCES

1. CATTELL, R. B., & WILSON, J. L. "Contributions concerning mental inheritance: I. Of intelligence." *Brit. J. Educ. Psychol.*, 8, (1938), 129–149.
2. OUTHIT, M. C., "A study of the resemblance of parents and children in general intelligence." *Arch. of Psychol.*, No. 149 (1933).
3. THORNDIKE, E. L., "The resemblance of siblings in intelligence." *27th Yrbk. Nat. Soc. Stud. Educ.*, Pt. 1, (1928), 41–53.

THE CAUSATION OF FRATERNAL RESEMBLANCE [9]

I have records of 409 pairs of brothers (plus four pairs of half-brothers, not used in this investigation), students at Columbia College, consisting of height, weight, age at entrance to college, and score made at or near the time of entrance in the Thorndike *Intelligence Examination for High-School Graduates.*

I have used these to compare the amount of resemblance in traits little subject to home environment with that in traits more subject to it. Weight is presumably more subject to home environment than height is; and age at entrance to college is subject to parental wealth and pressure to do well in school more than test-score is.

HEIGHT

We correct the actual heights to probable values at age 19 and later by adding 4 inches to those of age 15.1 or 15.2;

[9] *The Journal of Genetic Psychology*, Vol. 64, (1944), pp. 249–264.

3½ inches to those of age 15.3 or 15.4; 3 inches to those of age 15.5 or 15.6; 2½ inches to those of age 15.7, 15.8 or 15.9; 2 inches to those of age 16.0, 16.1 or 16.2; 1½ inches to those of age 16.3, 16.4 or 16.5; 1 inch to those from 16.6 to 16.9; and ½ inch to those from 17.0 to 17.4.

Table 1 [omitted here] shows the fraternal resemblance of the Columbia brothers in stature so corrected. They are obviously a selected group with a mean stature of 69.25 inches and with about three quarters of them above the mean of the general adult male population, which is 67½ inches.[10] The Pearson correlation computed by using deviations from their own mean is .50, but that computed by using deviations from 67.75 is .60. [I used 67.75 rather than 67.5 partly for convenience and partly to have a factor of safety against too high correlations.]

Using 67.75 as the mean for the general population and using the means of the 12 Columbia arrays under 76.5″, 76.0″, 75.5″, . . . 71″ as means of the arrays of all brothers of persons 76.5″, 76″, 75.5″ . . . 71″, we have values of the fraternal correlation in the general population as follows: [11]

By the array under 76.5, $n =$ 3, $r = .43$
By the array under 76.0, $n =$ 0
By the array under 75.5, $n =$ 1, $r = .56$
By the arary under 75.0, $n =$ 5, $r = .59$

[10] According to the monumental work óf Davenport and Love (The Medical Department of the United States Army in the World War, vol. XV, Statistics, 1921), the mean stature of the general male population of the United States draft in the first World War was 67.49 inches. The means for New York, New Jersey, and Connecticut were 66.72, 66.77 and 66.71 respectively. The corresponding standard deviations were 2.71 inches for the entire draft and 2.66 for the New York urban area, 2.66 for the New York eastern manufacturing region, 2.76 for the New York suburban territory, 2.77 for the New York urban area, 2.74 for the New Jersey densely populated area and 2.68 for the Connecticut near-metropolitan area. Rountree found 67½ inches as the average for 2,000,000 examined for the present draft. (Science, Vol. 94, p. 552 f.)

[11] The assumption that the resemblance of the 409 pairs of Columbia brothers in stature will equal the resemblance of brothers in the general population is not fully justifiable. Stature has a slight positive correlation with intelligence, so that if tall boys have dull brothers unable to enter college, the dull brothers will be somewhat shorter than the brighter brothers who do go to college. But the influence of the correlation between stature and intelligence is surely very slight.

By the array under 74.5, $n = 11$, $r = .44$
By the array under 74.0, $n = 12$, $r = .55$
By the array under 73.5, $n = 10$, $r = .63$
By the array under 73.0, $n = 27$, $r = .48$
By the array under 72.5, $n = 23$, $r = .80$
By the array under 72.0, $n = 30$, $r = .80$
By the array under 71.5, $n = 29$, $r = .73$
By the array under 71.0, $n = 51$, $r = .70$

The average is .61 if we give equal weight to each array; it would be .67 if we gave weights in proportion to n, but that is not desirable because, other things being equal, the arrays most remote from the general mean should have the most weight. Weighing each array by $\sqrt{n}$ we have .60 as the average r.

An independent estimate of the fraternal correlation for stature in the general population may be made by comparing the variability of an array of Columbia brothers with the variability of the general population, and using

$$\frac{\text{var. of an array}}{\text{var. of the gen. pop.}} = \sqrt{1 - r^2}.$$

The estimate from the reduction of the variability of an array is .52.[12] It is .523 from arrays for 68½ inches or higher, and .515 from arrays for 68 inches to 64 inches. The standard deviations in arrays for 64 inches or less vary according to how the means are smoothed, but a reasonable treatment of them gives $r = .52$. There are so few cases in these arrays that any reasonable estimate will not alter the general estimate of .52 by the reduction of the variability.

The fraternal correlation for stature by our data may then be set as .56. This is somewhat above the figures of Pearson and others. But the populations used by them may have been selected from the upper levels, economic and intellectual, of the population.

[12] I compute the SD's of the successive arrays from a series of smoothed means, 72½" for the array under 76½, 72 for the array under 75½ and 75, 71½ for the arrays under 74½ and 74, 71 for the arrays under 73½ to 72, and so on. If the actual means had been used, the estimated r would have been higher, of course.

WEIGHT

I correct the weights to probable weights at age 19.0 as given in Table A.

TABLE A

Age	Add	Age	Add	Age	Add	Age	Add	Age	Subtract
15.0	32 lb.	16.0	19 lb.	17.0	9 lb.	18.0	4 lb.	19.0 to 19.9	2 lb.
15.1	30 lb.	16.1	18 lb.	17.1	9 lb.	18.1	4 lb.	20.0 to 20.9	3 lb.
15.2	28 lb.	16.2	17 lb.	17.2	8 lb.	18.2	4 lb.	21.0 or >	4 lb.
15.3	27 lb.	16.3	16 lb.	17.3	8 lb.	18.3	3 lb.		
15.4	25 lb.	16.4	15 lb.	17.4	7 lb.	18.4	3 lb.		
15.5	24 lb.	16.5	14 lb.	17.5	7 lb.	18.5	3 lb.		
15.6	23 lb.	16.6	13 lb.	17.6	6 lb.	18.6	2 lb.		
15.7	22 lb.	16.7	12 lb.	17.7	6 lb.	18.7	2 lb.		
15.8	21 lb.	16.8	11 lb.	17.8	5 lb.	18.8	1 lb.		
15.9	20 lb.	16.9	10 lb.	17.9	5 lb.	18.9	1 lb.		

The fraternal correlation table is shown in Table 2 [omitted here].

The average weight at age 19.0 of the general male population whence these brothers are drawn may be set at 139.5. The average for the draft in 1917–18 for New York, New Jersey, Connecticut, and Pennsylvania was 139.5. The average for the draft in the present war is eight pounds heavier, according to Rountree. The average at age 19.0 would be less than that for the same persons at the draft ages. Using deviations from 139.5, the correlation is .41.[13]

We may check this correlation of .41 by using the variabilities of the arrays. The standard deviation of the general male population at age 19.0 is almost certainly not over 17.42 lb., the figure for the draft in the first world war. The standard deviations of the arrays, deviations being taken from smoothed means, are as given in Table B.

The average of these (weighted by the numbers in the

[13] The mean corrected weight at age 19.0 of the Columbia brothers is 143.4. If the mean weight of the general population at age 19.0 is higher than 139.5, the correlation will be lower (about .40 for 140.5, .39 for 141.5, and .38 for 142.53. If the mean weight of the general population is lower than 139.5 the correlation will be higher (about .44 for 138.5 and .45 for 137.5).

arrays) is 16.12, which would correspond to a correlation of .38. But if we omit the arrays for 180 or over, which may be unduly influenced by our process of correction, it is 15.84, which corresponds to a correlation of .42.

TABLE B

Array	Smoothed mean	N	Standard deviation
Under 93–101 lb.	124.5	4	21.20 lb.
Under 102–110 lb.	127.5	11	22.35 lb.
Under 111–119 lb.	130.5	54	13.32 lb.
Under 120–128 lb.	133.5	100	16.27 lb.
Under 129–137 lb.	139.5	151	16.05 lb.
Under 138–146 lb.	141.5	172	15.15 lb.
Under 147–152 lb.	145.5	104	13.83 lb.
Under 153–161 lb.	148.5	112	19.53 lb.
Under 162–170 lb.	151.5	63	13.59 lb.
Under 171–179 lb.	154.5	24	12.21 lb.
Under 180–188 lb.	157.5	13	19.77 lb.
Under 189–197 lb.	160.5	4	12.45 lb.
Under 198–206 lb.	163.5	4	23.80 lb.
Under 207–215 lb.		0	
Under 216–225 lb.	169.5	2	51.00 lb.

Since the 17.42 lb. is an outside estimate for the variability of the general population at age 19.0 we may be confident that the fraternal resemblance of all brothers in that population is as likely to be under .41 as above it, and has only one chance in 700 of exceeding .50.

INTELLIGENCE-TEST SCORE

We have two measures of "intelligence," the actual score made in the Thorndike *Intelligence Examination for High-School Graduates* a few days (or sometimes a few months), before the time of entrance, and an estimated score if the person had taken the test at age 17.75 years. The latter is computed from the actual score by adding amounts for the younger and substracting amounts for the older by the scale given in Table C.

We wish to know what the fraternal correlation would be in a random sample of the general population tested with the

Thorndike examination at age 17.75 years. We may use our data to estimate this in two ways. The first is to estimate the mean Thorndike score for such a random sample and to compute the regression toward it of the brothers of persons scoring 115, or 114, or 113, or any other very high score from the observed regression in the Columbia brothers. The second is to estimate the variability for such a random sample and to compute the reduction from it in the variability of arrays of Columbia brothers for scores of 115, 114, 113, . . . 95.

TABLE C

Age at entrance 15.1–15.2,	add 7.0 to the Intelligence Score
Age at entrance 15.3–15.4,	add 6.0 to the Intelligence Score
Age at entrance 15.5–15.6,	add 5.5 to the Intelligence Score
Age at entrance 15.7–15.8,	add 5.0 to the Intelligence Score
Age at entrance 15.9–16.0,	add 4.5 to the Intelligence Score
Age at entrance 16.1–16.2,	add 4.0 to the Intelligence Score
Age at entrance 16.3–16.4,	add 3.5 to the Intelligence Score
Age at entrance 16.5–16.6,	add 3.0 to the Intelligence Score
Age at entrance 16.7–16.8,	add 2.5 to the Intelligence Score
Age at entrance 16.9–17.0,	add 2.0 to the Intelligence Score
Age at entrance 17.1–17.2,	add 1.5 to the Intelligence Score
Age at entrance 17.3–17.4,	add 1.0 to the Intelligence Score
Age at entrance 17.5–17.6,	add 0.5 to the Intelligence Score
Age at entrance 17.7–17.8,	add 0 to the Intelligence Score
Age at entrance 17.9–18.0,	add 0 to the Intelligence Score
Age at entrance 18.1–18.2,	subtract 0.5 from the Intelligence Score
Age at entrance 18.3–18.6,	subtract 1.0 from the Intelligence Score
Age at entrance 18.7–19.0,	subtract 1.5 from the Intelligence Score
Age at entrance 19.1–19.6,	subtract 2.0 from the Intelligence Score
Age at entrance 19.7–20.6,	subtract 2.5 from the Intelligence Score
Age at entrance 20.7–21.6,	subtract 3.0 from the Intelligence Score
Age at entrance 21.7 or over,	subtract 3.5 from the Intelligence Score

It may be assumed that if we had every brother of those scoring 95 or higher in the Thorndike examination instead of only those who entered Columbia, the mean score and the variability for them all would differ little from the mean score and variability for those who did enter Columbia. This assumption was checked as follows:

There were 88 families in the group having one or more brothers scoring 95 or higher in the intelligence examination. With the coöperation of the Columbia Alumni Federation, the following request probably reached 77 of them, of whom 76 replied.[14]

Have you any brothers besides ....
If so, please give the following facts for each of them:
    First name and middle initial   ....
    Year of birth   ....
    Did he graduate from high school? ....
    If so, in what year?   ....
    Did he enter college?   ....
    If so, what college?   ....

Of these 76 families, 55 had no other brothers than those in my records, 21 had 25 brothers, 16 years old or older at the time of writing, besides those in my records. All of these 25 save one graduated from high school; all save four entered college; all save five graduated from high school before the age of 19.

Unless the one who failed to reply and the 11 who were not reached had brothers not on my list who were duller than the 25 reported by the 76 who replied, we must conclude that almost every brother in a fraternity containing one scoring 95 or higher, might have gone to Columbia so far as intellect was concerned, and that if all the brothers in these 88 families had taken the Thorndike examination at age 17.75 the means would have been only a trifle lower than the mean for our selection from them and the variability in each array would have been only a trifle greater than the variability for our selection from them.

If all males aged 17.75 in the general white population did the best that they could with the Thorndike examination, the mean score would probably be near 50. For there was a substantial percentage of high-school graduates in 1920 to 1930 scoring below 50, and the 5 percentile of high-school graduates of those years was near the 50 percentile of the total population of their age. Lorge found the following equivalents in a group of 80 adults all tested with *CAVD*, Army Alpha, Thorndike, Otis and other tests: Thorndike,

[14] No good address was available for six, and the letters for five more were returned to me by the postal authorities.

52.1 is equal to army Alpha, 128.0, and to *CAVD,* 400, and to Otis *A,* 42.4, and to Otis *B,* 32.3. By these equivalents Thorndike 52 represents a point above the mean ability of persons of age 17.75.

The standard deviation of Thorndike Examination scores of all white males at age 17.75 may be estimated as at least 20.0. The upper range surely extends past 115 and we may reasonably expect that 1½ persons per thousand of that age would score 113 or higher. The low range surely extends below zero, in the sense that the idiots and imbeciles would have to improve considerably to make any positive score in this examination. The standard deviation for the 80 W.P.A. adults measured by Lorge is about 21, a stretch of 49 being required to include 70 per cent (2.08 *SD*), a stretch of 54 being required to include 80 per cent (2.56 *SD*), and a stretch of 59 to include 90 per cent (3.29 *SD*). Robert Thorndike has found with a vocabulary test that the standard deviation of the Gallup-poll sample is twice that of Columbia and Barnard students. The standard deviation for Columbia College Entrants is at least 12. It is 14.2 for our group of brothers using the score corrected for age at entrance, but this may be a little high because of spurious variation introduced by the corrections. It is 11.6 if the uncorrected scores are used, but this is surely too low because the uncorrected scores of the younger and brighter pupils are reduced unduly toward the mean, and those of the older and duller are raised unduly toward the mean. These facts support the estimate of 20 as a minimum for the standard deviation of the general male population at age 17.75. . . .

Using 53 as the mean score of the general population at age 17.75 and the means of the arrays of Columbia brothers under scores of 95 or higher as the means of the arrays of brothers in the general population under similar scores, we compute seven estimates of the correlation as follows:

Array under   95– 98; $n = 59$, $r = .80$
Array under   99–102; $n = 23$, $r = .90$
Array under 103–106; $n = 30$, $r = .78$

Array under 107–110; $n = 18$, $r = .70$
Array under 111–114; $n = 15$, $r = .67$
Array under 115–118; $n = 6$, $r = .65$
Array under 119–122; $n = 2$, $r = .59$

Weighting each array equally the average of the seven is .73. . . .

The variability of each of the arrays in the double-entry correlation table for intelligence-test score corrected for age was as shown in Table D.

TABLE D

Arrays	N	Smoothed means	SD
Under 95– 98	59	89.0	13.5
Under 99–102	23	89.0	13.8
Under 103–106	30	93.0	12.7
Under 107–110	18	93.0	14.5
Under 111–114	15	97.0	15.1
Under 115–118	6	97.0 ⎱	16.0
Under 119–122	2	101.0 ⎰	

If the standard deviation of the general population at age 17.75 is set at 20, the correlations inferred from these variabilities are in order .74, .72, .78, .68, .65, and .61. They have an average of .71 if weighted equally and an average of .73 if weighted by the numbers in the arrays. The latter seems a much sounder weighting here. If the standard deviation for the general population at age 17.75 is 22, as it may well be, the correlation estimated from the variability of the arrays would be, not .71 or .73, but .73 or .76. . . .

A fraternal correlation of .73 for intelligence-test score is much higher than most of those that have been reported, but is in accord with results of Outhit, Raymond Cattell, and the writer. . . .

AGE AT ENTRANCE TO COLLEGE

The two procedures in estimating the fraternal resemblance in the age at entrance to college are in general the same as those used for Thorndike score, but the facts are more complex and less certain. The mean age at entrance for the general male population if all tried to get into Columbia may be set at 20.5 years, it being understood that most of those who did not get in at or before age 20.5 could never get in. Probably over half of the general male population could never get admitted to Columbia College, no matter how much their parents spent for schools and tutors. The standard deviation of age at entrance to Columbia may be set at 1.8 years for the top half of the general population in this respect since there are actually entrants at age 15.1 or younger $(20.5 - 15.1 = 5.4$, which equals 3 times the standard deviation of the upper half). The standard deviation of the bottom half is undetermined. The variability of an array of all brothers of persons who entered at 15.1, or at 15.2, or at any age up to 16.9 may be assumed to be little greater than the variability of an actual array of the Columbia brothers of entrants at these ages. There would doubtless be an occasional brother in the general array who was long delayed by economic conditions, or invalidism, and so on, or who did not enter at all. But as a rule, if one brother in a family enters college as young as 15.1 to 16.9, his brothers may be expected to enter college with few exceptions, and to vary from his entrance-age not much more than the Columbia brothers of such a young Columbia entrant vary from his.

The facts for Columbia brothers of young Columbia entrants are presented in Table 3 [omitted here]. The means and standard deviations of the five arrays are as given in Table E.

TABLE E

	Mean	Smoothed mean	SD from smoothed mean
Array under 15.1–15.2	16.55	16.20	.820 yr.
Array under 15.3–15.6	16.20	16.50	.535 yr.
Array under 15.7–16.0	16.90	16.80	.804 yr.
Array under 16.1–16.4	16.96	17.00	1.028 yr.
Array under 16.5–16.8	17.26	17.20	.955 yr.

If the means of corresponding arrays of brothers in the general population are the same as these we have the following as the five estimates of the correlation by the regression lines from 20.5 years through these means: .75, .86, .78, .84, and .85. . . . [The fraternal resemblance in age at entrance to college may then be set at .84 or .85 compared with .73 for resemblance in intelligence-test score.]

If the variabilities of corresponding arrays of brothers in the general population are the same as those for the Columbia group and if the SD of the general population is 1.8 years, we have .890, .956, .896, .821, and .847. . . .

I have additional data by which to compare the resemblance of siblings in intelligence-test score and in age at entrance to a certain grade in high school. All the pupils attending Grades IX, X, and XI, in May, 1922, in a certain city were tested with the *I.E.R. Test of Selective and Relational Thinking, Generalization, and Organization.* So also were all the pupils attending Grades X and XI in May, 1924. Among them were 812 pairs of siblings, all of whom were tested with another form of the test a year later. For 809 of these pairs, I have the age in months at the time of taking the test in May. Subtracting eight months gives the age at entrance for all save the few who were held back in that grade for a year or more. [The results for these 812 pairs of siblings and for 486 pairs in another city contradict those for Columbia College siblings. They show less resemblance in age at entrance to a given high-school grade than in intelligence-test score (about .60 compared with about .70).

On the whole this investigation presents a confusing picture. The college siblings are more alike in height than in weight, though similarity in home environment should influence weight more than height. The high-school sibs are more alike in test score than in age at entrance to a given grade. The conflicts in the evidence can be explained by assuming (1) that with identical environments height would show much greater resemblance of sibs than weight would, and (2) that such family actions as keeping a boy out of school for a half year or more to work, or striving to have him complete high school in less than eight semesters were much commoner in the families of the Columbia college boys than in the families of the two cities. But no reasonable explanation of them is consistent with any great influence of home environment upon stature, weight, intellect, or rate of progress in school. In the case of intelligence-test score, the investigation gives no reason for any upward revision of Shuttleworth's allotment of 15.4 per cent of the variation of individuals as due to differences between their home environments independently of their genes.]

[The fifth and sixth selections report measurements of the influence of the environment.]

THE INFLUENCE OF DIFFERENCES IN THE AMOUNT OF PRACTICE IN CAUSING DIFFERENCES IN ACHIEVEMENT [15]

One fruitful form of experimentation concerning the relative contributions of heredity and environment in the causation of individual differences is to measure the consequences of a partial equalization of the environments of certain individuals. This article reports the facts for ability to add columns of 10 one-place numbers like those shown in Table 1 in 69 college students. Each did 336 such columns (48 a day for seven days), which, apart from any checking on the one hand or additions by grouping on the other, meant about 400 additions of two one-place numbers and about 2600 additions of a two-place and a one-place number.

TABLE 1

7	8	6	6	4
5	7	8	7	8
9	9	5	8	7
8	2	9	4	6
8	6	4	9	5
3	5	9	6	9
7	9	7	8	3
6	7	7	5	8
9	3	2	3	7
4	8	6	9	7

[15] *The Journal of General Psychology*, Vol. 31, (1944), pp. 101–109.

The individuals may be grouped either according to their scores for the first day or according to their scores for the entire seven days. I shall use both methods, but begin with the grouping by the total scores for the entire period, because these are the more reliable measures of the ability.

Six persons completed the 336 columns, including 3024 additions, in less than 2800 seconds and with an average of 19 errors. At the other extreme were six who required over 7300 seconds and made an average of 27 errors. In between were Groups II, III, IV, V, VI and VII shown in Table 2. Table 3 shows the status of each group on Day 1 and Day 7, and its gain.

TABLE 2

Data for eight groups arranged according to total achievement

		Amount of practice per person (in seconds)	Per cent correct	Amount of practice per person from mid-point of Day 1 to mid-point of Day 7 (in seconds)
Group	I (6 persons)	2430	99.4	2055
"	II (7 persons)	3137	99.4	2652
"	III (9 persons)	3810	99.1	3330
"	IV (15 persons)	4611	98.9	3946
"	V (11 persons)	5373	99.2	4547
"	VI (6 persons)	5771	98.9	4938
"	VII (9 persons)	6406	98.6	5370
"	VIII (6 persons)	7820	99.1	6762

The amount of time spent on the additions used in the experiment previous to Day 1 is not known for any of our groups. If the time so spent was 5390 seconds more by Group I than by Group VIII, there was equalization of these groups by the end of Day 7. Similarly if the time so spent was 4683 seconds more by Group II than by Group VIII, and so on.

Whatever progress there was toward equalization, or beyond equalization to an excess of time spent by Groups V to VIII over that spent by Groups I to IV, the resulting progress toward equalization of ability was small. Table 3 shows that Group I, which on Day 1 did 3.1 times as much as Group VIII, did 2.8 times as much on Day 7. Group II, which on Day 1 did 2.2 times at much as Group VII, did almost two times as much on Day 7.

TABLE 3

Average scores on day 1 and day 7 and average gains for groups arranged according to total achievement

| Group | N | Day 1 | | Day 7 | | Gain | |
		Number of additions per 100 sec.	Per cent correct *	Number of additions per 100 sec.	Per cent correct *	In number per 100 sec.	In per cent correct
I	6	108	99.0	140	99.6	32	0.6
II	7	80	99.2	110	99.5	30	0.3
III	9	65	98.9	87	99.3	22	0.4
IV	15	56	98.2	75	99.3	19	1.1
V	11	45	98.9	63	99.5	18	0.6
VI	6	44	98.8	64	99.3	20	0.5
VII	9	36	97.8	57	98.9	21	1.1
VIII	6	35	98.8	50	99.2	15	0.4

* In computing the per cent correct, I assume that each wrong answer for the sum of a column is caused by one wrong addition. The degree of accuracy with which these college students worked was such that this will be true with very few exceptions.

We do not know that Group I or Group II had had any more practice or any better teaching in the addition of integers than Group VIII or Group VII. It may be that the entire difference between the achievements of Group I and Group VIII on Day 1 was due to differences in the persons.

There is in fact strong evidence that this is near the truth. If all the groups had had 6300 seconds of practice previous to Day 1 and had gained as much from each 1000 seconds of it as they gained on the average from 1000 seconds of practice during the experiment, the status of the ability in Groups I to VIII when that 6300 seconds began would have been as follows:

Group   I   10   additions per 100 seconds. 97.0% correct.
Group   II   9   additions per 100 seconds. 98.4% correct.
Group   III   23   additions per 100 seconds. 98.1% correct.
Group   IV   26   additions per 100 seconds. 96.2% correct.

Group   V   20   additions per 100 seconds. 98.0% correct.
Group   VI   18½   additions per 100 seconds. 98.1% correct.
Group VII   11   additions per 100 seconds. 96.4% correct.
Group VIII   21   additions per 100 seconds. 98.4% correct.

The average condition of Groups I to IV and the average condition of Groups V to VIII would then have been almost the same, 17 additions per 100 seconds with 97.4 per cent correct and 17½ additions per 100 seconds with 97.7 per cent correct.

Suppose that each of the eight groups had been taken at the time when each averaged 10 additions per 100 seconds with 97.5 per cent of them correct.[16] Suppose that each of them had thereafter 7700 seconds of practice during which they gained at the same rate per unit of time spent that they did in the experiment, and then began the work of Day 1. The scores for the groups in Day 1 would then have been as given in Table 4. These scores are close to the actual scores in Day 1, except for Groups I and II; these would have been even further ahead of Groups VII and VIII than they actually were.

TABLE 4

		Additions per 100 sec.	Deviation from actual	Per cent correct
Group	I	130	+22	99.7
	II	97	+17	99.4
	III	61	−4	98.4
	IV	47	−9	99.7
	V	41	−4	98.5
	VI	41	−3	98.3
	VII	40	+4	99.0
	VIII	27	−8	97.9

In general any shift toward increasing the practice time for Groups I to IV or decreasing it for Groups V to VIII will make the fit of expectation to actuality worse. . . . .

Our assumption of the same gain in number of additions

[16] This time would have been during the early stages of practice with additions of a one-place to a two-place number, probably somewhere in Grade 3 for most of these college students.

per 100 seconds from a status of 10 as from a status of 20 or 30 or 90 or 100 is unduly simple. Probably the gains per unit of time spent from a status of 10 or 20 are less than the gains from a status of 50 or 60. After a very high status is reached there may well be a reversal. But any reasonable assumption about the rates of gain that is based upon what is known of the actual gains during the experiment will give similar evidence that the superiority of Groups I to IV over Groups V to VIII is not caused by a greater amount of time spent in practice by the former. The number gained may increase with the progress of practice, or decrease, or increase and then decrease; but if the curve of gain from a status of 10 done in 100 seconds is alike for all eight groups, and is estimated from the facts of the experiment, the evidence will hold that the superiority of Groups I to IV over Groups V to VIII is not caused by more time spent in practice by the former.

Our assumption of 97.5 per cent correct at a rate of 10 per 100 seconds is unduly optimistic, except for schools which took unusual precautions to prevent practice in error. If we had the actual work of these groups at the periods when they had reached a rate of 10 per 100 seconds, the accuracy would probably have been much less. But there is no sufficient reason to suppose that the differences between Groups I to IV and Groups V to VIII in the percentage of accuracy would in any way weaken the argument. Let number done and percentage correct be combined into a single score in any reasonable way, and let Groups I to VIII be taken from a starting point of equality in this combined score, and let the progress in this score made by each group in the same amount of time be estimated in any reasonable way from the facts of Tables 2 and 3—then the result will show that the superiority of Groups I to IV over Groups V to VIII is not caused by more time spent in practice by the former. . . .

[If the 69 persons are divided into groups according to their ability as measured on only Day 1 of the experiment, the evidence against environmental influence is not so strong.]

The essential facts of the amount of time spent and the

gains for each of seven groups (A, B, C, D, E, F, and G) are presented in Tables 5 and 6. The six highest on Day 1 then averaged 3.6 times as many additions per unit of time as the six lowest, and with 1.2 per cent higher percentage of accuracy. On Day 7 they averaged 2.6 times as many and with 1.0 per cent higher percentage of accuracy, though in the meantime the latter group had spent nearly three times as many seconds in practice. The 17 highest on Day 1 averaged 2.7 times as many additions per unit of time as the 19 lowest, and with 0.8 higher percentage of accuracy. On Day 7 they

TABLE 5

Amount of practice per person from mid-point of day 1 to mid-point of day 7 (in seconds) for groups arranged according to score on day 1

A	(6 persons)	2130
B	(11 ")	2958
C	(17 ")	3868
D	(6 ")	4134
E	(10 ")	4498
F	(13 ")	5528
G	(6 ")	5941
A + B	(17 ")	2666
C + D + E	(33 ")	4104
F + G	(19 ")	5664

TABLE 6

Averaged scores on day 1 and 7 and average gains for groups arranged according to score on day 1

		Day 1		Day 7		Gain	
		Number of additions per 100 sec.	Per cent correct	Number of additions per 100 sec.	Per cent correct	In number per 100 sec.	In per cent correct
A	6	109	99.0	144	99.7	35	0.7
B	11	76	99.2	92	99.5	16	0.3
C	17	61	98.8	74	99.4	13	0.6
D	6	51	99.0	71	99.5	20	0.5
E	10	46	98.3	67	99.2	21	0.9
F	13	38	98.6	58	99.3	20	0.7
G	6	30	97.8	56	98.7	26	0.9
A + B	17	85½	99.1	110½	99.6	25	0.5
C + D + E	33	54	98.7	71	99.4	17	0.7
F + G	19	35	98.3	58	99.1	23	0.8

averaged 1.9 times as many, and with 0.5 higher percentage of accuracy, though in the meantime the latter group had spent over twice as many seconds in practice.

If all groups had been given 6000 seconds of practice beginning in the case of each group at the point where it scored 10 additions per 100 seconds with 97.5 per cent correct, and if the gain during the 6000 seconds of practice was at the same rate per unit of time as during the experiment, the abilities reached by the different groups at the end of the 6000 seconds would have been:

A	109	additions per 100 sec. with 99.5% accuracy
B	42½	additions per 100 sec. with 98.1% accuracy
C	30	additions per 100 sec. with 98.4% accuracy
D	39	additions per 100 sec. with 98.2% accuracy
E	38	additions per 100 sec. with 98.7% accuracy
F	31½	additions per 100 sec. with 98.3% accuracy
G	36	additions per 100 sec. with 98.4% accuracy

The expectations for Groups A, F, and G are close to the actual abilities on Day 1, deviating respectively 0, +6, and −6 from them. Groups D and E would need about 2000 seconds more of practice to reach 51 and 46, and Groups B and C would need about 6000 and 9000 more respectively, to reach 76 and 61.

Considering the results by both groupings of the 69 subjects of the experiment, it is probable that the individual differences among college students in the speed and correctness of the mental connections involved in single-column addition would be little or no less than they are if all had spent, up to the time of measurement, identical amounts of time in forming and strengthening those connections. . . .

[A superficial criticism of this investigation might assert that the number of repetitions of the additions should have been used instead of the amount of time spent. But individual differences in the number of repetitions per unit of time spent are primarily consequences of differences in the abilities of the persons at that time.]

There are many important cases where a greater native

ability obtains more repetitions from the same amount of time and opportunity, for example, reading the vernacular or a foreign language and typewriting. In such cases superiority in the amount of repetition comes primarily from superiority in the ability.

HEREDITY AND SCHOOL ENVIRONMENT [17]

Certain facts published in the *Educational Records Bulletin*, Number 20, of June 1937, can be used to measure the influence of the environment in cases which are important both for theory and practice. They concern the variations in the Coöperative Test Service Examination of 1937 of students in the same school grade who have studied a certain subject for a certain length of time.

Thus in the Latin examination in Grade IX, three hundred thirty-one pupils who had studied Latin seven months had an average deviation from their mean of 5.0; five hundred fifty-seven pupils who had studied Latin sixteen months had an average deviation of 5.4; one hundred seventy-five pupils who had studied Latin twenty-five months had an average deviation of 7.4. When all three groups are combined with equal weight the average deviation is increased only to 8.0. That is, the variation in a group with an average deviation of six months (two-thirds of a school year) in length of study of Latin is reduced by only twenty-six per cent when this variation is reduced to zero, or near zero. [In some of the schools Latin was begun in Grade VII, in some in Grade VIII, and in some in Grade IX. The amount of time spent in each grade in each school is not known.]

The pupils in Grade X who had studied Latin sixteen, twenty-five, and thirty-four months, respectively, showed average deviations of 7.2, 6.5½, and 7.3½. The variation when the three groups were combined with equal weight was 8.5. The reduction of the variation in length of study of Latin from

[17] From *The Journal of Educational Psychology*, Vol. 29, (March, 1938), pp. 161–166.

six months to zero or near zero causes in this case a reduction of seventeen per cent in the variation in test score.

Using in the same way the facts for pupils in Grade XI who had studied Latin twenty-five, thirty-four and forty-three months, respectively, I find a reduction of only seven per cent.

Students in Grade IX who had studied French one, two, and three years respectively showed AD's of 8.14, 7.34 and 9.22, averaging 8.23. When all three groups were combined with equal weight, the AD was 9.07. The reduction was thus only nine per cent. Using Q's it was eight per cent. The three populations numbered four hundred fifty-nine, two hundred forty-six, and three hundred seventy-nine, respectively.

Students in Grade XII who had studied French one, two, and three years, respectively, showed AD's of 6.8, 5.2, and 6.0, averaging 6.0. When all three groups were combined with equal weight, the AD was 6.71. The reduction was thus only ten per cent. Using Q's it was fifteen per cent.

Let us now observe the effect of the reduction to zero or near zero from a still greater variation in length of study.

By the courtesy of Dr. Ben D. Wood I have the records in the Latin and French examinations from college sophomores who had had one, two, three, and four (or more) years of study of the language in question. The populations are large enough for our purposes, being fifty-two, fifty, one hundred forty-one and one hundred twenty-nine, respectively, for Latin, and three hundred nineteen, five hundred seventy, two hundred twenty-nine, and thirty-eight for French.

[In the case of Latin when all four groups are combined with equal weight the AD is 13.4 points. For the separate lengths of study the AD's are 11.0, 10.9, 10.6 and 8.7. The variation in score is reduced by only twenty-three per cent when the variation in their length of study is reduced from an average deviation of one year to zero or near zero. It is reduced by only twenty-six per cent if Q is used.]

The same procedure applied to the eleven hundred fifty-six college sophomores who had studied French from one to four years gives a reduction of the variation (measured by the average deviation) of thirteen per cent (from 11.2 to 9.75). Using the semi-interquartile range, the reduction is twenty per cent.

The same procedure applied to four hundred twenty-five college sophomores who had studied German from one to three years gives a reduction of twelve per cent (ten by AD, fourteen by Q). Applied to three hundred seventy-three who had studied Spanish from one to three years, it gives almost no reduction, (two per cent and one-half per cent).

If a certain amount of variation in maturity and in the action of the selective forces which retain a pupil in school and advance him in grade is added to the variation in length of study, we can get high-school groups also in which the latter is a whole school year.

The facts for Latin, calling a school year nine months, are as follows:

Grade IX	7 months study	$Q=4.3$	$AD=5.0$	$n=331$
Grade IX	16 months study	5.05	5.4	557
Grade X	16 months study	5.55	7.2	504
Grade X	25 months study	5.45	6.55	642
Grade XI	25 months study	6.85	8.0	266
Grade XI	34 months study	6.1	7.4	291
Grade XII	34 months study	6.0	8.5	101
Grade XII	43 months study	6.2	7.2	162
Average		5.7	6.9	

All combined with equal weight, $Q=12.65$, $AD=13.2$.

Reduction in the variation in length of study from one year to zero or near zero produces a reduction in the variation in score of fifty-two per cent (fifty-five by Q, forty-eight by AD). Much of this reduction is, however, due to the factors of maturity and selection which are correlated with the length of study. This is shown by the following facts: When groups of two lengths of study in the same grade are combined (with equal weight) the variation is hardly increased at all over that of either group. So combining the seven-month and sixteen-month groups in Grade IX gives a Q of 4.3 and AD of 4.6; combining the sixteen-month group and the twenty-five-month group in Grade X gives a Q of 5.7 and AD of 7.1; combining the twenty-five-month and thirty-four-month groups in Grade XI gives a Q of 5.8 and AD of 6.6; and combining the thirty-four-month and forty-three-month groups in Grade XII gives a Q of 6.3 and AD of 8.0.

But when groups of the same length of study in two grades are combined (with equal weight), the variation is increased substantially. So combining the sixteen-month groups in Grade IX and Grade X gives a Q of 6.1 and AD of 6.9; combining the twenty-five-month groups in Grade X and Grade XI gives a Q of 7.1 and AD of 8.4; combining the thirty-four-month groups in Grade XI and Grade XII gives a Q of 6.4 and AD of 7.8. Of the reduction of fifty-two per cent at least half may safely be credited to the reduction of maturity and selection differences when the population of only one grade is used. The twenty-six per cent remaining is about the same as the twenty-four and one-half per cent found for the college sophomores.

The facts for French are as follows:

Grades X and XI	7 months study	$Q = 7.75$ AD = 8.7
Grade X	16 months study	$Q = 5.75$ AD = 7.2
Grade XI	25 months study	$Q = 5.4$ AD = 6.1
Grade XI	34 months study (or more)	$Q = 5.85$ AD = 6.8
Average		$Q = 6.2$ AD = 7.2
All combined with equal weight		$Q = 8.7$ AD = 11.0

Reduction in the variation in length of study from one year to zero or near zero produces a reduction in the variation in score a bit under thirty-two per cent, (twenty-eight and one-half by Q, thirty-four and one-half by AD). If a fourth of this is credited to the maturity and selection factors, we have twenty-four per cent to put with the sixteen and one-half per cent found for college sophomores.

From these various and mostly independent determinations we have the following reductions in the variation in score with reductions in the variation in length of study:

6 months (two-thirds of a school year) to zero or near zero
  Latin by AD, 26, 17 and 7; by Q, 21, 23 and 7; average 17.

French by AD, 9 and 10; by Q, 8 and 15; average 10½.
9 months (one school year) to zero or near zero
Latin by AD, 23, 24; by Q, 26, 27½; average, 25.
French by AD, 13, 26; by Q, 20, 21; average, 20.

Consider now the influence of variation in amount of school training plus the variation in maturity (and possibly in selective forces) in the case of the combination of abilities in English usage, spelling, and word knowledge measured by the Coöperative Test Service English Examination.

The variation in the various groups is as follows:

640 students in Grade VIII	AD $= 6.75$	$Q = 5.8$
2083 students in Grade IX	AD $= 7.5$	$Q = 6.6$
2402 students in Grade X	AD $= 7.53$	$Q = 6.35$
2767 students in Grade XI	AD $= 8.2$	$Q = 6.1$
2701 students in Grade XII	AD $= 7.4$	$Q = 6.35$
Average	AD $= 7.47$	$Q = 6.2$

All five groups combined with approximately equal weight, AD $= 8.5$, $Q = 7.32$.

Reduction of the variation in education from an average deviation of one and a quarter school years to zero or near zero, produces a reduction in the variation in English score of only thirteen or fourteen per cent (twelve by AD, fifteen by Q). After any reasonable allowance for the part of the variation caused by maturity, there is very little left to be credited to the differences in amount of school training, not a tenth of what must be allotted to differences in heredity and in other environmental forces than school training.

These facts are important for theory because they show the weakness of the environment as a cause of differences in abilities where it should be strong. Latin, French, English usage, spelling, and vocabulary are in large measure informational abilities, and presumably more susceptible to increase by training than such powers as strength, energy, memory, or intelligence. . . . Yet variations in these abilities are out of all proportion to variations in the amount of school training.

Let anyone make any reasonable allowances for the fact that the time spent in study is spent in part upon things not measured by the tests, for the fact that the students in the later years of study may spend less time on their Latin or French than they did in the earlier years, and for any other facts which make the average difference in *actual training* with the Latin or French in the combined groups less than the average difference in years, and make the average difference in *actual training* within a single year group greater than zero. There will still remain a notable lack of correlation between amount of training and amount of test-ability, a notable failure of the variation in training to account for more than a minor share of the variation in the ability measured by the test.

We are subject to a fallacy in arguments about the causation of individual differences in man, which leads us to suppose that what training of a special sort does under special conditions training of any sort does in general. At its worst this fallacy is as bad as arguing that differences in stature are due to the environment, because one of two identical twins became fourteen inches shorter than the other by having his legs cut off! So the resemblances (that is, reduced variation) of whatever sort among siblings were plausibly attributed to resemblances in their home environments. The facts for children reared in orphanages showed how weak this argument really was. So the environment of infancy when the mind was supposedly at the mercy of any Watson who might inflict a loud noise upon it when it was viewing a dog or snake, or of any mother who cuddled it too long or often, turned out in Bregman's extensive and careful experiments to be a very feeble modifier. It has been plausible to attribute the bulk of various resemblances and differences to schooling because we did not look to see just what the actual variations in schooling do do. The more one looks the more one is confronted by failures of the environment to do what has been expected of it.

CHAPTER XIV

Mental Fatigue

[In recent years psychologists have paid relatively little attention to what was once a subject for much experimentation. The meaning of the term *fatigue* is changing from "a condition caused by mental work done with inadequate rest" to "a condition caused by work, shock, emotional strains, and so on." Thus in World War II "combat fatigue" replaced the "shell shock" of World War I. However, the facts concerning mental fatigue in its older meaning are still important.]

I. FATIGUE IN A COMPLEX FUNCTION *

By the coöperation of eighty-nine students in a graduate course in educational psychology at Teachers College I am able to report measurements of the effect of about four hours of continuous work at writing poetry upon the quantity and quality of the product produced per unit of time and upon the satisfyingness of the process of producing it.

The work consisted of writing lines to complete 108 couplets, the first lines being given. These first lines were taken from Pope and Byron, the following being a random sampling.

Glittering with ice here hoary hills are seen
_____

The fourth day rolled along and with the night
_____

Self-love forsook the path it first pursued
_____

* From *The Psychological Review*, Vol. XXI, No. 6, (November, 1914), pp. 402–407.

What she has done no tears can wash away,

———————

Bid harbors open, public ways extend

———————

From the damp earth impervious vapors rise

———————

Mark first that youth who takes the foremost place

———————

Back to my native moderation slide

———————

But still he only saw, and did not share,

———————

In clouded majesty here dullness shone;

———————

But while he shuns the grosser joys of sense,

———————

But high above, more solid learning shone

———————

They were arranged in 9 sets of 12 lines each (called here-after sets *a, b, c, d, e, f, g, h,* and *i*). Eight sets were done without rest in the afternoon or evening of a given day; the ninth set being done after rest in the morning or afternoon of the following day. The individuals who engaged in the experiment were divided into nine squads (called hereafter squads *abc, bcd, cde, def, efg, fgh, ghi, hia* and *iab*). One squad did the sets in the order *a, b, c, d, e, f, g, h,* rest, *i;* the next squad did the sets in the order *b, c, d, e, f, g, h, i,* rest, *a;* and so on. I shall use Period 1, Period 2, Period 3, etc., to designate the nine periods of work. The arrangement of the work was then as in Table I.

Each individual recorded the time required to get the twelve couplets of each set, and also the degree of satisfying-ness of the work on each set. The scale for satisfyingness was arbitrarily defined as follows: Call 5 the amount of enjoyment or satisfyingness of mental work which represents your average condition; let 10 represent the greatest amount of enjoyment or satisfyingness which you have experienced from mental work; let 0 represent the greatest distaste or intoler-ance toward any piece of work which you have experienced. Let 6, 7, 8, 9 and 1, 2, 3, 4 represent intermediate conditions by equal steps. This scale is obviously crude and unduly subjective, but will suffice for such inferences as will be drawn here.

TABLE I

The set of couplets completed by each squad in each period

Squad		Period							
	1	2	3	4	5	6	7	8	9
abc	a	b	c	d	e	f	g	h	i
bcd	b	c	d	e	f	g	h	i	a
cde	c	d	e	f	g	h	i	a	b
def	d	e	f	g	h	i	a	b	c
efg	e	f	g	h	i	a	b	c	d
fgh	f	g	h	i	a	b	c	d	e
ghi	g	h	i	a	b	c	d	e	f
hia	h	i	a	b	c	d	e	f	g
iab	i	a	b	c	d	e	f	g	h

The quality of the poetry written was measured as follows: The various completions of one couplet (call it $a\,1$) were collated and graded by four judges. The same four judges would grade similarly the completions of another couplet (call it $a\,2$). A new combination of four judges would grade the completions of $a\,3$ and $a\,4$; a new combination would grade the completions of $a\,5$ and $a\,6$. In all about 80 judges shared in the work of grading the couplets for quality, each judge grading some hundred or more lines; and every line being graded by four judges. The grading was on a scale of 0 to 10, 0 being a line absolutely devoid of merit and 10 as good a line as, in the opinion of the judge, could be written to make that couplet. This again is obviously a very crude and unduly subjective scale, but will serve the purpose of the present argument sufficiently well.

We have then for each of eighty-nine individuals a record like the following of the time required for each of eight consecutively accomplished sets of 12 lines of poetry, and of one done the next day after rest, of the satisfyingness of the work at each of the nine periods, and of the quality of the product produced:

Individual M. D. F. did set f in period 1, 7.46.30 to 8.5.45 P. M., spending 25 minutes 15 seconds, the successive couplet-completions being rated as 16, 17, 21, 15, 14, 17, 17, 9, 6, 13, 13 in quality by the sum of four judges' ratings. M. D. F. rated the satisfyingness of the work as 4.

He did set g in period 2, 8.8.45 to 8.29.30 P. M., spending 20 minutes 55 seconds, the successive couplet-completions being rated as 14, 19, 20, 11, 14, 16, 20, 15, 12, 7, 18, 13 in quality by the sum of four judges' ratings. M. D. F. rated the satisfyingness of the work as 4.

And so on for the seven remaining sets.

These individual records are arranged in 9 squads so that each set (a, b, c, d, etc.) was done at each period, equalizing the effect of any differences in the difficulty of the sets of first lines to be made into couplets.

Examination of the individual records shows that for the problem under consideration there is no misleading in massing the results and presenting simply average or median achievements and degrees of satisfyingness by squads. This is done for time required, quality of product, and reported satisfyingness in Tables II, III and IV, [omitted here] which utilize all the records for Period 1, Period 8 (the last of the consecutive work-periods), and Period 9 (the work-period of the following day after rest).[1]

The facts are clear. The speed of work increases throughout the work-period and is not benefited by the rest. [The average time required to complete twelve couplets is 34.5 in Period 1, 23.0 in Period 8, and 23.2 in Period 9, after rest.] The average quality of the product produced falls off a very little, from 4.47 in Period 1 to 4.24 in Period 8, and is slightly benefited by the rest, from 4.24 in Period 8 back to 4.47 in Period 9. The reported satisfyingness of the work falls off greatly, from 5.38 in Period 1 to 3.56 in Period 8, and is greatly benefited (from 3.56 to 4.85) by the rest. The effect of continuous exercise of the function is to increase gross efficiency, but to decrease satisfyingness or interest. The effect of the

[1] Some of the eighty-nine individuals did not complete all of the 108 couplets within the approximate four hours set apart for the experiment. Some others by accident failed to complete the entire set of couplets or to score the time.

rest is a very slight gain in gross efficiency but a very great gain in satisfyingness or interest.

The average amount per unit of time and satisfyingness reported for each successive period of the total work period and the quality of the product in periods 1, 4, 6 and 8, were as follows:

Period	1	2	3	4	5	6	7	8
Couplets per 10 minutes	3.48	4.36	4.69	4.82	4.84	5.08	5.03	5.22
Quality of couplets	4.47	...	...	4.43	...	4.35	...	4.24
Satisfyingness	5.38	5.21	4.94	4.48	4.31	3.95	3.67	3.56

The changes from period to period were thus:

	1–2	2–3	3–4	4–5	5–6	6–7	7–8
Couplets per 10 minutes	+.88	+.33	+.13	+.2	+.24	—.05	+.19
Satisfyingness	—.19	—.27	—.46	—.17	—.36	—.28	—.11
Quality of couplets	—.04 from 1 to 4			—.08 from 4 to 6		—.11 from 6 to 8	

These facts are also clear. Speed improves, with fluctuations such as one customarily finds. Quality remains about the same. Satisfyingness falls off throughout.

II. THE DECREASE IN EFFICIENCY OF A SINGLE FUNCTION UNDER CONTINUOUS EXERCISE [2]

The term *efficiency* is used here to refer to the quantity and quality of the product produced. If the quantity per unit of time remains constant, decrease in efficiency is measured by the decrease in quality; with quality constant, by the decrease in quantity; with both varying, by some composite of the two changes.

The term *single function* is used in antithesis to "the mind as a whole," not to mean a function devoid of compoundness or complexity. I mean by it such functions as adding a column of figures, reacting to a signal by a movement as quickly as possible, the signal and movement being the same throughout,

---

[2] From *Educational Psychology*, Vol. II, Chapter II, *passim*, and *The Journal of Educational Psychology*, Vol. 2, (Feb., 1911), pp. 61–80.

judging which of two weights (all close to 100 grams) is heavier, memorizing the English equivalents of German words, or multiplying a three-place number by a three-place number, nothing being allowed to be written or spoken save the two numbers themselves. Each of these functions comprises different elements, not all of which are at work all the time. Exercise is continuous only in the sense that the subject does his best to make it so.

[If the efficiency at the end of a work period is compared with that at its beginning, as was done by Burgerstein ('91), Bettman ('95), Oehrn ('95), Bergström ('94), Lindley (1900), Bolton ('02), Heüman ('04), and Whipple ('10), losses from the exercise without rest are on the whole counterbalanced by gains from practice. It is better to define fatigue as a decrease in efficiency which is curable by rest, and compare the efficiency at the end of a work period with that shown after an adequate rest. The experiments of Weygandt ('97) and Kafemann ('02), when so treated, show a fatigue effect of 11 per cent for 90 minutes of addition; and the author ('12) found an effect of 6 per cent from approximately 100 minutes addition in the case of five adult subjects. These effects may be due largely to fatigue of the eye muscles.

As a function which taxes the mind far more than the functions used in the experiments referred to in the preceding paragraph, I chose mental multiplication of a three-place number by a three-place number, neither number having any 0's or 1's among its digits. These examples were typewritten; the subject looked at an example (say, $\frac{297}{465}$) and got the product in any way he chose, with the one condition that he must write nothing until he got the whole product. He could look at the example as often as he pleased. He was asked to work for 5 hours, and longer if he could. The subject recorded the time (to seconds or to the nearest 10-second point) of beginning an example. As soon as he got and recorded its product, he recorded the time and began on another example. Apart from these intermissions of a second or two to look at a watch and record the time, the work was substantially continuous.]

Such work is, as anyone will find by attempting it, very exacting and fatiguing in the popular sense. It is also very hard both in the sense that many individuals cannot do it at all, and in the sense that those who can do the work experience in most cases pronounced feelings of strain or effort.

Six subjects worked with no rest . . . from 2 to nearly 8 hours, respectively. Nine subjects worked from 4 to over 12 hours, respectively, with rests for luncheon of from 24 to 98 minutes. One subject worked over six hours, but was compelled by circumstances to make a stop of over three hours. All the subjects did from a half hour's to an hour's work on the following or a later day. . . .

Only 3 of the 16 individuals did apparently as well after the work as after the rest. Their work-periods were the shortest three of the sixteen. The variations in the amount of fatigue are very great, even if these three are left out of account. Three individuals require over twice the time per example after work as after rest, and one of these nearly thrice the time. The individual differences in general would remain nearly as great had all individuals worked, say seven hours without rest, for the greatest fatigue effect comes from a rather short work-period (300 min., 0 rest), and the next greatest from a short period with a moderate rest (388 min., 52 min. rest), and one of the smallest fatigue effects (except the three negative cases) comes from a very long work-period with a very short rest (734 min., 29 min. rest). . . .

The median increase in time required per example, with equal accuracy, at the end of the work over that required after a rest of 12 hours or more was 40 per cent for the entire group and also 40 per cent for the six persons who worked 7 hours or more with rests of 0, 0, 29, 60, 77, and 90 minutes respectively. If the persons who stopped before five hours had forced themselves to continue the median would probably have been higher. . . .

In considering the percentages showing the amount of

fatigue, the reader will bear in mind the significance of time as a measure of efficiency in this function. For a person to be able to multiply mentally a three-place by a three-place number *at all* means a rather high degree of efficiency in the function. A great diminution in efficiency should make a person unable to remember one partial product while getting another. For one to take twice as long means to be half as efficient only in one special sense of "half as efficient."

For Shakespeare to have required twice as long to write *Hamlet* as he actually did require would not have meant a loss of half the efficiency of the play-writing function! For Napoleon to have taken twenty instead of five minutes to plan a series of moves at Austerlitz would not have meant that his generalship was only one fourth as efficient!

The *degree* of difficulty that can or cannot be met is for many purposes a more satisfactory measure than the time required and the success attained in meeting *one given* degree of difficulty. With mental multiplication it would be practicable, though very laborious, to make the former measurement, by having interspersed in, and at the close of, a rigidly fixed long work-period of mental multiplication with two three-place numbers, tests in multiplying a four-place by a three-place number, a four-place by a four-place, a five-place by a four-place, and a five-place by a five-place. There should also be tests with three-place by two-place, two-place by two-place, and so on, in case an individual comes to fail utterly with the three-place by three-place multiplication.

There was a wide variation in the feelings of the persons and in the relations of these feelings to either the amount of work or the diminution of efficiency. The details appear below. After the number identifying a person there are three numbers giving the length of the work period (in minutes), the length of the pause for lunch (in minutes), and the per cent of increase in time per example with equal accuracy near the end of the work-period over that after 12 or more hours of rest. Then follows the person's report on his feelings.

The reports were as follows:

No. 1. 467 0 45 "Fatigue came suddenly to disappear again and recur suddenly. It came sometimes when the work was bad or went slowly; at other times poor work would occur and no corresponding fatigue would be felt."

No. 2. 428 0 36 "A strange feature entered in a few places. My mind seemed not able to grasp the figures, and the more I worked, the more confused I became." Very tired last hour. Eyes were strained.

No. 3. 300 0 197 "The principal fatigue which I felt was physical; resulting from sitting so long in one position and the eye-strain."

No. 4. 262 0 81 "I think my mind was clearer at the close than at the beginning in both (series of tests)."

No. 5. 212 0 −9 "At first I could remember only two figures with any certainty. About the middle of the test remembered the six. Gradually lost this ability and the mind finally refused to remember any. Fatigue was gradual until about the last hour; then I completely gave out. Feeling of heat in the back of the head, pain in the temples, exhaustion in the muscles, especially in the arms and fingers. The second day began the work with more confidence, but fatigued more quickly. After working about 15 problems the brain refused to get results until within a few of the end, when it 'sprinted' and remembered five or six of the numbers, then relapsed, leaving pain in back of neck and twitching muscles."

No. 6. 121 0 −15 "Work began at 1.25 P. M. I could not work steadily, as mental fatigue brought on severe headaches. Second attempt made 9.05 A. M. Fatigue came gradually. Being exceedingly dizzy and having headaches at the end of two hours I thought it best to discontinue."
Third attempt at 6.30 P. M. Dizziness and headache after a brief hour.

No. 7. 734 29 14 No report on feelings.

No. 8. 490 77 28 "After the first half-hour I found that it gradually became harder to concentrate my thoughts. After dinner I had great difficulty in forcing myself to go back to the task."

No. 9. 460 60 68 "I did not suffer any great strain in this test, though it was exceedingly tedious."

No. 10. 432 204 36 "I felt alternately tired and rested as I worked; sometimes my head ached. At the end of each period I did not feel specially tired. I had, however, a giddy feeling most of the time, and seemed to have to work faster than I wished."

No. 11. 420 90 55 "I commenced to work willingly enough, but at the end of the first hour I wanted to stop badly. My mind would seem to 'slip a cog.' I was too tired for expression during the seventh hour."

No. 12. 392 45 83 "Work difficult. Not hard to concentrate at first. Near end of third hour mind began to wander. Almost unconsciously grasped at distractions; listened for telephone bell; wished to be interrupted. At end of fifth hour almost exhausted. Brought out all will power possessed; did better for a short time; 6 hrs. 32 mins. became utterly exhausted; could not hold numbers at all. Mind a blank. Exhaustion came gradually.

"Next morning could get results much more quickly at first; mind seemed to tire more quickly."

No. 13. 388 52 152 No report concerning feelings.

No. 14. 314 98 118 "I worked from 9:35 A. M. to 1.20 P. M. I was interested in the effect of the experiment and was quite willing to continue for some time—not noticing how tired I had become by 1.20. After I had stopped for lunch I realized that my eyes were very tired. I began again at 2.58 P. M. and had worked only seven minutes, when I felt as if I could not continue. From 3.05 to 4.27 I worked with the greatest effort. At that time I was more exhausted than I ever have been before. * * * Fearing

that further application might be too much of an
eye-strain, I stopped work at 4.27."

No. 15. 240 24 5 "After an hour my eyes felt as burning
coals of fire, my hands trembled, the back of my
head had a 'drawing' feeling and felt uncomfortably
warm. ° ° ° When at 8 P. M. I stopped the
'feelings' didn't stop. My head continued its 'large as
a barrel' feeling, and in my head and down my spine
little hammers kept up a lively tune. Only after a
long time did sleep come.

"Great 'fatigue' was felt the next morning as well.
The second test was delayed till late the next day."

No. 16. 240 30 –39 "At end of third hour nervousness
began; at end of fourth, intense hatred of work.
Toward the end of the fifth hour fatigue diminishes
because of consciousness that task is nearly completed. Fatigue came more or less rapidly toward
the fourth hour, but before that there seemed to be
a gradual tiring out." . . .

III. THEORIES OF MENTAL FATIGUE [2]

[Two sorts of theories have been set forth to account for the
facts of mental fatigue in daily life in homes, schools, factories, offices, and so on.] The first consider mental work after
the analogy of the work of an engine, waterfall or dynamo,
supposing a quantity of mental energy to be used up as work
is done and reproduced during rest. They may be called
Mechanical Theories of mental work and fatigue. The second
consider mental work as the action of certain situation-
response bonds, supposing tendencies unfavorable to their
action to be produced as work is done and to die out during
rest. They may be called *Biological or Response Theories.*

According to the Mechanical theories, fatigue is *intrinsic*
or *direct* and *negative* or *subtracting,* in the sense that an

[2] From *Educational Psychology*, Vol. III, pp. 11–12 and 120–126; and
School and Home Education, Vol. 33, (Oct., 1913), pp. 44–47.

activity in and of itself weakens its own efficiency by being exercised without rest, as a reservoir by discharging water lowers its pressure. According to the Biological theories, fatigue is also *extrinsic* or *indirect* and *positive* or *additive*, in the sense that an activity, by being exercised without rest, produces certain by-products, or releases certain forces, external to it, which check it.

According to the mechanical theories, temporary deterioration is referred vaguely to a loss of some one thing—mental energy. According to the biological or response theory, the deterioration is referred specifically to changes in the strength of certain connections . . . and to changes in the readiness of certain conduction-units.

In the early discussions of mental work and fatigue, the use of the term *Work* led thinkers naturally enough to follow the train of thought suggested by physics and to conceive of mental work as the consequence of expenditure of mental energy, of fatigue as the consumption of a stock of potential energy, and of rest as an opportunity for its restoration. . . . Such theories were in harmony with the current faculty psychology.

Experimental studies gave results inconsistent with any such "Mechanical" or "Energy" theory. And the facts of daily life also fit a "Biological" or "Response" theory much better. In homes and schools we observe the enormous potency of interest in maintaining, and of repugnance in diminishing, efficiency in mental work. . . . Interest does not add to, nor does repugnance subtract from, a store of energy. By the mechanical theories rest and work monopolize these two functions. Interest could, at the most, only release the energy faster. But it is a fact easily verifiable that interest *does* add to, and that repugnance *does* subtract from, the amount of work done. The amount of work done then cannot depend closely upon the magnitude of a supply of mechanically conceived energy. . . .

Consider any representative samples of mental work— e. g., addition, solving geometrical problems, writing essays, devising arguments, correcting examination papers, reading proof. The work is the production of the *right* responses to certain situations. . . . There is always a *qualitative* demand and a variety of obstacles to be overcome, and a choice of ways and means. . . .

All that a supply of "mental energy" could properly mean would be a supply of power to make the required connections; and since what hinders making a connection in learning is its consequences, the reasonable expectation is that what will hinder making it in fatigue will be its consequences. An animal tends to repeat a connection when repeating it brings a satisfying state of affairs, and may be expected to discontinue it when repeating it annoys him. An animal would seem likely to discontinue or decrease mental work because continuing it annoys him rather than because some inner fund of impulsion, which might be likened to physical potential energy, was running low. The more promising theory would seem to be one that explained why mental work continued without rest became less and less satisfying.

This the Biological or Response Theory tries to do. Work without rest, it maintains, becomes less satisfying (1) by losing the zest of novelty, (2) by producing ennui, a certain intellectual nausea, sensory pains and even headache, and (3) by imposing certain deprivations—for instance, from physical exercise, social intercourse, or sleep.

That these facts of behavior are found where diminished efficiency as a result of work without rest is found, is a fact subject to verification by observation and experiment. Even the advocates of a mechanical theory will hardly deny it. That they cause the loss in efficiency is shown by the gain which follows their elimination. Varying the superficial form of arithmetical drills, while exercising the same mental function, will postpone the loss in efficiency by maintaining the force of novelty. The addition of a money reward, or of a demonstration that the work is useful for some desired end, or of competition for excellence, may temporarily abolish fatigue by abolishing the ennui. The common phrase that one is "tired of" certain work represents a certain stage of fatigue better than "tired by" it does.

The extreme condition where the mind seems literally nauseated—will not have anything to do with the problem—may be cured similarly by an increase in the value of the answers to be got. . . . It is harder to eliminate experimentally sensory pains and headaches, but it seems probable that if these incubi could be lifted off, efficiency would rise.

That eliminating the deprivations, or in clearer phrase, permitting the indulgence of certain impulses, increases the efficiency of work is almost a crucial experiment for decision between the two classes of theory. When a boy regains efficiency by being allowed to walk up and down the room, or when the presence of a friend to study with her doubles a girl's achievement, it is clear that the previous deficiency was but little due to a lower pressure from a lessened reservoir of energy.

The effect of mental work without rest in causing deprivations, and of rest in permitting the corresponding indulgences, has been little studied. Attention has been centred upon what happens in the function that is working in disregard of the other functions which are being denied exercise. It is the fact that we are fatigued by what we do not do as truly, and perhaps as much, as by what we do. For children *not* to run and jump and squirm and sing and laugh and talk is the essence of mental work. For us all *not* to indulge in our favorite occupations is, as hour after hour of reading legal reports, or adding columns, or whatever the task may be, progresses, a more and more impressive feature of the task. Cases of special theoretic interest are those where the deprivation is from opportunity to do other mental work. For, in some such cases, the other work, deprivation from which fatigues, and exercises at which rests, the individual, would be rated by men in general as very exhausting. By the ordinary energy-theories it would involve large expenditures of mental energy.

If one could count up all the cases where individuals have stopped mental work and could know the chief cause in each case, it seems likely that the plea of some contrary impulse for gratification, some game to be played, sensory pleasure to be enjoyed, or the like, would be by far the commonest cause. Rest, again, except when spent in sleep, is not as a rule devoted to replenishing lost mental energy. It is far oftener devoted to indulging wants which mental work proscribes. To read, to talk with one's family and friends, to hunt or fish, to play active or sedentary games, and to make or listen to music, are occupations that often require a large expense of "mental energy," however defined, and that almost never approximate to the mental inaction of *dolce far niente* or sleep. They rest us by relief from strain and irritation, but not by cessation of mental action.

No theory of mental work and fatigue should then fail to take account of what continued work prevents the worker from doing. The little child who complained "I am tired of not playing," expressed admirably one feature of fatigue. The strain of not giving way to certain tendencies to response is as important as the strain of continuing certain others. Work in the popular sense is distinguished from play or recreation less by the amount of positive action than by the amount of restriction. We are fatigued by what we do *not* do.

On the whole, the biological theory seems much more probable. The effect of continuous mental work may be in part to use up some store of a complex of patience, self-control, vigor and the like, which may be called mental energy, but it surely is to produce certain annoying states to which the natural response is a diminution or cessation of the activity which causes them.

The behavior which results in certain products such as sums done, dictations written, paragraphs translated, and the like, is subject to the laws of all behavior, and to no others. If a continuance of the productive responses at the same speed and in such a form as to give equal quality, is satisfying to the individual concerned, he will continue them. If such continuance brings discomfort, he will tend to stop them altogether, or to intermit them, or to make them in such altered form and speed as lets them bring relative satisfaction. Stopping the work outright does not of course occur in the great majority of experimental investigations of fatigue, but is very common in ordinary mental work. Intermitting the work, dropping it, taking it up as thoughts of rewards, punishments, duty and the like, make idleness even more discomforting than the work, dropping it again, and so on, are also, in the nature of the case, rare in the experimental studies, but very common everywhere else. Relaxing speed and care and tension to such a degree that the work is less annoying than is the condition of not working (with the consequences attached thereto) is the device to which the subjects of the experiments are restricted. Whether one relaxes, intermits or stops work, the immediate reason is not that he has not the "energy" to go on with it, but that he feels more comfortable to relax, intermit or stop it. Whatever parallel to a decreased store of energy there is, is effective chiefly by making the responses concerned in production less satisfying than they were before.

CHAPTER XV

Valuations of Certain Pains, Deprivations and Frustrations *

[I have from time to time gathered and reported facts about human activities, interests, desires and aversions. The selections printed in this chapter and Chapter XVI were chosen partly because they illustrate ways of measuring desires and aversions (preferences for and against) from an approximate zero point, and partly because their findings, which are somewhat startling, can easily be checked in a college class or in any group of fifty or more persons.]

Better knowledge of the attitudes of people toward prospective "disutilities" in the form of pains, discomforts, deprivations, degradations, frustrations, restrictions, and other undesired conditions is obviously important. The best approach is through direct observations and experiments; and we plan to make such. But the opinions of persons concerning their attitudes are by no means valueless, if used reasonably. For example, the answers reported to the set of questions printed below by various individuals are instructive in a number of ways. (The two numbers after each item did not appear on the list as it was read by the person; they are inserted here for economy's sake and represent the median demand by a group of 60 students and teachers of psychology and by a group of 39 unemployed men and women, under 30 years of age, mostly college graduates. . . .

Name .... Date ....

For how much money, paid in cash, would you do or suffer the following? Write the amounts on the dotted line. You must suppose that the money can be spent on yourself only and that whatever you buy

* From *The Journal of Genetic Psychology*, Vol. 51, (1937), pp. 227–239.

with it is destroyed when you die. You cannot use any of it for your friends, relatives, or charity.

.....1. Have one upper front tooth pulled out. [$5000; $4500]
.....2. Have all your teeth pulled out. [$1,000,000; $750,000]
.....3. Have one ear cut off. [No sum; $1,500,000]
.....4. Have your left arm cut off at the elbow (right arm if you prefer). [No sum; $2,500,000]
.....5. Have a little finger of one hand cut off. [$75,000; $200,000]
.....6. Have the little toe of one foot cut off. [$10,000; $57,000]
.....7. Become entirely bald. [$750,000; $75,000]
.....8. Have all the hair of your eyebrows fall out. [$100,000; $25,000]
.....9. Have one leg cut off at the knee. [No sum; $40,000,000]
....10. Have both legs paralyzed. [No sum; $40,000,000]
....11. Have small-pox, recover perfectly, except for about 20 large pock-marks on your cheeks and forehead. [No sum; $1,000,000]
....12. Become totally deaf. [No sum; $100,000,000]
....13. Become totally blind. [No sum; no sum]
....14. Become unable to chew, so that you can eat only liquid food. [No sum; $10,000,000]
....15. Become unable to speak, so that you can communicate only by writing, signs, etc. [No sum; $15,000,000]
....16. Become unable to taste. [$1,000,000; $5,000,000]
....17. Become unable to smell. [$300,000; $150,000]
....18. Require 25 per cent more sleep than now to produce the same degree of rest and recuperation. [$100,000; $37,500]
....19. Fall into a trance or hibernating state throughout October of every year. [$300,000; $325,000]
....20. Fall into a trance or hibernating state throughout March of every year. [$200,000; $400,000]
....21. Be temporarily insane throughout July of every year (manic-depression insanity, bad enough so that you would have to be put in an insane asylum, but with no permanent ill effects). [No sum; $2,500,000]
....22. Same as 21, but for two entire years now with no recurrence ever again. [No sum; $5,000,000]
....23. Have to live all the rest of your life outside of U.S.A. [$200,000; $150,000]
....24. Have to live all the rest of your life in Iceland. [No sum; $1,000,000]
....25. Have to live all the rest of your life in Japan. [$1,000,000; $500,000]
....26. Have to live all the rest of your life in Russia. [$1,000,000; $150,000]
....27. Have to live all the rest of your life in Nicaragua. [$1,000,000; $500,000]
....28. Have to live all the rest of your life in New York City. [$50,000; $25,000]
....29. Have to live all the rest of your life in Boston, Mass. [$100,000; $50,000]
....30. Have to live all the rest of your life on a farm in Kansas, ten miles from any town. [$1,000,000; $300,000]
....31. Have to live all the rest of your life shut up in an apartment in New York City. You can have friends come to see you there, but cannot go out of the apartment. [No sum; $60,000,000]
....32. Eat a dead beetle one inch long. [$5,000; $5,000]

....33. Eat a live beetle one inch long. [$25,000; $50,000]
....34. Eat a dead earthworm 6 inches long. [$5,000; $25,000]
....35. Eat a live earthworm 6 inches long. [$10,000; $100,000]
....36. Eat a quarter of a pound of cooked human flesh (supposing that nobody but the person who pays you to do so will ever know it). [$1,000,000; $100,000]
....37. Eat a quarter of a pound of cooked human flesh (supposing that the fact that you do so will appear next day on the front page of all the New York papers). [No sum; $7,500,000]
....38. Drink enough to become thoroughly intoxicated. [$100; $50]
....39. Choke a stray cat to death. [$10,000; $10,000]
....40. Let a harmless snake 5 feet long coil itself round your arms and head. [$500; $100]
....41. Attend Sunday morning service in St. Patrick's Cathedral, and in the middle of the service run down the aisle to the altar, yelling "The time has come, the time has come" as loud as you can until you are dragged out. [$100,000; $1,000]
....42. Take a sharp knife and cut a pig's throat. [$1,000; $500]
....43. Walk down Broadway from 120th Street to 80th Street at noon wearing evening clothes and no hat. [$200; $100]
....44. Spit on a picture of Charles Darwin. [$20; $10]
....45. Spit on a picture of George Washington. [$50; $10]
....46. Spit on a picture of your mother. [$10,000; $25,000]
....47. Spit on a crucifix. [$300; $5]
....48. Suffer for an hour pain as severe as the worst headache or toothache you have ever had. [$500; $250]
....49. Have nothing to eat but bread, milk, spinach and yeast cakes for a year. [$10,000; $25,000]
....50. Go without sugar in all forms (including cake, etc.), tea, coffee, tobacco, and alcoholic drink, for a year. [$1,750; $2,000]
....51. Lose all hope of life after death. [$6,500; $50]

I shall discuss first the reports made in April, 1934, by a group who had been employed for three months by the C.W.A. as subjects in experiments in adult learning, and who were accustomed to taking all sorts of tests and answering all sorts of questions. They consisted of males under 30, females under 30, males over 40 and females over 40, and covered a wide range of intellectual ability and amount of education, though the majority were college graduates of much above average intelligence.

In spite of their wide experience as subjects in psychological tests and experiments, some were so overcome by the novel task that they would make no estimates or only for a very few of the 51 injuries, deprivations, repulsive acts, and so on. Some reported that no amount of money would induce them to do or suffer any of them. These reports, though apparently absurd, may be sincere.

The most striking fact about the reports in general is the absurd magnitude of the bids. The loss of one little toe is put as priceless by one-fifth of the group, and at from $50,000 to $10,000,000 by another fifth. The median valuation is near $25,000! An hour of the severest pain known to the person is put at $250 or over by half of the young men, and at $500 or over by half of the young women. Half of the group required over $50,000 for eating a beetle or worm (average for living and dead). Only a fifth make bids under $1000. The impairment of physical attractiveness by the loss of one ear and both eyebrows, total baldness, and the presence of 20 pock marks totals a million dollars for over three-fifths of the group. The deprivation from sugar for a year is put at $1000 or more by three-fourths of the group. Similar utterly unreasonable estimates appear throughout. The median estimates for 19 men and 20 women under 30 appear as the second of the two numbers printed after each item.

Why did these persons put these absurdly high valuations upon suffering these imagined injuries, deformities, degradations, and so on? The first possibility to consider is that many of them did not take up any of the suppositions seriously, that their estimates were given carelessly and represented only a general pronounced negative attitude. There is this much truth in this supposition: namely, that (a) voluntary acceptance of some of the suggested calamities is to many individuals so utterly intolerable that they cannot bring their minds to consider it, and that (b) this attitude occasionally transfers to act and sufferings which, had they been presented alone, would have been rated much more reasonably. The first fact is important. It illustrates a strong tendency in mankind to refuse to face personal calamities in imaginative bargaining in any straightforward, intellectual way, other than to utterly eschew them.

There were two flippant reports and probably some careless ones, but the reports of persons whose characters guarantee their coöperation and sincerity are not observably different from those who might be suspected of carelessness. Moreover, as will be shown later, reports from members of the Psychology Club of Teachers College show the same general facts as these.

There is also internal evidence that most of the reports are genuine expressions of opinion. For example, the requirements to balance personal disfigurement of 3, 7, 8, and 11 are higher for young women than for young men and are very much lower for old men than for the others. The requirements to balance eating beetles and worms are enormously higher for the women than for the men. The payment for spitting on a crucifix ranges from 0 to infinity. The relative payments required are reasonable within any group of comparable items (such as 1, 2, 3, 4, 5, 6, 9, and 10; or 12, 13, 16 and 17; or 24, 25, 27, and 29). There is little or no concealment of unorthodox traits; for example, a quarter of the group reported less than $10 for their hope of immortality. It may be objected that all the bids of over a half a million are proof of carelessness, since the assumption was to be that the money could be spent only on one's self, and since for that purpose an annuity of $25,000 or more would be as good as any larger amount. But a neglect of this fact in the process of making comparative estimates is not a proof of general carelessness. We must, I think, accept the great majority of the absurdly high bids as genuine expressions of the persons' attitudes.

How well these attitudes prophesy what the persons would do if real money offers were made can only be surmised. Doubtless there would be many changes, mostly downward, but I believe that essentially uneconomical refusals and requirements would remain for many items. It may seem incredible that any persons needing money as much as these recipients of public funds did would not gladly sacrifice one toe for $5000, or endure an hour of pain for $100, or eat a beetle for $500, or cut a pig's throat for $100, or eat ¼ pound of cooked human flesh secretly for $10,000. It is, however, credible to the writer because of two facts. First, a person may know that a certain course of conduct is to his advantage and ardently wish to do it, but be prevented from doing so by an inner compulsion. Second, the essence of the transaction may not be the temporary nausea or misery, but the permanent remorse, loss of self-respect, or other torment. These two facts are of general importance. The obsessional power of certain tabus, notions, habits, and so on, is widespread. Just as certain persons simply cannot take the wiggling worm and chew it up, so certain workers simply cannot change their trade, certain farmers cannot give up their profitless farms and work under orders in a factory, certain artists cannot do as they are told. They may wish to do so, but their natures must be changed in radical ways to make it possible. The force of self-approval is enormous because it acts incessantly and is inescapable. Some psychiatrists believe that it is literally true that persons will become insane in order to retain it. The approval of others operates in large measure by making a person content with himself. The serf could endure his lot in large measure because he could respect himself in his status as the lord could in his. We are all prone to blame luck or favoritism or the government rather than our own ineptness. Whatever its supernatural powers may be, religion as a natural phenomenon has had much of its power because it could put man at peace with himself.

A third important fact is suggested by the high prices set upon the various acts and sufferings: namely, the undervaluation of insurance against hunger, cold, and exposure. Among the items were some which would (at least in ninety-nine persons out of a hundred) entail no conflict with any obsession and no loss of social approval or self approval. Any penniless person who had a realizing fear of physical miseries would presumably gladly buy insurance against them at the cost of a finger and toe, or of being unable to smell, or of eating only bread, milk, spinach and yeast cakes for a year. But even for the last we have over a third of the persons demanding $50,000 or more! The realizing fear was probably absent in

many of the group. They probably had never had any pro-
tracted experience of hunger and cold, and took it for granted
that somehow the world would feed and clothe them as it always had done. And this is true of a very large proportion of
the population of the United States. Many of us are so used
to food, clothes, and shelter that we do not thank either God
or the social order for them, nor even consider that the provision might fail.

To the extent that the reports represent genuine attitudes
toward reality, we may use them as indications of real motives. For example, items 3, 7, 8 and 11 (*have one ear cut off;
become entirely bald; have all the hair of your eyebrows fall
out; have small-pox and recover perfectly, except for about
20 large pockmarks on your cheeks and forehead*) concern
personal appearance primarily. Items 14, 16, 17, 48, 49, and
50 (*become unable to chew, so that you can eat only liquid
food; become unable to taste; become unable to smell; suffer
for one hour pain as severe as the worst headache or toothache you have ever had; have nothing to eat but bread, milk,
spinach and yeast cakes for a year; go without sugar in all
forms—including cake, etc.—, tea, coffee, tobacco, and alcoholic drink for a year*) concern sheer discomfort primarily.
Item 18 (*require 25 per cent more sleep than now to produce
the same degree of rest and recuperation*) concerns loss of
time. The difference between the obnoxiousness of 31 and 28
(*have to live all the rest of your life shut up in an apartment
in New York City. You can have friends come to see you there,
but you cannot go out of the apartment; have to live all the
rest of your life in New York City*) is an indication of the
dislike of confinement.

If the reports do not represent what the persons would do
if real money offers were made, they at least represent attitudes of the persons toward imagined offers. The relative
magnitudes will be instructive in either case.

I therefore report in Table 1 the median estimates and the
lowest estimates for 19 young men and 20 young women for
certain items and combinations of items. The highest esti-

mates are ∞ or some enormous number in all cases save 43, which one woman offers to endure for $100,000.

The reader may draw his own conclusions from the facts of this table. He should note the ultra-realism which demands

TABLE I

ESTIMATES OF THE AMOUNTS OF MONEY WHICH WOULD INDUCE
THE PERSONS IN QUESTION TO DO OR SUFFER THE THING IN QUESTION

| | Young C.W.A. workers | | | | Graduate students and teachers median |
| | Median | | Lowest | | |
	M	F	M	F	
1. Average of 44 and 45 (spit on pictures of Darwin and Washington).	10	10	0	0	40
2. 38 (become thoroughly intoxicated).	25	98	0	0	100
3. 43 (walk 2 miles on Broadway in evening clothes at noon).	125	75	0	5	100
4. 40 (let snake coil around arms and head).	100	400	0	10	500
5. 41 (run yelling down aisle of cathedral during Sunday service).	1,250	1,000	20	15	10,000
6. Average of 39 and 42 (choke a cat, cut a pig's throat).	1,250	105,000	2	25	7,500
7. 18 (lose time by need for 25 per cent more sleep).	25,000	2,500	20	500	100,000
8. Average of 48, 49 and 50 (1 hour pain; year on bread, milk, etc.; year without sugar and alcoholic drinks).	33,000	10,700	100	233	3,000
9. 46 (spit on a picture of one's mother).	25,000	22,500	1	5	5,000
10. Average of 32, 33, 34, and 35 (eat dead beetle, live beetle, dead earthworm, and live earthworm).	12,500	62,500	4	2,200	5,000
11. Average of 3, 7, 8, and 11 (lose an ear, become bald, lose hair of eyebrows, acquire 20 pock marks).	31,000	1¾ mill.	1,000	7,600	1 mill.
12. Average of 28 and 29 (restriction of habitat to New York or to Boston).	40,000	30,000	0	0	75,000
13. 36 (eat human flesh secretly).	50,000	100,000	40	1,000	1 mill.
14. Average of 5 and 6 (lose little finger, lose toe).	200,000	75,000	500	2,800	300,000
15. Average of 19 and 20 (fall into a trance for a month every year).	1 mill.	100,000	2,500	750	200,000
16. Average of 23 to 30 (restriction of habitat to outside U.S.A., Iceland, Japan, Russia, Nicaragua, N.Y. City, Boston, Kansas, farm).	1½ mill.	500,000	5,500	13,300	500,000
17. 37 minus 36 (eat human flesh publicly instead of secretly).	6½ mill.	325,000	0	0	?
18. 21 (be insane one month every year).	5 mill.	1½ mill.	20,000	35,000	∞
19. 37 (eat human flesh and have the fact widely known).	10 mill.	1 mill.	250	5,000	∞
20. 31 minus 28 (confinement indoors).	2 mill.	100 mill.	100	0	—500,000
21. Average of 14, 16, and 17 (become unable to chew, taste, smell).	6 mill.	41,000	12,000	12,000	1½ mill.
22. Average of 2, 4, and 9 (lose all teeth, left arm, one leg).	36 mill.	6 mill.	1,900	26,000	∞
23. 12 (lose hearing).	∞	52 mill.	40,000	10,000	∞
24. 15 (lose speech).	∞	100 mill.	75,000	75,000	∞
25. 13 (lose vision).	∞	100 mill.	100,000	100,000	∞

a thousand times as much for suffering an hour of pain as for spitting on Darwin's or Washington's picture, and eighty times as much for baldness or pock marks (in women), as for spitting on the picture of one's mother. He should note also the relative tolerance of disgracing oneself, and the great aversion to minor and almost harmless mutilations of one's body and limitations to one's freedom.

The same 51 questions were asked in November, 1934, of 58 students and teachers of psychology, mostly between 25 and 35 years old, and about equally divided between men and women. The answers were written anonymously. About five-sixths of the group were students; and it may safely be assumed that three-fourths of the group had no present or future income beyond earnings. Very few, however, were destitute or receiving public relief as all in the other group were.

All the general characteristics of the returns are the same for this group as for the other. They too make extravagant demands, expressing the aversions which they feel rather than reasonable balancing of the pain, deprivation, or frustration against what money can buy. They too suffer from inner compulsions. They too probably undervalue security from hunger, cold, and exposure.

The medians for various items are presented in the last column of Table 1. They are of the same general magnitude as those for the other group, and hold much the same relative positions. The chief differences are:

1. Greater aversion to spitting on pictures of Darwin and Washington (40 to 10).

5. Greater aversion to causing a disgraceful disturbance in church (10,000 to 1,125).

7. Greater aversion to losing time by sleep (100,000 to 14,000).

8. Less aversion to sheer pain and discomfort (3,000 to 22,000).

9. Less aversion to spitting on a picture of one's mother (5,000 to 24,000).

10. Less aversion to eating the worm or beetle (5,000 to 3,800).

13. Greater aversion to eating human flesh secretly (1,000,000 to 75,000).

No one of these by itself has much reliability because of the great variation within both groups. If they agreed in supporting some one explanation of themselves, it would be worth consideration, but they do not. Though 8 and 10 suggest greater reasonableness in the psychology group, 13 and 14 oppose this. Though 1 and 5 suggest greater sensitiveness, or greater conventionality, 9 and 3 oppose this.

On the whole, it is safest to treat the differences between the two groups as unimportant. . . .

The sciences of man are tempted to describe and measure the causes of conduct by some simple and logical scheme. Bentham's is the most famous of such. Lewin's is the latest. Any scheme must, I think, take account of certain positive wants (desires, drives, impulses or preferences *pro*) and of certain negative wants (aversions, or preferences *con*) which are infinitely strong in the sense that the person in question in the situation in question does not treat the status or tendency in question as a quantity to be weighed in comparison with others, but as something utterly desirable or intolerable. To a thirsty infant a drink is worth everything in the sense that he craves it wholeheartedly and irrespective of all else. Even after many years of training in quantifying the force of all sorts of desirables and undesirables by thinking of their consequences and of other alternative possibilities, much obsessional activity remains. A hedonic calculus, or any other calculus of motivation, must reckon with it.

Students of valuation disagree about the extent to which values are commensurate, so that for any given person in any given situation the relative magnitudes of the values to him of, say, a feeling of safety, a compliment, the beautiful sunset, a long-deferred smoke, and the cessation of a toothache can be computed. A safe step toward a solution is to realize that if the person does in fact prefer A to B, then he has set A as greater in value than B no matter how disparate they may be.

Our experiment illustrates both the wide range of such valuation and some of its difficulties, in the case of negative values. Using money as their measure, some persons can in thought, and probably could in reality, readily put our 51 mutilations, pains, deprivations, degradations and frustrations into an order of preference. Some persons rebel against the task. But their rebellion occurred not in proportion as the undesirables are unlike but in proportion as they are great. The more convincing illustrations given in arguments against commensurability are likely to be cases of great beauty, great elevation of spirit, great bodily pain, great shame, and so on. The very man who insists that one scale of value for literary delights and smoking is impossible will admit that he preferred to use sixpence for Punch rather than cigarettes, or vice versa. It may be hard for him to decide whether he prefers to give up all reading for two months or to give up all smoking for ten years. But that may not be because of the incomparability of the satisfactions, but because both are intolerable. . . .

[Here followed certain facts concerning intercorrelations.]

CHAPTER XVI

Valuations of Achievements, Acts, and Persons *

VALUATIONS OF TWENTY
ACHIEVEMENTS, a to t

THE ranking of the achievements a to t listed below was done by a group of 22 persons of superior intelligence, nine of whom were psychologists, and six of whom were advanced students of psychology, and by a group of 44 unemployed of the white-collar and professional classes.

The first number after each achievement is the median rank for the group of 22, and the next two numbers joined by a dash show the range of ranks required to include 20 of the 22. The next number is the median rank for the group of 44 unemployed, and the two following numbers joined by a dash show the range of ranks required to include 40 of the 44. The variation is very great in both groups for all the items except curing cancer and converting Roman Catholics to Presbyterianism. The unemployed agree in many respects with the superior and psychological group, the correlation between the two rank orders being .82. If items n and o are omitted, the correlation is .94.

A remarkable fact in these rankings of achievements is the large majority assigning less value to the conversion of a hundred Roman Catholics, Jews, or Buddhists to a highly respected Protestant faith than to making a sick dog happy for an hour. q is ranked higher than a by 16 of the 22 psychologists and other superior intellects, higher than b by

* From Chapter VI of the *Albert Schweitzer Jubilee Book,* 1946.

Write 1, 2, 3, 4, etc., before each of the achievements listed below according to the value you set upon them. Write 1 before the one you would like best to achieve, 2 before the one you think next most valuable, and so on to 20 for the least valuable. If two or more of the achievements seem equally valuable, write the two or more appropriate numbers before each.

a.	Convert a hundred Roman Catholics to Presbyterianism	19	15—20	19	16—20
b.	Convert a hundred Jews to Presbyterianism	19	13—20	19	15—20
c.	Convert a hundred Buddhists to Presbyterianism	18	11—20	18	14—20
d.	Convert ten millionaires to giving up all their property to the poor and spending their lives in literal obedience to the teachings of Jesus	9½	1—17	12	1—17
e.	Convert ten political bosses to using all their skill and wealth and influence to do what the clergymen of their cities want done	9	3—16	11	3—18
f.	Cure ten children of habitual thieving	9	5—14	7½	3—14
g.	Cure ten children of habitual lying	10	7—15	8½	4—13
h.	Cure ten children of occasional auto-erotic indulgences	12½	5—17	10	5—16
i.	Discover a means of preventing cancer	1	1—4	1	1—7
j.	Discover a means of preventing influenza	2	1—7	2½	1½—9
k.	Induce a hundred women to use the time and money they now spend in beauty shops in the serious study of social and political problems	9½	5—16	12½	4—19
l.	Induce a hundred women to use the time and money they now spend in playing cards in telling poor people in the slums how they should bring up their children	16	7—19	12½	5—18
m.	Induce a hundred men to use the time and money they now spend in playing golf, fishing, or hunting in attending public forums and group discussions on "How a Christian should run his business"	13	9—17	13½	6—17
n.	Induce a hundred students in a teachers college to be as impartial in thinking about the merits of social and political questions as they are in thinking about physical or chemical problems	4	3—12	10	3—16
o.	Induce any hundred of the wives of the thousand most promising young men in the U.S. to have four children instead of two or less	6½	2—15	13	2—18
p.	Make a sick child happy instead of miserable for an hour	11½	6—19	9½	3—16
q.	Make a sick dog happy instead of miserable for an hour	16½	11—20	14	4—20
r.	Make a hundred sick children happy instead of miserable for an hour	9	5—16	7	3—12
s.	Make a thousand sick children happy instead of miserable for an hour	7½	4—15	6	2—14
t.	Make a million sick children happy instead of miserable for an hour	5½	2—14	4	1—14

16 of them, and higher than *c* by 15 of them. *q* is ranked higher than *a* by 38 of the 44 unemployed, higher than *b* by 38 of them, and higher than *c* by 37 of them.

The values set upon making children happy in comparison with making them good are also noteworthy. Ten hours of happiness is set above being cured of habitual thieving or lying. In the group of 22, *r* is rated as more valuable than *f* by 12, and as more valuable than *g* by 14. In the group of 44 unemployed *r* is rated as more valuable than *f* by 29 and as of equal worth by 1. It is rated as more valuable than *g* by 31, and as of equal worth by 1. The cure of occasional erotic indulgences is set clearly below the cure of habitual thieving or lying, such cure of one child being set as less valuable than making a sick child happy instead of miserable for six minutes!

Among the reformations *d, e, k, l, m, n,* and *o,* that in the direction of more scientific and impartial thinking (*n*) leads by a clear margin. The others are of nearly equal merit in the opinion of the 44 unemployed, and rank clearly below giving a sick child an hour's happiness and not far above doing the same for a sick dog. The psychologists and others in the group of 22 rate *o* (production of offspring by superior families) much higher than *d, e, k, l,* and *m.* They value the addition of one such child somewhere between five hours and five thousand hours of happiness. They rate *m* and *l,* especially *l,* much lower than *d, e,* and *k.* They rank the conversion of one woman from playing cards to giving advice to parents in the slums as about equal to making one sick dog happy for one minute.

Using well-known formulae and certain assumptions, it is possible to compute the amount of value attached to any of these achievements as a plus over the value of one hour's happiness for a sick dog in terms of the variability (I shall use the standard deviation) of the group in valuation, and also approximately as a fraction of the difference in value between one hour's happiness for a sick dog and one hour's happiness for a million children.

For example, h has more value than q by a vote of 15 to 7, which corresponds to 47½ hundredths of the variability of opinion (standard deviation) of the 22; g has more value than h by a vote of 16 to 6, which corresponds to 60½ hundredths of the standard deviation of opinion of the 22; t has more value than g by a vote of 18 to 4, or 91 hundredths of the standard deviation of opinion of the 22. Letting x equal the value of q, we have as the values of h, g, and t, x + .47½, x + 1.08, and x + 1.99. Since the value of x is less than a millionth of the value of t, we may disregard it and use .47½, 1.08, and 1.99 as the relative values of h, g, and t.[1]

Taking h as .24 t and g as .54 t, we may equate h to 240,000 happiness hours and g to 540,000 happiness hours. The values of any other item (except i,) can be determined in a similar manner by using the votes about it in comparison with q, h, g, or t. Using the opinions of the 44 and the variability of opinion of the 44 in a similar manner, we find h valued at 385,000 happiness hours, and g at 670,000.

If the 22 judges were replaced by 100 or more representing a high quality of knowledge and impartiality and all important points of view, and if the 20 achievements were increased by 20 or 30 wisely chosen achievements, such measurements as those given above would be not only a convenient expression of valuations in terms of happiness units, but an excellent feature of a textbook on morals or guide for human activities. They would, of course, be subject to amendment by the advancement of knowledge about the consequences of, say, d, or i. Perhaps it would be discovered that the common good was benefited more if the millionaires kept their property and used it to make more than if the poor received it while the millionaires tried to do the Lord's will empty-handed. Perhaps the discoverer of a cure for cancer would only hasten by a few years what the course of events would surely produce sooner or later if he spent his life growing potatoes or playing pinochle. Certain sociologists suggest this in their criticisms of the "great-man" theory. Until so

[1] Using m instead of h in the computations, we find $g = 1.10$ and $t = 2.01$.

amended, however, they would be enormously superior to the adulteration of common sense by ignorance, superstitions, prejudices, and wishful thinking that now characterizes human valuations.

VALUATIONS OF FIFTY ACTIVITIES

Twenty-two persons of superior intelligence, 14 of whom were psychologists, and 42 unemployed persons of the white-collar and professional classes, assigned values to each of the 50 activities listed below. The number preceding each activity identifies it and gives its position in the list given to each of the 64 subjects of the experiment. The first number following the description of the activity is the median value assigned by the group of 22. The second number is the range required to include 20 of the 22. The third number is the median value assigned by the group of 42. The range required to include 38 of the 42 is not reported, but would equal or exceed the range for the 22.

John Smith, college graduate, a chemist aged 40, married to a woman of average health, beauty, intellect, morals and temperament, with three children, aged 12, 10 and 4, worth $40,000 and earning $3600 per year, is let off from work for Thursday afternoon so that he has three hours at his disposal. This being all you know about him, consider the following ways of spending the time by him, rating each for its probable value, or merit, or goodness. Use 0 if the activity would do as much harm as good. Use 10 for the best of the first page of the list. Use −10 for the worst of the first page of the list. If you later find something better than what you called +10, or worse than what you called −10, you may use 11, 12, 13, etc. and −11, −12, −13, etc., as seems necessary.

1. Studying chemistry.	5.5	14	5
7. Reading a standard work on history.	2	7	5
48. Reading *Harpers Magazine*.	3	8	5
49. Reading the *Literary Digest*.	2.5	6	3
50. Reading the newspaper.	2	9	5
5. Taking his wife for a walk, a thing of which she is very fond. He cares very little about walking.	5.5	10	5
15. Relieving his wife of care of the four-year-old by taking it to play in the park.	5	10	3
47. Telling his wife to choose what she would most like to have him do and doing it cheerfully.	3.5	12	4.5

17. Taking a young woman who works in his office to the movies.   —2   9   0.5
2. Going to a prostitute.   —10   15   —10

34. Getting the two older children excused from school and taking them to the Natural History Museum.   3   10   5.5
3. Making out his income-tax report.   3   7   1
19. Working in his garden.   5.5   9   5
28. Making repairs and improvements in his home.   5   10   5
46. Cleaning out the cellar of his home.   2.5   6   3

4. Visiting his aged mother.   6   10   6
40. Going with his wife to call on two poor maiden aunts.   2   9   1.5
6. Taking a nap.   2   8   2.5
14. Playing solitaire.   0   8   0
20. Playing golf with his brother.   5   10   5

24. Going to a baseball game.   3.5   10   5
27. Listening to the radio at home.   2   9   4.5
44. Playing the piano.   3.5   7   5.5
29. Getting a hair-cut, shampoo, and manicure and shopping for clothes.   3   6   3.5
9. Gambling (roulette, with small stakes, losing $4.00 in all).   —2   11   —1

13. Taking a quart of whiskey home to his room and getting thoroughly drunk there.   —8.5   11   —8
8. Doing extra work for $25 which he donates to the local hospital.   5   11   5
31. Helping a neighbor who has asked advice about some chemical problems.   6   8   5
41. Going to the office of a friend who has been ill and helping him to catch up with his work.   6   11   5
43. Analyzing the water from the well of a farm which a friend is thinking of buying.   5   8   5

10. Loafing with men friends.   1   9   1
12. Reading a detective story.   1.5   4   2
11. Praying and reading the Bible.   1   16   0
16. Going to the park alone and talking encouragingly to unemployed men found there.   2   11   3
18. Writing letters to the newspapers complaining about the noisiness of the streets.   —0.5   12   0

42. Making calls to solicit subscriptions for the city's Community Chest.   2.5   12   0.5
45. Writing a set of good resolutions for the New Year.   0   9   0.5
32. Shooting squirrels in the woods.   1   11   0

35. Reading literature issued by the Communist Party.   2   11   3
36. Reading literature issued by the Socialist Party.   2   15   2
37. Reading literature issued by the Republican Party.   0   15   0

38. Reading literature issued by the Mormon church.	1	*14*	0
21. Writing and sending anonymous defamatory letters to several men about their wives.	—10	*8*	—10
33. Sitting in the park, trying to frighten any children who came near by making horrible faces at them.	—6.5	*11*	—9.5
39. Teasing the monkeys in the zoo by holding out food and pulling it back when they reach for it.	—4	*11*	—8
22. Writing and sending anonymous insulting letters to prominent clergymen.	—8	*9*	—10
23. Writing and sending anonymous insulting letters to prominent politicians.	—5	*10*	—9.5
26. Going to stores and stealing small articles.	—8	*7*	—10
25. Going to a symphony concert.	5	*9*	8
30. Writing poetry.	2	*7*	3

The variation even among the 22 individuals is very great —14 or more for six of the activities, from 8 to 12 for thirty-five of them, 6 or 7 for eight of them. Getting drunk is rated as an innocent indulgence (0) by two, shooting squirrels as worse than frightening children by two, and reading literature issued by the Republican party as worse than writing and sending defamatory letters to prominent politicians by three! Gambling is put above giving the man's wife her chosen pleasure by two. Our chemist could find among the 22 one or more defenders of any of the 50 activities except writing and sending defamatory letters to men about their wives.

The great variation among individuals is, however, consistent with a consensus of the 22 which probably approximates closely to a consensus of the opinions of, say, all American college graduates, or all American doctors, lawyers, teachers, engineers, and labor leaders.

The medians present this consensus of the 22. The medians for the 42 are in general similar, the correlation between the two being over .90.

This consensus lacks such surprises as characterized the consensus valuations of the achievements *a* to *t*, but the low valuations of praying and reading the Bible (1 for the 22 and 0 for the 42) and the opprobrium cast on the Republican party (0 and 0 as compared with +2 and +2 for the literature of the Socialist party) may seem remarkable to some, and almost surely would not have been the consensus of the intelligentsia of two generations ago. The valuations are, I think, the resultants of both impersonal considerations of the consequences of the activities, and more personal judgments of what one would do or ought to do in the chemist's place. There is also some acceptance of conventional opinion about whether the activity is praiseworthy.

The individual opinions reveal many prejudices or doctrinaire notions such as that one should use leisure to get far away from one's specialty (as in a rating of −10 for studying chemistry, −5 for doing extra work for $25 and giving that to the local hospital, and −5 for helping a neighbor with chemical problems). Taking a nap is put as −10; talking encouragingly to the unemployed as −9; listening to the radio as −6; writing poetry as −8. These doctrinaire notions and individual prejudices are in part counterbalanced by opposite ones, and exert an appreciable influence on the medians only when several of them act alike upon the rating of an activity.

The general assignment of value in accord with consequences is adequate to account for a large fraction of most of the median valuations. The consequences primarily of benefit to the chemist himself are given weight, the self-improvement of activities 7, 48, and 49 being valued at 2, 3, and 2.5, the innocent indulgences of 6, 14, 20, 24, 27, and 44 averaging 2⅔, and those of 10, 12, 32, and 50 averaging 1.4. Consequences benefiting others at some sacrifice to the chemist are set much higher; the activities in behalf of his wife, mother, aunts, neighbor, friends, and the hospital have medians from 3½ to 6, and average almost exactly 5.

The influence of more personal judgments about what is fit and proper for a man to do with an unexpected half-holiday appears in the ratings of 5.5 and 5 for "working in his garden" and "making repairs and improvements in his home," as compared with 3 and 2.5 for making out his "income-tax return" and "cleaning out the cellar of his home." "Playing golf with one's brother" (5) also seems much better than "playing solitaire" (0), over and above its greater value for health. "Telling his wife to choose what she would most like to have him do and doing it cheerfully" seems somewhat unreal and silly, and perhaps as setting a bad precedent, and so is ranked low in spite of its superior consequences.[2] The degradation of oneself by anonymous insults to clergymen seems greater than that by similar insults to politicians.

How far the low ratings for acts of religious devotion and for informing oneself about the programs and arguments of political parties are caused by low estimates of the value of the consequences of so doing, and how far by the absence of personal impulses in their favor as proper uses of a holiday, I do not know.

The influence of conventional opinion may be seen in the rating of 6 for the visit to an aged mother but only 2 for the visit to two poor maiden aunts, and in the high rating for going to a symphony concert. On the whole, the median ratings fit rather closely a happiness-welfare calculus in which the happiness or welfare of another is credited at about two and a half times the happiness or welfare of oneself. . . .

VALUATIONS OF A PERSON

A person may be valued on hundreds of scales—qua producer, consumer, citizen, neighbor, friend, husband, immortal soul, carrier of genes, bundle of habits, source of infection, and so on.

Twenty-five men and women of high intelligence, 17 of whom were psychologists or advanced students of psychology, and 42 unemployed men and women of the white-collar and professional classes assigned ranks to the 25 persons, a to y, described on p. 258, as husbands. The letter preceding each description is unimportant. It merely shows the order in

_____

[2] The average for the three activities in favor of the wife (5, 15, and 47) are in order 5.2, 5.2, and 2.9 for the group of 22, and 3.9, 3.3, and 3.0 for the group of 42.

which the candidates were listed on the sheets given to the 67 persons who made the ratings. The first number following the description is the median of the ranks assigned by the 25; the next two numbers joined by a dash show the range required to include 23 of the 25 ratings; the next number is the median of the ranks assigned by the 42 unemployed; the next two numbers joined by a dash show the range required to include 38 of their 42 ratings. The meaning of the last two numbers will be explained presently.

The rankings by the two groups are much alike, the correlation between them being .96. The 25 in the more intelligent group value the Chinese, the headwaiter, the undertaker, and the Methodist clergyman higher than the 42 do; and value the Christian Science healer, the working man, and the two men with Catholic affiliations lower than the 42 do. But even these differences are not large or very reliable.

In the seventh and eighth numbers the valuations of the two groups are combined, equal weight being given to the more intelligent 25 and the less intelligent 42. The seventh number is the valuation in units of the variability of opinion expressed as a deviation from the valuation of the architect a and high-school teacher (v). The eighth number is the same quantity expressed as a deviation from the valuation (3 standard deviations below a, v) which the great majority of the 67 persons would probably regard as no better for their daughter or sister than going without a husband. . . .

All these reported valuations of achievements, acts, and persons may differ considerably from the preferences shown by the actual behavior of the reporting groups in doing or avoiding, stimulating or repressing, rewarding or punishing, and other concrete treatment of concrete cases. The observations and experiments that would tell how great such differences would be are lacking. I conjecture that there would be a close parallelism (say a correlation of .90 or more) between the valuations reported by either group and the valuations shown by the actual behavior of that group. For an individual the correlation would, of course, be less. The

Write 1, 2, 3, 4, etc., before the following to show which you would choose for your sister or daughter to marry. Use 1 for first choice, 2 for next, 3 for next, and so on to 24 for next to worst and 25 for worst. If two or more seem equal in merit write the two or more appropriate numbers before each of them. The age of all is supposed to be 30 years. The amount of money in parentheses is the person's annual earnings.

...f.	A factory owner, a college graduate ($7000)	2.5	1–9	2	1–13	+.21	3.2
...a.	An architect ($2500)	3.5	1–8	3	1–8	0	3.0
...v.	A teacher in public high school ($2500	3	1–6	4	1–7½	0	3.0
...j.	A librarian ($2500)	5.5	1–8	6.75	2–12	−.73	2.3
...m.	A musician ($2500)	6	2–12	7.5	1–14	−.73	2.3
...i.	A Jewish lawyer ($3000)	8	1–20	8.5	1–20	−1.06	1.9
...y.	A writer of advertisements ($2500)	7.5	4–14	7.25	2–17	−1.06	1.9
...k.	A life-insurance agent ($2500)	9	4½–15	9.25	5–16	−1.43	1.6
...l.	A Methodist clergyman of liberal views who earns $2000 as a pastor and $500 by writing	10	4–22	14	2–19½	−1.47	1.5
...p.	A poet of undoubted genius, but who earns only $1400	11	1–20	11	1–20	−1.47	1.5—
...t.	A secretary of the Non-Partisan Voters' League ($2500)	10	5–14	11	5–16½	−1.54	1.5+
...q.	A policeman ($2800)	13.5	9½–18	13	5½–21	−1.86	1.1
...h.	A head-waiter in a hotel earning (with tips) $6000	13.5	7½–21	16	5–22	−1.88	1.1
...o.	An officer in the Eastern Catholic Publishing Company ($2500)	14	7–22	14	6–23	−1.88	1.1
...w.	An undertaker earning $3000	12	9–20	15	5–21	−1.88	1.1
...r.	A professional stage dancer ($2500)	15	7–21	15	6½–20½	−2.02	1.0
...s.	A secretary of the Knights of Columbus ($2500)	15	10–24	12.5	6–23	−2.02	1.0
...x.	A working-man ($1800)	16	10–22	14.5	3½–22½	−2.02	1.0
...e.	A Chinese mandarin's son aged 25 (Christian convert) with an income equivalent to $10,000	17.5	4–24	21.5	12½–25	−2.50	.5
...c.	A Baptist clergyman believing literally in the Bible ($2000)	20	14–24	18.5	9–24	−2.60	.4
...d.	A Christian Science healer ($4000)	20.5	14–24	18	12–24	−2.70	.3
...b.	An agitator employed by the Soviet Republics to encourage dissatisfaction among American workers	20.5	16–25	21	13–25	−2.90	.1
...n.	A Negro physician, a college graduate ($3000)	21	16–25	23	13–25	−3.20	−.2
...u.	A son of an old American family who is a lawyer and also an illicit seller of drugs. He makes $600 a year from the law and $1900 from the traffic in morphine, etc.	23	17–25	23	17–25	−3.50	−.5
...g.	A feebleminded man (IQ 70) with an income of $12,000 from trust funds	25	23–25	23.75	20½–25	−4.13	−1.1

group of unemployed were accustomed to experiments, tests, and questionnaires of all sorts and descriptions, were very coöperative, and to give internal evidence in their replies of great frankness. There was probably relatively little harm done by deliberate efforts to show oneself in a favorable light.

CHAPTER XVII

Personality

[AMONG the "personality" tests used up till now the great majority are autobiographic questionnaires. The questions may (A) consist of, or include, directly relevant ones such as a psychiatrist might ask a patient, or an employer a candidate for employment; and the answers if true may be important as a condensation of parts of a life history or present profile. Or (B) they may consist of such as the framer of the questionnaire has reason to think will not arouse the subject to suspect the questionnaire's purpose and will still be productive of important facts about him. The record of autobiographic questionnaires up to 1946 was unpromising. Ellis reported then that only 91 of 162 showed positive correlations with the criterion (26 of these being questionably positive), the relation being negative or zero for 71 of them. The future must do much better than that, or prudent students of personal traits will abandon these questionnaires.

At the opposite extreme from asking persons questions about themselves is the method of submitting them to genuine opportunities to cheat in school work, to cheat in games, to steal, to help the suffering, and the like, so arranged that fear of detection or hope of acquiring merit is absent. The two volumes of Hartshorn and May are the best illustration of this method. It is sound and should be used often in the future. The necessary equipment and arrangements are likely to be too expensive in money, or time, or both to encourage wide use of such genuine opportunities to display personal qualities. However, a bonding company might, in my opinion, profitably use such tests for honesty with money; a private school might well use the Hartshorn-May techniques for cheating at school work and in games; Moreno's genuine choices among persons could be used to reveal personal qualities as well as improve social arrangements in schools, camps, factories, and so on; the number and nature of inter- personal contacts in kindergartens is a small but worthy item in an estimate of budding personality.

In between the testimonies of persons about themselves and their behavior in situations that are both genuine and crucial, may be put tests such as (1) free association, (2) the completion of sentences, (3) the interpretation of ink blots, (4) the writing of what is suggested by pictures, (5) drawing pictures, (6) arranging little tiles to form mosaics, and (7) answering questions about what certain imagined persons would do in certain circumstances, and other so- called "projective" tests.

The first two seemed promising but my own experience with them has been rather disappointing. Dr. Irving Lorge and I got scanty results from a free association test with 200 words selected by Professor Truman Kelly; and not much more from 200 completions of incomplete sentences selected by me.[1] Such tests are revealing, but they do not reveal much. Nor would 200,000 of each reveal a person's entire personal- ity. A person's responses in these tests are determined too much by what he has heard and read, too little by what he has been and done. It may even be doubted whether all that a person ever wrote or said or thought in words would do that. Many cravings, urges, and satisfactions act without verbalized parallels.

The first article quoted here reports the use of a 4000-word record from each person. Its results were meager. The second article studies the degree of liking or disliking reported by each of 22 persons for each of 437 experiences.]

[1] Irving Lorge and E. L. Thorndike, "The value of responses in a com- pletion test as indications of personal traits," *Journal of Applied Psychology,* Vol. 25, (April, 1941), pp. 191–199.

TRAINS OF THOUGHT AS SYMPTOMS OF INTERESTS AND ATTITUDES: AN EXPLORATORY INVESTIGATION [2]

Each of sixty-five adults, mostly of intellect and education much above the average, wrote one hundred sets of forty words. The stimulus starting each set was a word (such as *afraid* or *angry* or *baby* or *bath*) and the persons were asked to write the words that came into their minds until the forty spaces on the sheet provided were filled. The experiment was spread over a month, five sets usually being written on any one day. The starting stimuli were the words of the Kent-Rosanoff list. [We thus have 4000 words written by each person.]

Various features of such written lists are presumably indicative of the natures of their authors to some extent and in certain respects. It is the purpose of this report to present facts concerning the indications furnished by the words which appear in the lists, regardless of their particular contexts.

Suppose, for example, that we count for each person the number of occurrences in his 4000 words of the following common words: *ballad, banjo, bass, bugle, carol, Caruso, chant, chime, choir, chord, chorus, clang, concert, cymbal, discord, discordant, flute, guitar,* etc., etc.; and of such rarer words as: *adagio, Aida, allegro, alto, Amati, andante, anthem, aria, baby grand, Bach, bassoon, baton, Bayreuth, Beethoven, Bori, Brahms.* What correlation is there between this number and his interest in music as measured by some reasonable criterion?

Or suppose that we count the occurrence for each person of the following and check the results against some criterion of his interest in the church and religion: *altar, baptism, Baptist, baptize, bible, blaspheme, blasphemy, censer, chapel, Christ, Christianity, church, churchman, clergy, clergyman, cloister, divinity, God,* etc., etc.: *archimandrite, asceticism,*

[2] From the *Proceedings of the American Philosophical Society*, Vol. 77, No. 3, (March, 1937), pp. 439–445.

atheism, Ave Maria, biblical, canonized, catechism, Deuteronomy, etc., etc.

I have made such counts for fifty-four of the persons, for twenty-one of whom certain criterion scores are available, using the rubrics listed below.

2. Interest in things and mechanisms
3. Interest in persons and feelings and acts
4. Interest in animals
5. Interest in words
13. Interest in art
14. Interest in music
15. Interest in beauty
24. Interest in neatness
31. Interest in church and religion
54. Interest in food
64. Interest in clothes and personal adornment
61. Tendency to think of the bright side, pleasant facts, etc.
62. Tendency to think of the dark side, unpleasant facts, etc.
100. Self-indulgence
111. Puritanism

No word was ever counted for more than one rubric. [For reasons of practical convenience the counts of common words (i. e. those in Thorndike's *Teacher's Word Book,* edition of 1921, containing 10,000 words) were kept separate from the counts of rarer words.] Words of the Thorndike 10,000 list of the most used words in books, newspapers, etc., were scored by a uniform key. Words outside it were scored (for 25 of the 54 persons) by one person, preserving approximate uniformity.

THE RELIABILITIES OF THE SCORES

Words from A through K were used to provide one random half-score, and words from L through Z to provide another.[3] It would have been well to use also scores made from the writings on alternate days. But the labor of such double entering seemed prohibitive. Scores of two sorts were recorded: (1) the gross number of words, and (2) the per cent which this was of the sum of the person's counts in all rubrics.

[3] The dividing point was put earlier or later if the above method gave a very uneven division.

As I have shown elsewhere, the words written by some persons on some occasions are largely determined by the person's intent to have ideas and write words all related to the starting stimulus word. There is also a widespread tendency, as the experiment progresses, to change from thinking in strings of names of things, persons, qualities, acts, and events to thinking in sentences. This dilutes the 4000 words by many relational or colorless words (such as *a, and, as, be, if, in, of, it, the, when, who*). Persons vary greatly in the strength of this tendency, and also in the strength of the tendency to insert quotations. The second sort of score mentioned above frees the records from the influence of these last-named tendencies, and is the better one to use. It does, however, have the demerit of eliminating the influence of genuine differences in total average score in *all* rubrics.

Using these percentage scores, the correlations of half-score with half-score range from 0.2 to 0.7, indicating reliabilities of from 0.3 to 0.8 from the use of all the 4000 words written that were inside the Thorndike 10,000.[4] These results are very disappointing. The reliabilities could be improved somewhat by multiple scoring, as by counting the response of *piano* under 2 (things) as well as under 14 (music), or counting *cathedral* under 15 (beauty) as well as 31 (church and religion). But this enrichment of the material will not avail much. We have with single scoring a median of 826 (range from 460 to 1157) words per person written that are inside the Thorndike 10,000 and are in one or another of our scoring keys. Multiple scoring might raise the 826 to 950 or even 1000, but the reliabilities would still be low.

The effect of the inclusion of the words a person writes which are outside the Thorndike 10,000 commonest words will be considered after the facts concerning the validity of the scores for words within the 10,000 (i. e. their significance

---

[4] The reliability coefficients are as follows: things, 0.7; people, 0.6; animals, 0.3; words, 0.5; art, 0.7; music, 0.7; beauty, 0.5; neatness, 0.6; church and religion, 0.5; food, 0.8; clothes and adornment, 0.7; pleasant rather than unpleasant ideas (61/62), 0.8; self-indulgence, 0.7; Puritanism, 0.3.

as indicators of the person's real interests) have been presented.

THE VALIDITY OF THE SCORES

I have used two checks on validity. The first is the correlations with the scores for interests obtained from the extensive questioning reported later in this chapter. By this check, the free-association scores are disappointing; the correlations average very low (near 0.10). The blame doubtless lies in part with the scores obtained from questioning, which have only a dubious validity; but the lack of agreement is disappointing.

The second check is the correlations with ratings for the traits in question by two men who had been working with the persons for some months.[5] I use interest in animals, interest in art, interest in music, interest in words, and interest in the church and religion. The correlations are very low, from 0 to 0.3. Here also part of the blame doubtless lies with the ratings of the two men, but only a part.

The plain fact is that when we take, from 4000 words written by a person in 100 sets of 40 each spread over a month, those included in the commonest 10,000 words, and score them reasonably as indicators of interests, the scores show very little correspondence with either the scores obtained from questions such as are used in tests of interests, or those obtained by ratings made by acquaintances. Nor would increasing the associations and questions and raters a hundred-fold raise the amount of correspondence to more than 0.3 or 0.4.[6] Such trains of thought written in formal tests are revealing, but they do not reveal much. The correlations with other measures of interests tend to be positive, but extremely low. Words written as serial associations reveal the nature

[5] They correlate one with another about 0.8, but the two raters may well have been afflicted by similar errors.

[6] The reliability coefficients from the questions were as follows: things, 0.9; people, 0.6; animals, 0.8; words, 0.8; art, 0.8; music, 0.8; beauty, 0.6; neatness, 0.9; church and religion, 0.7; food, no data; clothing, no data; indulgence, 0.5; Puritanism, 0.6.

of a person only in part and confused by irrelevant factors. Some gluttons may not think much about foods when they are writing words; the actual presence of foods or hunger may be necessary to evoke their interest. Love of music may not cause a person to think much of music when he is writing words or sentences, and similarly for other interests.

Indeed our results cast some doubt upon the assumption that a person's natural, ordinary thinking reveals his interests perfectly. In so far as it is in the form of words, it, too, may be an imperfect index. It is not certain that "as a man think-eth in his heart, so is he," in the sense that so will he behave *in toto*. Some of our cravings and motives may be dumb, or at least inarticulate; conventionality and insincerity may direct our secret thoughts as well as our observed deportment.

Nothing of what has been said so far requires alteration if the words written by a person which are not in the commonest 10,000 are included in his score. Using the records from 25 persons, I have computed reliability coefficients and correlations with the question-test criterion (but this was available for only 10 of the 25). The number of words which were taken as indicative of one or another of the interests studied (and also the interest in books) ranged from 65 to 800 with a median of 188. Using the percentages obtained by dividing the score for each interest by the sum of all such scores, the reliability coefficients are higher than they were for the commoner words in spite of the smaller numbers of words. The validity measures are a little higher, but still very low. The correlations between the scores for the same interest by words inside and by words outside the 10,000 are approximately as high as their reliabilities permit, showing that the two scores measure the same functions.

The use of long serial associations is less promising as a result of our study than it seemed *a priori*. We are led to conclude that the nature of the words written in such tests will be useful in the practice of measuring interests, attitudes, and other personal traits only as one feature of a team of tests, not as a sole reliance, and that the yield for a given expenditure of time in testing and scoring will be smaller than naïve deductions from the psychology of trains of thought would predict. Such tests do have the great merit of being relatively free from certain limitations and dangers which attach to a person's rating of his likings for music, art, etc., and to his answers to detailed questions of the sort found in the instruments devised by Strong, Thurstone, Woodworth and others. But the scores give small returns for much labor.

Free associations in the form of single responses or very short series may differ in important ways from those in the series of forty each studied by us. Moreover, we have used words occurring anywhere in the person's thinking, not words as evoked by specific words.[7] It would not therefore be right to take our results as a condemnation of the ordinary verbal association test as a diagnostic instrument. . . . Certain associations do testify to intelligence; others to abnormality; others may indicate "conflicts," or at least give clues useful in locating "conflicts"); others may give evidence of the strength of interests. The one stone may injure many birds. I fear, however, that it rarely kills any of them. And the cost in time and need of special ability in scoring such a test are serious defects. Psychologists should continue to explore the possibilities of 200 or 400-word association tests as *candidates* for inclusion in a general inventory and appraisal of a person. But it will be prudent not to expect as much from them as we have in the past.

[7] It would be possible to investigate the significance of the associations evoked by specified words in these serial-association records. If, for example, the word *orchestra* occurs five times in A's record and also in B's and is followed in A's record by *beautiful, conductor, out of tune, Beethoven* and *Brahms,* and in B's by *tedious, pay, dance, school* and *club,* we should expect A to have a stronger musical interest than B. The arrangement of scoring keys and of systems of computing scores for the general use of this method, would be very difficult, and their operation would be well-nigh impracticable. This type of scoring should probably be restricted to single associations, as in the work of Rosanoff and Kelley. Consequently, I have not explored its possibilities or determined its values in the case of the 4000-word records.

THE VALUE OF REPORTED LIKES AND DIS-LIKES FOR VARIOUS EXPERIENCES AND ACTIVITIES AS INDICATIONS OF PERSONAL TRAITS [8]

The lists which will be studied here comprised 250 items, 187 items, and 150 items, concerning each of which certain persons reported by symbols (1, 2, 5, 8, and 9) meaning:

(1) I am sure that I like it
(2) I think I like it but am not sure
(5) I neither like nor dislike it
(8) I think I dislike it, but am not sure
(9) I am sure that I dislike it

We also had by the courtesy of Dr. Lorge three complete records for each person with the Strong Vocational Interest Blank. . . .

We begin by grouping items. In proportion as the items that we put together as presumably (that is to say, in our judgment) related by a fair degree of common causation continue to show substantial individual differentiation after summing, and substantial self correlation between two random halves of each sum, our grouping is justified. We may then proceed to check the summed scores for groups of items with such criteria as are available.

In groups 7 to 35 (Nos. 1 to 6 refer to measures to be described later) we never [except once by an inadvertence discovered too late] used an item in more than one group, because we wished, in case the records gave sufficiently reliable and valid measures of interests, to have each of these measures derived from independent sources. We also left many items unassigned to any group, in the hope of later checking them against groups of known significance before placing them.

Our groupings were as shown below for some of the items in the lists of 250 and 187. The items in the list of 150 and in

[8] From the *Journal of Applied Psychology*, Vol. XIX, No. 3, (June, 1936), pp. 285–313.

the Strong blank were used (1) as an independent check, (2) to determine reliability coefficients, and (3) for certain special purposes and need not be shown here.

In the 250 set, items numbered from 21–50 refer to school life, at age 13–19; items 51–100 refer to life outside school at age 13–19; items 101–250 refer to age 20–25. All items in the 187 set refer to age 20–25.

7 Things.

250 set.
38. Manual training
39. Shop-work
40. Trade work of any sort
46. Cooking
47. Domestic science (in general)
119. Repairing an automobile
124. Working with tools
187. Sharpen a knife
188. Take a clock apart and put it together
225. Do picture puzzles
227. Do mechanical puzzles

187 set.
4. Be a cabinet maker
9. Be an electrician
10. Be an inventor
12. Be a plumber
14. Be a repairer of typewriters
37. Spend an afternoon visiting a shoe factory
52. Make ship models
106. Clean a bicycle
113. Oil a sewing machine

8 People.

250 set.
104. Bargaining (also in item-group 22)
105. Selling to a customer
127. Going on errands
186. Go around applying for a job
241. Working as a guide on a sightseeing trip

187 set.
1. Be a book agent
2. Be a life insurance agent
3. Be an ambassador or diplomat
6. Be a chief clerk in an office
7. Be a conductor on a railroad
13. Be a politician
16. Be a secretary to a senator
17. Be a social secretary to a society lady
26. Read the personal column in a newspaper
31. Spend an afternoon making social calls
58. Take pictures of insane people

9 Animals.

    250 set.   33. Studying zoölogy
                56. Taking care of animals
             174. Play with a dog or cat
             192. Feed the horses and cows
             193. Feed the hens and chickens
             200. See a beautiful horse

    187 set.   43. Teach a parrot to talk ·
                44. Teach a dog tricks
                56. Take pictures of domestic animals
                57. Take pictures of wild animals
                68. Have a pet canary
                69. Have a pet monkey
                86. Washing a dog
             116. Raise fancy pigeons

10 Words.

    250 set.   23. Latin
                24. French, German or Italian
             217. Try to write a poem
             226. Do cross-word puzzles

    187 set.   25. Read a page of a dictionary
                51. Make puns
                53. Make slang words or novel expressions

11 Reading.

    250 set.   25. English literature
                57. Reading stories (in elem. school)
             128. Reading stories (20 to 25)
             130. Reading serious books

    187 set.   29. Spend an afternoon in a library
                83. Reading in bed
                84. Reading on a train
                85. Reading while music is being played
             141. Learn that if you can study for three years you can have a great career as a writer

12 Bodily Exercise.

    250 set.   43. Gymnastics
                51. Athletics (in teens)
                64. Doing heavy work, chopping, digging, etc.
                74. Swimming
             138. Athletic sports not competitive: hiking, bicycling, hunting, skating
             169. Take a walk in the city

    187 set.   82. Wrestling
             126. Walking to and from work or school
             146. Do a daily dozen of physical exercises
             160. Saw wood

13 Art.

250 set. 41. Art (in elem. school)
       67. Drawing (in teens)
       68. Painting (in teens)
     132. Drawing (20 to 25)
     133. Painting (20 to 25)

187 set. 28. Spend an afternoon in an art gallery
      38. Spend an afternoon watching a famous painter paint
      39. Spend an afternoon watching a famous sculptor model
      59. Take pictures of landscapes
    129. Spend $500 for a friend for pictures for his home
    136. See an exhibit of modern French paintings
    183. Try to learn to make etchings

14 Music.

250 set. 42. Music
      69. Singing
      70. Playing piano, violin or other instrument
      88. Going to concerts
    134. Singing (20 to 25)
    136. Listening to music
    179. Go to a good concert

187 set. 30. Spend an afternoon listening to Chinese music with explanations
      63. Go to an organ recital
      64. Go to a concert by a college glee club
      79. Listening to bird songs
    135. Take a trip to Mexico to collect phonographic records of Indian music
    140. Learn that if you can study for three years you can have a great career as a singer
    182. Try to learn to play the flute

15 Beauty.

250 set. 58. Reading poetry (in teens)
      63. Doing fancy sewing or embroidery (in teens)
    114. Doing fancy sewing or embroidery (20 to 25)
    129. Reading poetry (20 to 25)
    197. Seeing a beautiful sunset
    198. Seeing a beautiful painting
    199. Seeing a beautiful dancer
    236. Visit the art museum

187 set.   8. Be a dress designer
      22. Read books on lace and embroidery
      40. Watch an expert appraise antiques
      47. Make a collection of 50-cent objects that are really beautiful
    130. Spend $20,000 in making a collection of rugs for a museum

131. Spend $40,000 in making a collection of pottery for a museum
134. Take a trip through Eastern Europe buying old furniture, ikons, etc., for a museum
137. See an exhibit of Chinese porcelain
147. Earn your living as a jewel expert

16 Responsibility.

250 set. 110. Showing others how to do their work
161. Cook a fancy dinner
221. Plan for a party
245. Working on a committee to secure money for a good cause

187 set. 19. Be a vocational counselor
88. Be a buyer (i. e. head of department) of china and glass for a big department store
89. Be a buyer (i. e. head of department) of dress goods for a big department store
90. Be a buyer (i. e. head of department) of furniture for a big department store
91. Be a buyer (i. e. head of department) of sporting goods for a big department store
93. Be mayor of a small city
98. Manage a small bookstore of your own
99. Manage a small drugstore of your own
100. Manage a small grocery store of your own
101. Manage a small factory of your own
102. Manage a small farm of your own
117. Read manuscripts and advise a publisher whether to publish them

17 Detail.

250 set 66. Washing dishes (in teens)
125. Washing dishes
126. Making beds
191. Darn stockings

187 set. 74. Addressing letters
108. Copy quotations and references
161. Sort mail

18 System.

250 set. 182. Clean and arrange your bureau
183. Put everything in order in a room or office

187 set. 46. Make a card catalog of persons, books, etc.

19 Neatness.

250 set. 62. Doing plain sewing (in teens)
106. Filing papers
123. Cleaning house
189. Mend clothes

190. Shine your shoes
223. Clean up after a party (given by you)

187 set. 18. Be a street-cleaner
72. Have your hands manicured
75. Brushing your clothes
76. Brushing your hair
111. Keep neat and accurate accounts
119. Set a table
144. Clean up a yard or garden
155. Polish brass on a boat or car

20 Sum of scores in 17, 18, and 19.

21 Approval.

250 set. 201. Rescue a child from danger, and have the crowd cheer you
202. Stop a panic in a theater that gets on fire, and be praised in the newspapers
206. (Reversed). Have a waiter look sour because you did not tip him
208. (Reversed). Have your boss blame you when you didn't deserve it
212. Be elected to an office
213. Win a prize at a party
214. Be praised by your boss
219. Tell a funny story
229. Think what you would do if you were famous

187 set. 77. (Reversed). Having a crowd of beggars jeer at you because you give them nothing
109. Have clerks in stores comment on your good taste and judgment
118. Receive applause when you speak at a meeting
148. Find that your opinions on a subject are held also by noted writers
149. Get mentioned in the Atlantic Monthly as a promising poet
150. Have children admire your skill in swimming, diving, gymnastics, etc.
151. Have men in a garage admire your car
152. Help a rich drunkard throw money for a crowd to catch
169. Be surrounded by a crowd who mistake you for a popular actor or actress
174. Have people compliment you on your new clothes
179. Tackle a thief who is running away and hold him till a policeman comes

22 Mastery or Domination over Persons.

250 set. 104. Bargaining
111. Keeping others at work
204. (Reversed). Have people give you orders who have no right to

205. (Reversed). Have people give you advice when you did not ask for it
209. Make a cruel man stop beating a horse
210. Make a bully stop teasing a child
211. Call down somebody who is fresh to you

187 set.
48. Make a person who has insulted one of your friends apologize to her
96. Be strong enough to knock down anybody who pushes you on the street, and do so
104. Boss a gang of boys and make them do useful work
105. Catch a man stealing from a child and make him give back the thing plus a dollar
154. (Reversed). Let a policeman bawl you out without answering back
162. Stop a landlord from evicting a poor family with a sick father, by bluffing him into the fear that you and your gang will beat him up
175. Lead a disturbance against a militaristic lecturer and break up the meeting
176. (Reversed). Obey a teacher to save making a fuss although the teacher is in the wrong
178. Stop boys who are fighting in the street and make them go home

23 Religion.

250 set.
84. Going to church
155. Going to church (20 to 25)
172. Attend a religious service.
173. Read a religious book (Bible, Talmud, etc.)

187 set.
5. Be a clergyman
11. Be a missionary
15. Be a secretary to a bishop
45. Teach boys of sixteen in Sunday School
115. Pray for the sick and afflicted
120. Sing hymns
158. Read the Bible or Talmud to a poor blind man

24 Display; Public Attention.

250 set.
45. Dramatics (in high school)
102. Getting dressed for a party
203. Have people stare at you because your clothes are queer
207. Have people gossip about you
218. Make a speech to an audience of 100 people
220. Take part in a play
242. Be usher or bridesmaid at a wedding
246. Have your teacher tell the other pupils that you are a model pupil
247. Have your boss tell the other employees that you are best

187 set.
73. Have your picture taken
78. Introducing a speaker at a meeting

   92. Be a head-waiter
   97. Be toastmaster at a banquet
  103. Advertise a new style of bathing suit by appearing in a
        store window wearing it
  112. Lead a procession
  143. Address a meeting
  157. Read aloud to a group
  159. Rise up in a meeting and say "That is a lie" to a person
        who has uttered an outrageous lie

25 Novelty.

250 set.   85. Going on automobile trips
           131. Reading the newspaper
           139. Traveling and seeing new places
           163. Eat dog biscuit
           164. Eat a live beetle
           178. Go to a good talkie

187 set.   33. Spend an afternoon visiting a divorce court
            34. Spend an afternoon visiting the Ford factory
            35. Spend an afternoon visiting an insane asylum
            36. Spend an afternoon visiting the United States Senate
           133. Take a trip by yourself in a car
           170. Be hidden in a closet where you can see and hear a meeting
                of President Roosevelt's cabinet
           171. Be hidden in a closet where you can see and hear a talk
                between Henry Ford and his son
           172. Be hidden in a closet where you can see and hear the
                private life of a movie star
           173. Be hidden in a closet where you can see and hear a crimi-
                nal being electrocuted

26 Security.

250 set. 240. Spend the evening with your mother

187 set. 95. Be a traffic policeman (in contrast to 94)
          124. Travel by train (in contrast to 125)

27 Danger.

187 set. 60. Go from New York to Boston in a small sail-boat
          94. Be a regular policeman
          125. Travel by airplane
          138. Shoot tigers

28 Human Surroundings: Gregariousness.

250 set. 177. Go to a baseball game

187 set. 27. Spend an afternoon at Coney Island
          70. Have dinner in a big restaurant
          132. Take a trip in a sight-seeing bus
          166. Work in the reading room of a library
           71. (Reversed). Have dinner in your room alone
          167. (Reversed). Work in your own room
          177. (Reversed). Spend a day alone in the woods

29 Social Intercourse (commonly friendly).

250 set.
- 80. Going to parties (in teens)
- 83. Playing around with a group of friends (in teens)
- 86. Visiting relatives (in teens)
- 142. Making new acquaintances
- 145. Going to parties
- 146. Visiting relatives
- 154. Being with a group of friends
- 158. Going to weddings
- 222. Give a party
- 237. Go to a card-party
- 238. Go to a dance
- 239. Go to a picnic

187 set.
- 61. Go to a class reunion
- 62. Go to a club meeting
- 67. Go on a yacht for a week as a guest of a rich friend
- 107. Camp out in the Catskills with 10 to 12 friends or acquaintances
- 168. Be pleasant to strangers
- 185. Being snowed in for a week in a country hotel with a dozen strangers
- 186. Having the strangers be friendly to you
- 187. Living in a social settlement for a week

[The original does not state what items constituted group 30 and I am unable now to discover what they were.]

31 Children.

250 set.
- 65. Taking care of children (in teens)
- 120. Taking care of children
- 175. Play with a little child (baby up to 4 years)
- 176. Play with a child 5 to 10
- 194. Take care of a baby

187 set.
- 41. Teach children of six to read
- 42. Teach children of eight to sing
- 54. Take pictures of babies
- 65. Go to visit a day nursery
- 55. Take pictures of little children
- 121. Sing a little child to sleep
- 163. Tell stories to a group of children 8 to 10 years old
- 180. Take six or eight city children for a day in the country
- 181. Bring six or eight country children for a day in the city to see the sights

32 Conflict.

250 set.
- 95. Fighting (in teens)
- 184. Visit people who owe your firm money and try to collect it
- 185. Write letters to people who owe your firm money and get them to pay up
- 232. Complain to your landlord about something

233. Call a policeman and have him arrest somebody who has cheated you
248. Hearing and adjusting complaints
249. Convincing an opponent that he is wrong

187 set.   49. Make a man give you back your money for an article which he misrepresented
50. Make a professor raise your mark in a course
114. Persuade a person that he or she should resign from candidacy or from office in your favor
123. Tell somebody whom you dislike just what you think of him or her
145. Dispute with a friend over politics, religion, the merits of automobiles, etc.

33 Friendly Rivalry.

250 set.   20. Indoor games (at age 10–14)
54. Card games (in teens)
137. Competitive athletic sports and games
143. Sedentary games like cards and chess

34 Plants and Gardening.

250 set.   55. Working in a garden
89. Growing flowers
90. Growing vegetables
117. Growing vegetables (20 to 25)
118. Growing flowers (20 to 25)
196. See a beautiful garden

187 set.   66. Go to a flower show
80. Picking berries
81. Picking flowers
127. Water a flower garden
128. Weed a flower garden
156. Prune shrubs
164. Water plants in a vegetable garden
165. Weed a vegetable garden
184. Transplanting ferns from the woods to your rock garden

35 Self.

250 set. 144. Your regular job
147. Writing your diary
148. Making plans for the future

In Groups 36 to 42 there was some duplication of items *inter se* and with item-groups 7 to 35. In 36 (called "Reality") were included items of activity or experience concerned exclusively or chiefly with real things and people. In 38 (called Imagination or Fiction) were items such as (from the 187 set): Spend an afternoon in an art gallery (also in 13), Spend an afternoon in a library (also in 11), Make a card catalog (also in 17), Copy quotations and references (also in 17), Make puns (also in 16). In 37 (called Talk) were items where speech by the person was prominent. In 39 (called Indulgence) and 40 (called Moral) were respectively items commonly thought of as done chiefly for pleasure and done chiefly for duty. Group 41 included only Sedentary Games (3 items) and 42 included only Dancing (5 items).

For each person for each group we have then a record of so many likes, probable likes, indifferents, probable dislikes and sure dislikes reported. These can be turned into a measure of the person for that group by scoring the indifferents as O, the likes as plus values of any approved amount (we have used +2 for a sure like and +1 for a probable like), and the dislikes as minus values (we have used —1 and —2).

. . . [There follow in the original article measurements of the reliabilities of these thirty-six scores and of all their intercorrelations. These are disappointing. The reliabilities were rarely above .80. The correlations do not suggest the causation of personality by any dozen or more observable traits or inferable factors.] How far is this due to my selection of items? How far is it due to the failure of persons' reports of their likes and dislikes to reveal their personalities? How far is it the fault of human nature itself, especially those features of it which we refer to as "personality"? I hope someone will make a similar investigation with more and better items, but I fear that the results will not be very much improved thereby. The combination of reports made several weeks apart, and special precautions to secure honesty and uniformity in the use of the scales of liking and disliking would doubtless improve the results considerably. But I fear that the complexity and specialization of human beings with respect to character, temperament, and whatever else is included in personality would still prevent the results from providing consistent and clear, not to say simple and useful, profiles of personalities and theories of the organization and causation of personality.

Indeed, even if we had accurate and complete life histories of a thousand persons, supplemented by many tests of actual conduct, I suspect that the profiles and theories which psychology derived therefrom would not be simple or easily usable. [This is not to say, as Allport seems to say, that personality cannot profitably be analyzed, but only that the analysis will be difficult and its results complex.]

CHAPTER XVIII

The Origin of Language [*]

NOBODY knows when, where or how speech originated, and I am stepping in where wise scholars in linguistics and psychology fear to tread. My colleagues in psychology will, I beg, permit this divagation into speculation by one who has labored long in the less exciting fields of experiment and statistics. I ask and expect no mercy from experts in linguistic science, but only that they build a better theory on the ruins they make of mine.

We must first glance at three time-honored and then dishonored theories, now known by these opprobrious names: ding-dong theory, bow-wow theory and pooh-pooh theory.

The ding-dong theory assumed a mystical power of certain things to evoke certain sounds from men. Since each such sound was associated with the experience of the thing, it came to mean it. And since men were alike in their responses to things by sounds, one of these sounds meant more or less the same thing to all in the group, and easily became a vehicle of communication. All the evidence is against the existence of any such mystical power, and only extremely strong evidence would induce any scientific student of psychology or of language to put any faith in so extremely unlikely an origin of language.

The bow-wow theory supposed that men formed habits of using the sounds made by animals, things or events to mean the respective animals, things and events and that these habits

[*] A lecture given on November 5, 1942, as one of the series of the William James lectureship at Harvard University, and published in *Science*, (July 2, 1943), pp. 1–6.

started them on the road to inventing other sounds as signs of animals, things or events. For various reasons this theory is discredited. Doubtless after man has language, he will often make the sounds that animals and things make, but it is doubtful how often he will do so in a languageless group. Possibly he will do so only accidentally as a part of his general vocal play. There might be little agreement in the ideas evoked in the members of a human group by hearing the varying sounds which its various members made when they thought of a dog, a cow, thunder, and the like.

Even if a group got a sufficient agreement in the case of forty or fifty sounds for these to be used commonly in the group, an advance by the addition of non-mimetic sounds as signs of things and events would be difficult. If the mimetic sounds remained fully mimetic, it might well be impossible. But the opponents of the bow-wow theory have not considered sufficiently the possibility that a human group might modify their vocabulary of mimetic sounds by slurring, abbreviation and other processes that make speech easier for the speaker without losing the old meanings of animals, things and events in the hearer. If close imitations of a dog's barking, cock's crowing, baby's crying, lamb's bleating, etc., became conventionalized within a human group into sounds no more like the originals than *bow-wow, cockadoodledoo, mama* and *bah-bah,* or *urr-urr, uk a duk a duk duk, na-na* and *buh-buh,* that group could in a few generations progress to a set of sounds many of which would mean primarily certain animals or things and only secondarily or not at all the sound made by the respective animals and things. The group's vocabulary would all be about things that had distinctive sounds, but could be in the form of sounds different from these and in some cases hardly suggestive of them. The invention of a non-mimetic sound for some thing hitherto nameless would then be easier. The use of such an invention would, of course, spread somewhat slowly within the group and very slowly outside it to groups accustomed only to mimetic words.

The pooh-pooh theory, or interjectional theory, supposed that the instinctive unlearned cries of man as a wordless animal, which already are sounds that are evoked by certain situations and evoke in human hearers certain equally unlearned responses of action and feeling, came to possess meanings also, and that on the basis of this vocabulary of familiar sounds meaning pain, surprise, fear, affection, and the like, early man here and there used other sounds to mean other facts.

Nobody should doubt that part of this is true. To a mother whose baby cries and seeks her breast that cry probably means that the baby wants to be fed if anything means anything to her. If she can think of anything she will think of that, as well as react appropriately to it. But for various reasons students of language have decided that the attachment of meanings to the hearing or the making of these sounds of instinctive nature is not adequate to originate articulate speech. So-called animal language plus the power of thinking meanings would not produce human language.

An ingenious theory has been set forth by Sir Richard Paget, a physicist and student of phonetics, who argues that the total behavior of a man to a situation includes characteristic movements of the tongue and lips and other organs of speech. These gestures of the mouth parts became specially important when a man's hands were "in continual use . . . for craftsmanship, the chase, and the beginnings of art and literature," so that he could not gesture with them. Sounds were added to these "mouthings," and finally came to play the leading rôle. In Paget's own words:

Originally man expressed his ideas by gesture, but as he gesticulated with his hands, his tongue, lips and jaw unconsciously followed suit in a ridiculous fashion, "understudying" (as Sir Henry Hadow aptly suggested to me) the action of the hands. The consequence was that when, owing to pressure of other business, the principal actors (the hands) retired from the stage—as much as principal actors ever do—their understudies—the tongue, lips and jaw—were already proficient in the pantomimic art.

Then the great discovery was made that if while making a gesture with the tongue and lips, air was blown through the oral or nasal cavities, the gesture became audible as a whispered speech sound. If, while pantomiming with tongue, lips and jaw our ancestors sang, roared or grunted—in order to draw attention to what they were doing—a still louder and more remarkable effect was produced, namely, what we call voiced speech. . . .

In this way there was developed a new system of conventional gesture of the organs of articulation from which, as I suggest, nearly all human speech took its origin. . . .

We can now form a mental picture of how the process of speech-making actually began, but an example or two will make the argument clearer. If the mouth, tongue and lips be moved as in eating, this constitutes a gesture sign meaning "eat"; if, while making this sign, we blow air through the vocal cavities, we automatically produce the whispered sounds mnyΔm–mnyΔm (mnyum), or mnIΔ–mnIΔ (mnyuh)—words which probably would be almost universally understood, and which actually occur as a children's word for food in Russian, as well as in English. . . .

Another adult example may be given, namely, in connection with the beckoning gesture—commonly made by extending the hand, palm up, drawing it inwards towards the face and at the same time bending the fingers inwards towards the palm. This gesture may be imitated with the tongue, by protruding, withdrawing, and bending up its tip as it re-enters the mouth and falls to rest.

If this "gesture" be blown or voiced, we get a resultant whispered or phonated word, like eda, eda or edra (according to the degree of contact between tongue and upper lip or palate) suggestive of the Icelandic hadr, the Hindustani idhar and the Slavonic ıdeı—all of which bear much the same meaning as our English word "hither." If the same tongue gesture be finished more vigorously, the resultant word will end in a *k* or *g*, owing to the back portion of the tongue making a closure against the soft palate.

Thus, by unconsciously using the tongue, lips, jaw, etc., in the place of the head, hands, etc., pantomimic gesture would almost automatically produce human speech.[1]

Paget fabricated words by moving his own jaws, tongue and lips in ways which seemed to him likely to have been used as oral gestures of primitive men accompanying manual or other gestures meaning reach up, draw back suddenly, scrape, wave aloft, shoot with a bow and arrow, sew, blow, plough, strip grains from the stalk, pick berries, collect them and bury them in the ground, and many others. He finds substantial correspondences between his fabricated sounds and

[1] R. Paget, "Human Speech," pp. 133–138, *passim*, 1930.

certain words in old languages. Of the famous Aryan roots he considers that 77 per cent are clearly pantomimic. For example, "tank—contract, compress—as in thong, is due to two compressions in succession fore and aft the palate." "da —give—seems to be an offering gesture made with the tongue." [2]

Paget's book "Human Speech" is so recent (1930) that his theory has not yet received a pet name. Using the first illustration that he gives we might call it the yum-yum theory. This, however, really misrepresents and unduly favors it; for the theory requires the mouth parts to pantomime not eating, drinking, sipping, blowing and other acts of the mouth parts themselves (nobody doubts that), but movements of other parts of the body. A truer nickname would be the "tongue-tied" theory, meaning that the tongue is yoked with the body by subtle bonds of mimetic kinship. The theory has been accepted by at least one psychologist, Eisenson, but it has not been acceptable generally. Personally, I do not believe that any human being before Sir Richard Paget ever made any considerable number of gestures with his mouth parts in sympathetic pantomime with gestures of his hands, arms and legs, still less that any considerable number of men in any local community made the same oral gestures in such pantomime.

And now for my theory, which is a humdrum affair compared with any of these four.

Let us assume a group of one or more human families living together at least as continuously as one of the groups of chimpanzees studied by Nissen in their natural habitat. Let us assume that their environment includes, besides the untouched objects of nature, a few objects chosen and preserved as tools, say a few pounders, a few cutters, a few gourds, shells or other dippers and holders, and perhaps a few stabbers and scrapers; and also some natural objects chosen and preserved as playthings, things that one can chew on, roll or throw, make a noise with, and the like.

[2] *Ibid.*, p. 149.

We may safely assume further that these humans made a wide variety of movements with their hands, much the same as the human infants of today instinctively make, pushing, pulling, tearing, putting into their mouths, dropping out therefrom, dropping, throwing, picking up, and so on.

We may safely assume further that these humans made a variety of sounds like the meaningless prattle of infants, letting their mouth parts play with their voices in the same multifarious way that their hands play with any obtainable object. The variety of sounds made may indeed have been greater than that made by an infant of today, whose vocal play may be narrowed by the elimination of sounds which are alien to the language which his environment favors. And we know that an infant of to-day makes a much wider variety of articulate sounds than the language of his parents contains.

Such a person in such a group would at an early age have a memory image or expectation or idea of the appearance of the person who nursed him, which her voice or smell or caress could evoke though she was unseen. By having been experienced in so many different contexts, some image or expectation or idea referring to her would have acquired an existence independent of any particular sequence of behavior. In a similar manner he would have an image or expectation or idea referring to each object that had been associated with many varying concomitants in his uses of it or play with it.

Such a person would prattle while he worked or played much as a child of a year or two now prattles as he plays. If his making a certain sound became connected with his experiencing a certain object or act and having an image or expectation or idea of that object or act, he would have a language. That sound and the act of making it would mean that object or act to him. It would be a private language useless as yet for communication. It would be a narrow language consisting of only a few words referring mostly to his own acts and possessions, to the persons in the family group and to their acts and possessions. But it would be genuine language.

And it would be a valuable intellectual tool for its possessor, enabling him to replace the somewhat cumbrous and elusive images or expectations by sounds that he could make and arrange more or less at will. If he did connect *ik* with his digging stick, and *üg* with his large turtle-shell container, *yum* with truffle and *kuz* with clam, he could plan an expedition to get truffles or one to get clams more easily and conveniently than he could with only pictorial memories. Consequently, we may safely reckon that any person who made these connections that gave sounds meanings and gave things symbolic equivalents would keep them, even though he alone understood them.

What now is the probability that a person brought up in a languageless family group would form one such connection whereby a sound (not an instinctive cry of pain, delight, triumph, etc.) meant an object? What is the probability that he would form two such? Three? Four? A dozen? A score?

Properly planned experiments with enough infants brought up in a languageless environment for ten years (perhaps for a much shorter time) would give a decisive answer. I have long wished to make systematic observations of infants in linguistically under-privileged environments, but have never been able to find the time, and must rely upon memories of casual observations of my children and grandchildren in making my estimates.

I think that the probability that a person in the top half of the species for intelligence by birth would make four or five such connections is very high, say seven out of ten. Consider a child of early man playing with a large shell used as a container in the household and prattling as he plays. Let us take the state of affairs least favorable to connecting the sound *üg* with that shell.

Let his prattling possibilities consist of a thousand syllables all equally likely to occur, and all as likely to occur in any one situation as in any other. Then the chance that he will utter *üg* as he puts a pebble in the shell is 1 in 1000 if he prattles at all. And unless that connection between the manual act and the vocal act is somehow strengthened, he will be as likely the next time that he drops a pebble into that shell to utter any other sound in his repertory as to utter *üg*. Very often he will utter other sounds and no progress will be made toward the attachment of meanings to his utterances.

But there are forces which tend to cause progress away from purely miscellaneous vocal play. First of all the child who puts one pebble in the shell is likely to put another in then and there. His enjoyment of the act makes him repeat it, that is, strengthens its connection with the mental set in which he did it first. Now that mental set happened at that time to evoke also the vocal play of saying *üg*, and the confirming reaction which the enjoyment of the manual play set in action tends to spread or scatter so as to strengthen also the connection of the situation with the utterance.

In the second place, saying *üg* to the shell and pebble may be itself enjoyable and the connection may thereby be strengthened. Consequently, the probability that the child will drop a second pebble is substantial and the probability that he will utter *üg* therewith if he utters anything is far above 1 in 1000.

Let us assume provisionally that some active-minded Homo Sapiens did thus connect *ma* with the mother who nursed and fondled him, *ba* with the round black thing that rolled and tossed, *unk* with the club with which he knocked down his prey, and similarly for a dozen or more "words," as we may truly call them. If he did this, what would be the probability that some second person in the group would come to understand these words? And if he did come to understand them, what would be the probability that the first person would come to use them with the intent of having the second person understand them, and so attain the condition of possessing speech as a social tool?

If one person in a hitherto languageless group of two or three dozen souls has reached the stage of a private language of a score of words the probability that some other person in the group will come to understand three or four of his words is much more than infinitesimal.

His companions might well hear him say *kuz* as he dug up a clam or opened a clam or ate a clam, a hundred times in a week. Even if they paid no more attention to his speech than to his personal play, vocal or non-vocal, the sound *kuz* would tend to make them think of a clam more often than of any other one object. And under certain conditions they would be attentive to his speech. For example, in a group digging for clams together, if one cried *kuz* whenever he found a clam, the cry would become interesting to others.

If the group had a dozen or so "bow-wow" (that is, mimetic) words that they used as signals, they would be thereby the more disposed to attend each to the other's vocalizations. If a second person of the group had a private language of his own, though unlike that of the first person in every particular, the second person would be thereby the more disposed to attend to the first person's vocalizations. If the group had a system of mutual influence by gestures, even one utterly devoid of any vocal accompaniments, its members would be thereby a little more disposed to attend to the vocal behavior one of another.

So I would set the probability that in a group of thirty souls, one of whom had a private language of twenty words, some one other person would come to understand five of these words in the course of a moderate lifetime of thirty-five years as well above one in ten thousand, and probably above one in a thousand.

If the family group of say thirty souls has an inventor of a private language of say twenty-five words, and say ten of the thirty understand say eight of the words, what is the probability that any one of these ten will use any of the eight words that he understands, use it, that is, to mean to himself the thing or act or event in question? This probability is substantial, but it is not 100 out of 100. Some persons in such a group will hear and understand a word hundreds of times, but in all probability never say it at all, except accidentally as an element in their meaningless chatter. But some will, when they themselves utter this word in their meaningless chatter or for any reason, understand it as if it were spoken by A. And this act of saying a word and having it mean something will tend to be satisfying rather than annoying. Meaningful prattle is more satisfying than meaningless and will therefore be more frequently repeated.

If A, the original inventor, hears B or C or D say one of the words to which he, A, attaches meaning when he himself says them, what is the probability that he, A, will understand the work spoken by B? It is not 100 out of 100. The connection $kuz \rightarrow clam$ may remain confined to kuz said by A, because A is stupid or by nature an extreme introvert or what William James called a lonely thinker, or because of the general tendency of connections to operate only in the way in which they are formed. But A has, by hypothesis, an IQ of 100 or better, and if B goes about saying kuz repeatedly and as if he meant something, A is likely to notice what B says, and will at least be more likely to attach the thought of clam to the sound kuz when made by B than to attach any other one meaning to it. I should conjecture that the probability of A's understanding B would be well over 25 in 100 and under 90 in 100.

It is perhaps time to attach a name to the theory which I am expounding. Let us save everybody trouble by giving it an opprobrious name from the start! Since it relies on the miscellaneous vocal play of man instead of his alleged mimetic or emotional utterances, it could be called the "babble-babble" theory. Since it starts with languages private to single persons, and progresses gradually toward speech in the full speaker-hearer relation (which, indeed, my exposition has not yet reached) it could be called the "onety-twoty" theory. Since it depends on successive selections of chance variations in sound-reality connections, it could be called the "chancey-chance" or "luck-luck" theory. Or we may combine its two main dynamic features and call it the babble-luck theory.

Let us continue with the luck-luck course of the babble-luck theory.

If B understands *kuz* as spoken by A and A understands *kuz* as spoken by B, what is the probability that A will come to *use* the word as a means of influencing B? What is the probability that B will come to *use* the word to influence A?

It is not 100 out of 100. A and B might continue for years to get meaning from one another's use of the word, but never use it for any purpose other than as a self-reminder or as an aid in personal plans or for self-entertainment. However, if A said *kuz* when he was about to set forth to dig clams, and B was moved by hearing *kuz* to set forth to dig clams also, and so accompanied A on several occasions, there might fairly easily be built up a habit in A of saying *kuz* when he wanted B's company on a clamming trip. (The formation of this habit would not be as simple as this sounds or by one direct linking, but by various coöperating associative links which I could describe if necessary). Or if A had already a habit of purposive communication with B by means of a gesture such as pointing to a clam and to B's mouth when he wished or permitted B to eat it, A might well happen to say *kuz* along with the two gestures and eventually in place of the former gesture. (Here again the substitution would not be as simple as it sounds, but could come to pass.)

A and B thus reach a stage where a word is used by one of them, say by A, with the expectation that his saying it in the presence of the other will produce or favor certain behavior in the other, and where A has the habit of saying it to the other as an appropriate thing to do when a certain desire or purpose moves him. This is genuine human language used in the speaker-hearer relation. But the relation is, as yet, unidirectional, from A as speaker to B as hearer.

Speech need not progress further to full two-way, give-and-take speech, but it could, and often would. I will not run the risk of wearying you with the probabilities that the normal operations of repetition and reward would lead men to this final stage. They are high.

Each of the stages that I have described, from that of words used privately to purposive use of speech in the full speaker-hearer relation, was self-sustaining, by adding something to the group's balance of satisfactions, or to its chance of survival, or to both. A one-man language could make that man remember, anticipate and plan better. In so far as others understood A's words, each of them had some profit from A's experience in addition to their own. In so far as they used his words, each had a private language without originating it. When they reached the stage of understanding one another certain experiences of any one were of profit to all. The stage of purposive use of words to modify the behavior of another gave the possibility of increasing costless coöperation and decreasing costly interference of person with person. Even if the words used were few and the occasions of their use limited to a very narrow round of suggestions, commands, invitations and reports, the benefits would still be enough to maintain the linguistic activities.

Nothing in all this so far requires that either A or B thinks of the other as imagining or meaning clams when he says *kuz*. Such imputation of an inner life to another may arise later and regardless of communication, though of course it can not progress far without communication. How it arises is a fascinating problem, but to discuss it would make far too long an interruption of our present task.

Let us turn rather to some possible criticisms. First it will be said that the speech which I have derived from babble by luck is a pitifully small, crude affair in comparison with the speech of any known group present or past. This criticism is true. Even after a dozen or more words had been used purposively hundreds of times by a third of the family group and understood after a fashion by two thirds of the group, the use and understanding would be nowhere nearly as clean-cut as that of a modern man or child. A person could use words more or less appropriately in certain situations in the sense that the use of the word was much more appropriate on the average than saying nothing, or than saying some other word of those in his active vocabulary. He could understand words in the sense that what he did to the total situation including the word was on the average different from what he would have done if some other word had been there, and better than what he would have done if no word had been there. But when the imperfect appropriateness of a speaker's uses was combined with a hearer's inadequate understandings, a perfect result could not be expected. If the speaker went much beyond the regular routine uses, he would arouse misunderstanding, neglect or perplexity. The group's linguistic activities might be clumsy as well as extremely narrow.

It will be said that the evolution of any language worthy of the name from such crude beginnings is problematic. This criticism also is true, but it is not very damaging. The problems are no harder than the problems of the evolution of mechanical tools from their crude beginnings. The evolution of a vocabulary of two hundred names of acts, objects and events from a vocabulary of twenty is a problem, though a rather easy one.[3] The evolution of a language that can mean qualities and relations as well as objects and events is a further problem. The evolution of a language that can by sounds ask questions, distinguish orders from statements and date events has further problems. Refinements of meaning, as by our adjectives and adverbs, and abbreviations of speech, as by our pronouns, involve further problems.

I have not solved these and other problems. But I think they are all soluble. If the facts which I have related account for how men came to use articulate words with the purpose of influencing other men, to understand such words and to cooperate in the speaker-hearer relation, they can fairly be said to account for the origin of language, but to leave us with many problems of its development.

[3] One generation having reached the linguistic status I have described, the second generation can learn from it and spend most of its linguistic activity in adding its inventions to the parental stock. The custom of naming things and acts by sounds may, after a certain number of such sound-meaning connections has been reached, become a conscious deliberate habit. Some early linguist may then devote his spare time to naming every person in the group, every animal that frequents the locality, and every tool or weapon that he uses.

A third possible criticism is that the babble-luck doctrine should have produced dozens, maybe hundred of different languages of this beggarly sort. Origin from miscellaneous babble would cause a multiplicity of primeval languages unless one family group got so great a head start that its language spread to all other tribes before they had invented any languages of their own, which is unlikely. I see nothing objectionable in this. It seems to me sure that any continuing group of intelligent human beings would in time get a language from "babble and luck" if they did not get it earlier from neighbors or visitors who already had it. In many cases they would get it so. Inter-group learning would be of the same general nature as the intra-group learning.

A fourth possible criticism is that hundreds of generations seem to be required to get even this beggarly language if the group has no aid from outside. This seems to be really an argument pro rather than con. Surely the notion that primeval men who were wordless got words as quickly as modern men got Mohammedanism or Christianity or steam engines is fantastic. The length of time from selecting and using flints that were sharp to chipping flints to make them sharp, and the length of time from chipping them roughly to chipping and polishing them in the elegant neolithic styles are both reckoned in many thousands of years.

Whatever may be the value of this account of the origin of meaningful speech, one thing is certain. The human animal's miscellaneous play with his vocal apparatus and the articulate sounds he thereby produces and the associations he makes of these with things and events independently of, and especially contrary to, his linguistic environment deserve much more attention from psychology and linguistic science than they have hitherto received.

CHAPTER XIX

The Psychology of Semantics *

I. THE MEANINGS OF WORDS TO HEARERS AND READERS

MEANINGS are in persons' minds, not in words, and when we say that a word has or possesses such and such meanings, we are really saying that it has evoked, or caused, those meanings. Until it gets into a mind, a word is only puffs of air or streaks of ink. What a word, sentence, or other expression means to hearer or reader is mainly what it makes him think or feel or do as a fairly direct consequence of hearing or seeing it, and, more narrowly, what it makes him think or think of as the direct and almost immediate consequence of hearing or seeing it. Consideration of the rarer operations in which a hearer asks the speaker for explanations, or a reader consults dictionaries, would add little of value. Consideration of the still rarer cases in which all or part of a meaning bursts upon the mind after an appreciable interval, perhaps of hours, would add little of value.[1]

At least ninety-nine per cent of meanings depend upon the past experience and present attitude or "set" of the hearer (or reader). But it is desirable to clear the way for the facts about them by considering certain cases where single sounds

---

* From *The American Journal of Psychology*, Vol. 59, No. 4, (October 1946), pp. 613–632.

[1] Certain philosophers have found it possible to treat declarative sentences apart from speakers, hearers, and the speaker-hearer relation, as a part of what they call pure semantics, which, however, they would not regard as a part of linguistic science. R. Carnap's *Introduction to Semantics*, 1942, 1–263, is an authoritative presentation of their extremely abstract and subtle doctrines.

or serial combinations of sounds have inherent meanings or influences on meaning apart from what they have been associated with in a hearer's experience.

The first case of this sort is the alleged inherent pleasantness of hearing certain phonemes and inherent unpleasantness of hearing certain others. . . .

I have reported elsewhere experiments in which students recorded their likings and dislikings of the sounds of nonsense words differing in only a single phoneme (e. g. *zanto, santo, shanto, lanto*) heard among a long list. There are differences. For example, *l, d, t,* and *r* do carry more pleasantness than *f, g,* and *sh.*[2] But the differences are small; and they may not be entirely free from influences from past experience.[3]

The second case is Orr's recent hypothesis that the front vowels contrasted with the back vowels carry a meaning of "minuteness, slenderness, and, other kindred notions," and in the case of names of sounds carry a meaning of little volume and high pitch.[4] I have verified Orr's hypothesis as regards modern English words by a comparison of monosyllabic words having *I* (as in bit) or *i* (as in machine) as their vowel sound with monosyllabic words identical with them save in the vowel sound. I have made less extensive comparisons using Greek, Hungarian, and Finnish words. All agree in showing *I* and *i* to occur in a disproportionately large number of words meaning small things or sounds of high pitch and small volume, though the differences are much less than in modern English.[5]

The third case is the well-known one of words, called by lexicographers "onomatopoetic," "imitative," "echoic," or "formed from the sound." We are here concerned with the

[2] E. L. Thorndike, "Euphony and cacophony of English words and sounds," *Quart. J. Speech,* 30, (1944), 201–207.

[3] The evidence to this effect is reported in Thorndike, "The association of certain sounds with pleasant and unpleasant meanings," *Psychol. Rev.,* 52, (1945), 143–149.

[4] J. Orr, "On some sound values in English," *Brit. J. Psychol.,* 35, (1944), 1–8.

[5] E. L. Thorndike, "On Orr's hypothesis concerning the front and back vowels," *ibid.,* 36, (1945), 10–13.

contribution to meaning in the minds of hearers of these words that is made by the mere sound. This may be small even if the imitational origin is fairly certain. For example, how many of these ten words would Arabs, Finns or Chinese define correctly from merely hearing them—*blob, chatter, chuckle, flick, giggle, ping, slap, swish, thump, yap?* Per contra, a slight, even an imagined, similarity of a word's sound to its meaning may make the meaning easier to get and remember. If it seems as fit and proper that maladroit persons should bungle and ebullient persons blurt, as that dogs should bow-wow and cannon boom, then the mere sounds of bungle and blurt may help to carry their meanings as much as do the mere sounds of bow-bow and boom.

The sum total of help from the most helpful sounds like *baa* or *quack* to the least helpful like *jerk* or *loll* is not great. An Arab or Chinese would probably not require one half of one per cent more time to reach an equal degree of knowledge of English meanings if the sounds of all English words were entirely devoid of likeness to their meanings. The help in the case of other European languages is probably even less. It certainly is less in classical Greek and Latin.

A fourth case concerns sounds to which human beings may possibly have instinctive (*i. e.* unlearned) responses, such as they probably do have to threatening and soothing tones of voice. Perhaps guttural sounds so differ from liquids, but any such influence is surely extremely small.

In what follows I shall disregard all four of these causes of meaning. Except for them, words get their meanings for a hearer by their connections with real things, qualities, acts, events, and relations in his past experience. The connections may be direct, as when one learns what *two, three,* and *four* mean, or indirect via the meanings of other words, as when one learns what *million* and *billion* mean. They may be fairly simple as when one learns that *Bobby Dix* means the little playmate who lives next door, or very elaborate, as when one learns what *street,* or *neighbor,* or *citizen* means. They often have to be elaborate in the case of adequate meanings of words that name classes of things, acts, or events like *animal, house, pull, follow, storm, summer,* or qualities like *white, good, dangerous,* or relations like *with, for, because.*

The connections may be within a fairly isolated group as in those that have given meaning to *twenty, andante,* or *chiaroscuro,* or may be spread over much of a person's experience, as in those that have given meaning to *ability, govern, emotion,* or *social.* Connections may operate leading from a part of a word instead of the whole word or from some word like the word, especially when the given word has itself never or rarely been experienced.

The connections operate in a mental "set" and under the influence of more or less of the hearer-reader's entire mental equipment. Consequently, any word is interpreted by the hearer-reader with the aid of the real situation or verbal context in which it occurs, and of his knowledge of the relevant facts of the universe present and past.

The connections that words have in a person's experience produce modifications in his brain, but we cannot say with surety what these are. The neurones or nerve cells which are modified are receivers, selective or resonant in ways that we cannot yet describe. They are conductors, but transmitting we do not know what. They are also probably glands, but secreting we do not know what. The orthodox theory is that the modifications in them by experience consist of changes at the points where one neurone transmits to another, but some psychologists would question this. A man has billions of neurones. Millions of them are modifiable in some way by his experiences with words; and the various combinations of them and their modifications are practically infinite in number, able to parallel all the complexities and subtleties of a man's understanding and use of words. We cannot observe or infer what goes on in the brain in even so simple a case as when hearing "Come here" causes him to approach and hearing "Go away" causes him to depart. What we observe are the probabilities of occurrence of certain acts, thoughts, and feelings as consequences of certain hearings, seeings, and thinkings of words in certain contexts (of realities, or of other words, or of both).

The connections may operate with much, little, or no awareness by the hearer or reader. A good way to demonstrate this is to observe what takes place in one's mind when one thinks of synonyms or antonyms for a set of words. For example let the reader write antonyms for the list below.

(Write after each word the word which means most nearly the opposite of what the given word means.)

(1) sour	(5) day	(9) weak ....
(2) inside	(6) up	(10) sacred ....
(3) horizontal	(7) short	(11) equatorial .....
(4) parallel	(8) good	(12) rectilinear .....

To write the correct opposite of *sour* one must know what sour means but many persons will write 'sweet' with no images of sour tastes, or memories of sour substances, or ideas about sourness. There will surely be cases among (5), (6), (7), (8), and (9) where the reader had little or no awareness of anything telling him what *day, up,* and so on, mean. There may be cases among (3), (4), (11), and (12), where he did have images, memories, ideas or other conscious tendencies that stemmed from past experiences with the words in question, or with parts of them.

Books on language have greately exaggerated the rôle of mental images as components in meaning or causes of meaning. The essential is always what the word has been connected with in sensory experience and thought, not the images which it evokes when heard or seen. These may be entirely absent; they may come after the meaning; they are often irrelevant. In reading or hearing "The United States has assumed important responsibilities for the present and future of Germany, Japan, and other nations," or any other ordinary statement or question, the meaning may be understood fully and exactly enough to guide thought and conduct in less than ten seconds with no awareness of anything in between the words and their meanings, or attached to the words or the meanings in any way.

This is not to say that the meaning of this sentence was got by simple addition of meanings given inevitably by its constituent words. On the contrary, there had to be a rejection of the geographical meaning of *United States* in favor of a human and political meaning, a choice among meanings of *assumed* and *present*, an attachment of adequate weights to *great, for,* the first *and,* and *other,* and a proper relating of the elements of the sentence one to another. That certain brains can do this smoothly and without conscious awareness of anything but the final product does not mean that the physiology involved is simple.

In the workings of the brain in "solving" a sentence to get its meaning the attachment of proper weights to each element has been unnoticed by the science of semantics. It is important; errors and inadequacies in getting the meanings which a sentence was intended to arouse are often caused by overweighting or underweighting.[6]

Some sequences of words are connected as totals directly with meanings, without consideration of the words singly. For example: "Come here." "It is raining." "What time is it?" "―― is sick." "―― went home." "―― if you want to." "On account of." We may call these routine sequences. There are also routine patterns like, "―― plus ―― make ――,"or "if ―― had ――, ―― would have ――," or "When ―― ――, ―― will ――," which direct the flow of meaning more or less inevitably. But many of the sentences that we hear, and still more of those that we read, are in the form of novel combinations of words, routine sequences, and routine patterns. In such sentences the meaning given to each word or "routine sequence" except the first is determined in part by the preceding words, and contributes to the meanings of those that follow, all together giving a meaning to the sentence as a whole. The sentence is often a part of a still larger

---

[6] Facts concerning the meaning of sentences and paragraphs and especially the influence of the weighting of elements are available in the following: E. L. Thorndike, "The psychology of thinking in the case of reading," *Psychol. Rev.,* 24, 1917, 220–234; "Reading as reasoning," *J. Educ. Psychol.,* 8, 1917, 323–332.

unit the preceding parts of which set the mind toward or away from, in favor of or against, certain meanings of one or more words in the sentence.

Except for purely mathematical and scientific terms most words are multimeaning at least to the extent of varying shades or emphases. If a hearer is familiar with a word in any of its meanings, his past experiences and present set of mind will evoke some one of that word's meanings when he hears it; and he will make what sense he can of the sentence therewith. He has no time to consider alternative meanings among those in his repertory, or variations of them to fit the communication to which he is listening, and would do so rarely if he had the time. The reader, who could easily take the time, rarely does so unless the meaning he first thinks of for the word is very unpromising. It is more comfortable for most people to have questionable or foggy meanings for a sentence than to scrutinize what their minds provide word after word.

For these and other reasons there is a strong tendency to jump at the meaning of a word or of a sentence rather than suspend judgment or confess ignorance to oneself. Suppose, for example, that the sentence noted above (The United States has assumed important responsibilities for the present and the future of Germany, Japan, and other nations) were read slowly four or five times to a representative sampling of adults in the United States every one of whom gave it his full attention and was then asked the following questions: (1) What did the sentence that I read to you mean? (2) What did it say were important? (3) What nation did it group especially with Japan? (4) What did the word *assumed* mean in the sentence? Among the dullest tenth of the population there would be many wrong answers, even if they were urged to say "I don't know" to any question that puzzled them.

As a consequence of the facts of the last two paragraphs, experience in listening and reading is a less dependable means of extending or refining knowledge of the meaning of words than experience of words in direct connection with realities.

II. THE MEANINGS OF WORDS TO SPEAKERS AND WRITERS

In the speaker or writer meanings come first and words are found for them. For the most part a word that he uses has for him some one of the meanings which it has had when he has heard or seen it, and the causation is as stated in the previous section. But if the repertory he has from his experience as hearer and reader does not supply what is satisfactory to his purpose, he need not be silent; he can invent new words or use old words in new meanings. Writers who supply information or entertainment do so freely. Indeed they create new words or new meanings in situations where old ones would do as well, except for interest, or some nuance of meaning.

The speaker-hearer or writer-reader relation is an agent-patient or giver-recipient relation. The speaker or writer leads. The words he uses are not drawn out of him by the desires of his audience, but put forth by his impulses. He may, indeed, speak or write to please himself with little or no consideration of what his outpourings will mean to anybody. When he has an option he may choose the word or phrase that pleases him by being easier to say, or by attracting more attention, or by distinguishing him as learned, intelligent, and clever.[7] He originates semantic variations in language. Hearers and readers can only select from these variations, or modify them when they in turn assume the rôle of speaker-writer.

[7] In the choices of words to express the meaning in his mind, a speaker or writer may make slips of the tongue and pen. There may also be, as Freudians believe, slips motivated by unconscious hates, fears, etc., as when a person writes, "My father has always been my *fiend*." There may be blunders, as in Scott's well-known misuse of *warison*. But these are of very little importance for semantic theory.

III. THE ADDITION OF WORDS AND MEANINGS

Every year names are given to hitherto unnamed things, acts, events, qualities, and relations.

There has been an almost universal reluctance to coin new words out of sounds or letters.[8] In spite of the notable value and success of the word *gas* coined by Van Helmont three hundred years ago, scientists produced very few between *gas* and *radar* (made from "radio detection and ranging"), surely less than one half of one per cent of the scientific terms added during the period.[9]

The aversion to coining new words out of sounds or letters and the pressure toward more convenient designations have, especially in recent years, made a reasonable compromise in certain cases by pronouncing abbreviations as in *wī em′ sē ā′, ū″ es′*, or *em dē*. If the meaning of an abbreviation as a whole is known but the meanings of its letters are lost (as for many persons in the case of A. D., B. C., D.D., S.E.C., C.I.O.) the abbreviations are new words to them. If the pronunciation and writing treat the abbreviation as a single word as in *sec* (sek) for Securities and Exchange Commission or *NEP* (nep) for New Economic Policy, the words are comparable to *radar*.

The procedures used in naming something hitherto un-named because unexperienced are the product of (1) a law of least effort by which a person tends to call it by some name that comes easily to his mind and (2) a desire to do what is fit and proper, or at least customary, and has no risk of bring-ing scorn or ridicule upon the namer. The latter cause is predominant when names are made from Latin or Greek words, or by compounding two or more vernacular or foreign words. The former is predominant when a familiar word is

---

[8] The main exceptions are young children in their vocal play, makers of trade names for commodities, and entertainers after the fashion of Lewis Carroll. The coining of these groups is often from longer parts of words than single sounds or letters.

[9] Even Van Helmont's *gas* is said to have been suggested by the Greek χαος.

used with or without some modification, or when the name of some person, place, and so on, that is connected in reality or in thought with the to-be-named is used.

I may note that the general turning of modern science from Latin to Greek involved a sacrifice of ease of understanding to precise designation and the avoidance of confusion; and that for many years both Latin and Greek have been used to name novelties less because they were known to many learned persons than because they were different from the vernacular and so more suitable for precise designation and the avoidance of confusion. When *aqua fortis* displaced *strong water, nitric acid* displaced *aqua fortis,* and HNO_3 displaces *nitric acid,* the main reason was and is to have a more exact description.

Naming novelties by the compounding of vernacular words is perhaps best studied in Greek words. An abbey was named a Κοινοβιον, its head Κοινοβιαρχης. Even when the novelty (to them), had a name in its country of origin, they often made a Greek compound to name it. The new African animal was named a *riverhorse;* the lictors of Rome were named *rodholders.* Making two vernacular words into one semantic unit is really more frequent in English than superficial observation has led many to think.[10]

Cases where a familiar word is used to name something hitherto unnamed account for a large percentage of the added meanings of the same words that all living languages display. They range from apt choices to very inept ones. It is profitable to examine some samples.

Chemists aptly chose *nascent* to differentiate a substance at the moment of formation, and especially a gas when it has free atoms instead of the less active gas molecules. The added burden of meaning put on *nascent* is not great. *Cross-over* for a certain act or event in the genes of chromosomes is a specially apt choice, being very descriptive and subject to

---

[10] Semantically it makes no difference whether such a compound is printed as one word without a hyphen, or with a hyphen, or as two words.

little confusion with other uses. (No others are reported in the O.E.D. though there may be such in connection with dancing, embroidery, or other arts.)

The fairly common choices of *cat, dog,* and other names of familiar animals to mean various novelties that came into use in various occupations and activities are much more casual and inept. "A machine consisting of a heavy hammer or ram working vertically in a groove and used in pile-driving, etc." was called a *monkey.* "A grappling-iron for raising the monkey of a pile-driver" was called a *dog.* These two names might better have been shifted. The choice of *monkey* rather than *horse* or *ox* shows how careless the naming probably was.

Naming animals, plants, minerals, and so on after their discoverers or creators, naming machines, processes, products, and so on after their inventors, and naming minerals, fabrics, and so on after the places where they are found or made or were found and made at some early date are widespread customs. They turn what were previously proper names into common nouns, adjectives, and verbs, and thus do the equivalent of adding many new words. They never give more than slight help toward learning or remembering what they mean, and usually none at all. The choice of such names saves the time and trouble of thinking of a better name, and is treated as fit and proper by past and present customs.

It is useful to distinguish additions more or less forced upon language by new facts of science, invention, government, etc., from additions more subject to the impulses of speakers, as Darmesteter did long ago. However, the psychology is closely the same for the naming of something hitherto unnamed or named only by a long description as for the naming of genuine novelties. In both cases the speaker or writer tends to do what is pleasing and comfortable to him by present ease, or by future satisfaction, or by both. In both there is a range from aptness to ineptness. Some uses of flat may serve as an illustration.

Writers about painting seeking a name for the quality of

showing little or no relief or projection made a fairly apt choice of *flat* [1755]. The musicians' choices of *sharp* and *flat* instead of *high* and *low* show much the same readiness for a person to use an inept word that happens to come to mind, and for others to follow his lead, that the choices by workingmen of *dog, cat,* and so on as names for new tools show.

The causes that determine what word or words a fact hitherto unnamed or named only by a rather long description will make a person think of when he is impelled to name the fact in question are hidden in the person's brain beyond any present means of observation by science. But it is known that they correspond to (1) connections made in the person's experience with that fact as a whole plus (2) connections made with some part or feature of the fact.[11]

The first three examples below show potency of approximately the whole fact; the last three show potency of parts or features of it.

Fact to be expressed	Word used to express it
(1) hair as on the head	head
(2) head-dress	head
(3) antlers	head
(4) rounded leafy top of a tree	head
(5) foam or froth on a glass of beer	head
(6) thick end of a wedge	head

The difference resembles in some ways that between association by contiguity and association by similarity, but is truer and more useful. In fact, semantics may well avoid the terms association by contiguity and association by similarity. Contiguity when first used meant contiguity in space or time, which is irrelevant, the effective contiguity being in experience or thought. Similarity as such is irrelevant; a fact or idea does not tend to recall others in proportion to their similarity to it. If it did a person would tend strongly to keep on thinking the same idea which is perfectly similar to itself; the

[11] There often are contributing causes, corresponding not to associations with the fact to be expressed, but to the wider "set" of mind or brain at the time of expression, as in humorous and ironical usages.

thought of black would often arouse the thought of a very dark gray; good→bad, long→short, yes→no, and the like would almost never appear in tests of free association.

The word which the fact to be expressed makes the speaker-writer think of will often come to his mind devoid of some of the details which would give full and exact knowledge of its meaning, such as its derivation, its applicability to persons or things, whether it is singular or plural, whether it is transitive or intransitive, whether (especially in the case of English words) it is a substantive, an adjective, or a verb. Unless the speaker-writer is very well informed about such details, he may use the word without considering them. He may thus make adjectives out of substantives, transitives out of intransitives, passives out of actives, qualities of mind out of qualities of matter, and other transferences of meaning. Even if he is well-informed about such details he may disregard them in order to produce what seems to him a good effect, "Blow, bugle, blow" satisfied Tennyson, and probably ninety-nine out of a hundred of his readers.

Speakers and writers may use a word with a new meaning even though the thing, quality, act, event, or relation that they use it for has already been otherwise named. A speaker (writer) may use *laugh* to mean a person who is much laughed at because he does not know the word *laughingstock*. He may know *laughingstock* but not think of it at the time. He may think of laughingstock, but prefer *laugh* because of its brevity, novelty, or special fitness to his context. The third case is by far the commonest. His new use of *laugh* becomes a part of the experience of his hearers (or readers), and may cause some of them to use it also. Other speakers or writers may be moved to use it independently of him, and their followers may increase its vogue.

Cases like *laugh* for laughingstock, *head* for bundle, rise, excel, and butt, *foot* for sum, footing, pay, refrain (of a song), *mouth* for kiss and grimace, and *stagger* for unsettle, where the added meaning is already expressible with equal brevity and with little ambiguity are likely to be precarious additions of meanings unless they add interest.[12]

Speakers and writers prefer attention to neglect, as a means to communication, and also as a tribute to their personal worth and power. Their main means of getting attention is the content of their messages—the facts if the message concerns reality, the events, plot, situations, and characters if the message is fiction. Sometimes they make no use at all of the choice of specially interesting words. The gossip bearing the news that Mary Jones has run away from home does not need to embellish it by inventing a new variant of "flown the coop" or "taken a powder." The authors of Superman do not rely on inventions of metaphors to enliven their text and pictures. But some speakers and writers, especially literary men, make much use of the choice and invention of words and phrases to get and hold interest. They will therefore tend to favor words that are interesting by novelty, vividness, emotional attachments, and the like. Their minds may even be set *against* the first word that comes to mind to express a fact as likely to be commonplace, and be set rather to find something extraordinary, in the hope that it will add interest to their speech or writing.

They are on the lookout for interesting ways of stating ordinary facts, such as that a thing is big, little, good, bad, desirable, undesirable. So a big lie becomes egregious, gigantic, monumental, astronomical, Gargantuan, a whale-of-a-lie, a Munchausen. They are on the lookout for interesting ways of portraying certain sorts of persons. So a man according to the nature they attribute to him is an ape, a dog, a fox, a snake, a skunk, a lounge-lizard, an angel, a prince, a dynamo, a magnet, a live wire.

The addition of new meanings to words has been studied by scholars from the time of the Greek grammarians and

---

[12] Of those just named *foot = sum, refrain, footing,* and *mouth = kiss,* though added after 1600, are already obsolete and *laugh = laughingstock* is very rare.

rhetoricians. Their classification into synechdoche, metonymy, and metaphor is still alive, though it was replaced in the O.E.D. by the broader one of "transferred meanings and figurative meanings." The detailed classification into genus for species, species for genus, part for whole, whole for part, cause for effect, effect for cause, container for contents, contents for container, symbol for thing, thing for symbol, and so on, has been enriched by cases of agent for patient, patient for agent, active for passive, passive for active, intransitive for transitive, transitive for intransitive, done by persons for done by things and vice versa, and so on.

A study of each of these classes would not, we may be confident, refute anything in the account of the causation of added meanings given in this article. It would probably extend and improve the statement (see page 306) concerning the freedom from grammatical and other restrictions of a word evoked in a speaker's mind by a fact to be expressed. I conjecture that the insensitivity of ordinary people to these restrictions is rooted in the grammarless language of infants. I conjecture that the disregard of them by poets is aided by a general freedom of a poet's fine frenzy from the inhibitions imposed by convention. It is a fact that such freedom given to hypnotized subjects can turn halting producers of respectable "compositions," into daring adventurers in description or narrative.

In two respects the customary treatment of transferred and figurative meanings has been unfortunate. It encourages the notion that the speaker-writer thinks, "How else might one use this word? What else could it mean?," and as a consequence makes some innovation. On the contrary the "What else" is usually the prime mover. The customary treatment also makes the addition of meanings a more logical matter than it usually is. For example, the O.E.D. said (1883, General explanation, p. xxi) "If the historical record were complete, that is, if we possessed written examples of all the uses of each word from the beginning, the simple exhibition of these would display a rational or logical development." If *rational* and *logical* have any of their commoner meanings this simply is not true. "Natural and comprehensible" would have been safer than "rational or logical." If it means only that such a complete history would display a natural and fairly continuous development, with nothing incomprehensible by a competent student of language, it still is not entirely true. The causation of some semantic changes lies in events in certain persons' brains hidden from observation by linguistic science and only inferred dubiously by psychology.

IV. THE SELECTION OF WORDS AND MEANINGS

We lack records of the words originated by speakers or writers but not selected for extensive use and not recognized as parts of the language. Still rarer are records of old words used in new meanings, but by few or unimportant speakers or writers and not selected for extensive use. A certain sort of machine or weapon may well have been called by one or another workman or soldier a dog, a mule, a kicker, a hooker, a jimmy, a tommy, or any one of a hundred names none of which became a recognized name in the trade, much less in dictionaries.

On the other hand a favorable chain of circumstances may cause the name evoked in one workman's brain to be adopted throughout one neighborhood, and then in wider and wider circles. Other things being equal, most people will follow the usage of any speaker rather than think up an alternative. As noted earlier, very inept names may thus be selected for wide use.

The fundamental axiom of the psychology of language that if a thing, quality, act, event, or relation is worth thinking about, any name for it is better than none, applies to the selection as well as the origination of semantic variations. In general, however, semantic selection does cause a survival of the fit among the words and phrases used by speakers and writers to express and evoke a certain meaning. Other things being equal, the shorter the word is, the better. Other things being equal, the more surely it evokes the meaning, the better; the more exactly it evokes the meaning the better; the less chance there is of confusion with other words, the better.

If brevity is attained with no loss in comprehensibility, it is favored by both the speaker-writer and the hearer-reader. Even at some cost to the latter, the former will favor abbreviations that are easier to think of, say, or write as names for the meanings in his mind.

The influence of abbreviations ranges from the omission of sounds, as in *can't,* to the omission of words as in *Methodist* (for member of the Methodist Episcopal Church). It aids and abets in adding new meanings for words as in *water the horse* for give the horse water to drink, or as when *run* means compete in a race, compete as a candidate for office, move rapidly, make a fairly rapid journey, spread rapidly, move easily, peel off easily from a tree, continue operating, keep occurring, spread in a fabric if it gets wet, discharge mucus, and so on.

Certainty and exactitude in evoking the desired meaning are prime desiderata for words and phrases in mathematics, science, and law. In general intercourse they are often sacrificed; though not to the extent of making entire sentences ambiguous. If a usage is ambiguous in spite of the verbal context and real situation in which it operates, that usage will not fully satisfy hearers and readers, and is likely to be supplanted by another that does.[13]

V. COMMUNITY AND DIVERSITY IN SEMANTIC VARIATION AND SELECTION

Semantics would be enriched if some competent scholar would make a list of features common to all the languages for which adequate data have been published, extending even

[13] There may, however, be cases in language used for entertainment where the charm of a sentence depends on a certain vague and changeable quality in the meaning of some word, being reduced if the word in question is pinned down to any one definite meaning.

to such details as whether the language has words for head, mouth, eye, hand, foot, bite, swallow, shed tears, and run, and what secondary meanings these words have. The many notable diversities suggest that such a list would be very short. Sapir, indeed, seems to have been a bit surprised to find that all languages have stable units fitly called words. A similar expectation by ethnologists concerning the activities common to all "cultures" has, however, been proved erroneous by Murdock. He finds the following in every culture known to history or ethnography:

"Age-grading, athletic sports, bodily adornment, calendar, cleanliness training, community organization, cooking coöperative labor, cosmology, courtship, dancing, decorative art, divination, division of labor, dream interpretation, education, eschatology, ethics, ethnobotany, etiquette, faith healing, family feasting, fire making, folklore, food taboos, funeral rites, games, gestures, gift giving, government, greetings, hair styles, hospitality, housing, hygiene, incest taboos, inheritance rules, joking, kin groups, kinship nomenclature, language, law, luck superstitions," and twenty-nine more.[14]

The simple experiment of having persons of widely different languages and "cultures" name certain facts will provide useful information concerning community and diversity in semantic variation and selection. The facts to be named might include things, qualities, and events such as "something very highly valued"; "a man who is bossed by his children"; "a complaint of the eyes such that they are always twitching"; "very desirous of having the last word in a dispute or argument"; "a message from the spirit of a dead man"; plane figures such as semicircle, star, crescent and spiral; and novel tones, squeaks, bangs, and rumbles.

Experiment—I report here the results of such an experiment, but in a very restricted form. Four hundred fifty-five students of psychology in Dartmouth College and Queens College wrote words as requested on sheets like that reproduced below.[15]

---

[14] *The Science of Man in the World Crisis,* by various authors, (1945), 124.

[15] I am greatly indebted to the members of the Departments of Psychology at Dartmouth and Queens, and especially to Dr. T. F. Karwowski and Dr. Anne Anastasi, for their generous and efficient coöperation.

Write after each of the 22 facts listed below that one of these 12 words (dog, donkey, fox, horse, monkey, snake, eye, foot, hand, head, leg, mouth) which is the best name for the fact.

(1) act or deed ....
(2) agent or servant ....
(3) arrow ....
(4) beaker ....
(5) bottom of a ship ....
(6) close proximity ....
(7) a complaint of the eyes such that they are always twitching ....
(8) a creeping plant ....
(9) edge or point of a weapon ..
(10) flying squirrel ....
(11) lewd woman ....
(12) long walls parallel to another *
  ....
(13) member of a sentence ....
(14) overreach ....
(15) part of a surgical bandage .....
(16) phantom ....
(17) rudder ....
(18) spasmodic distortion of the mouth ....
(19) the upper millstone ....
(20) windlass ....
(21) a wood louse ....
(22) the worst throw at dice ......

* *walls* instead of *wall* was left on the test sheets by inadvertence.

The results are given in detail in Table I, which lists also words used for the 22 meanings in ancient Greek. As shown there 45 per cent of the Americans agree with the Greeks in choosing *hand* as a name for "act or deed"; 66 per cent in choosing *foot* as a name for "bottom of a ship"; 89.5 per cent in choosing *snake* for "a creeping plant"; 37 per cent in choosing *leg* for "long wall(s) parallel to another"; 26.5 per cent in choosing *foot* for "rudder." The other seventeen names average 8.31 per cent, almost exactly what mere chance would give.[16]

There is a wide variation in the choices of names for a fact. The number of names chosen is 9 in one case, 10 in two, 11 in 7, and all 12 in 13 cases. Each of the words *dog, snake, eye,* and *hand,* was accepted as a name for all of the twenty-two facts by at least 2 of the 455 Ss. *Horse* and *leg* were so accepted for twenty-one of the twenty-two facts. *Donkey, fox, monkey, head,* and *mouth* were so accepted for twenty of the twenty-two.[17]

[16] I assume that if 455 Athenian epheboi had taken this test 2400 years ago, a substantial majority would have agreed with Liddell and Scott's dictionary!

[17] If we use 10 of the 455 Ss as the criterion, it is met by *dog* for 12 of the 22 facts, by *donkey* for 10 of them, by *fox* for 12 of them, and by *horse, monkey, snake, eye, foot, hand, head, leg,* and *mouth* respectively for 13, 11, 16, 17, 10, 16, 15, 13, and 15 of them.

Even if a generous allowance is made for students who became bored with the task and wrote certain words at random, a wide variation would remain. To include three-quarters or more of the choices, there are needed *hand* and *head* for "act or deed"; *donkey, horse,* and *hand* for "agent or servant"; *snake, hand* and *head* for "arrow"; *hand* and *mouth* for "beaker"; *snake, foot,* and *leg* for "bottom of a ship"; *eye, hand, mouth, dog,* and *monkey* for "close proximity"; *eye, head, monkey,* and *snake* for "complaint of the eyes"; *head, hand, eye,* and *fox* for "edge or point of a weapon"; *monkey* and *fox* for "flying squirrel"; *dog, fox, snake, leg,* and *mouth* for "lewd woman"; *leg, horse, snake, eye,* and *foot* (or *hand*) for "long wall, parallel"; *head, eye, foot, leg,* and *mouth* for "member of a sentence"; *hand, monkey,* and *eye* for "overreach"; *head, hand, foot,* and *leg* for "part of a surgical bandage"; *fox, snake, eye,* and *head* for "phantom"; *foot, hand, head,* and *leg* for "rudder"; *mouth, monkey, donkey,* and *horse* for "spasmodic distortion of the mouth"; *head, donkey, horse, mouth,* and *foot* for "the upper millstone"; *hand, donkey, horse, leg, snake,* and *eye* for "windlass"; *snake, fox, dog, monkey,* and *mouth* for "a woodlouse"; and *snake, eye,* and *hand* for "the worst throw at dice."

The choices are caused (1) partly by positive associations and judgments of fitness, as when "beaker" suggests drinking, or when "worst throw at dice" suggests (to those familiar with the current vocabulary of dicing) snake's eyes; and (2) partly by a negative choice of the lesser evil when none of the twelve words strikes any very responsive chord in connection with the specified fact, as when "a wood louse" is called a snake rather than a donkey or horse, or is called a mouth rather than a hand, foot, or leg.

(3) A third cause which may adulterate the significance of the results for semantics is the idea that all of the twelve test-words were intended to be used. This is probably not an important cause. Only 32 per cent of the Americans used all of the twelve words; 27 per cent used eleven; 26.5 per cent used ten; and 14.5 per cent used nine or fewer.

TABLE I

Percentages of college stuents choosing each word

							Comparison words								
Facts	Ancient Greek word	dog	don-key	fox	horse	mon-key	snake	eye	foot	hand	head	leg	mouth	Omitted	% agreeing with the Greeks	Identification
(1) act or deed	hand	6.4	.7	2.4	1.1	3.7	.9	.7	.7	44.9	33.5	1.3	3.5	.2	44.9	1
(2) agent or servant	dog	9.7	22.0	.4	28.4	.9	0.0	.9	4.8	24.0	2.4	3.1	3.5	0.0	9.7	2
(3) arrow	snake	1.1	0.0	6.4	2.0	0.0	14.3	37.2	2.0	19.1	14.7	2.4	.4	.2	14.3	3
(4) beaker	donkey	2.0	1.1	1.3	.4	0.0	.4	4.6	.9	13.9	2.0	.7	72.2	.4	1.1	4
(5) bottom of a ship	foot	1.1	2.4	0.0	4.0	1.3	8.1	1.5	65.8	1.5	1.5	8.4	3.5	.7	65.8	5
(6) close proximity	foot	7.9	.7	1.8	1.1	7.7	5.7	33.7	3.7	14.7	7.3	3.7	11.9	0.0	3.7	6
(7) a complaint of the eyes such that they are always twitching	horse	3.1	2.9	6.2	6.4	19.8	10.1	32.3	0.0	1.3	13.0	.7	4.0	.2	6.4	7
(8) a creeping plant	snake	.4	0.0	2.2	0.0	.7	89.5	1.1	2.0	2.4	.2	1.3	0.0	0.0	89.5	8
(9) edge or point of a weapon	mouth	1.8	1.3	13.6	1.1	.4	4.8	13.2	4.2	19.6	34.3	.7	4.0	.9	4.0	9
(10) flying squirrel	fox	1.8	.7	24.4	3.1	56.8	.7	2.4	1.3	2.2	1.3	4.4	.4	.4	24.4	10
(11) lewd woman	horse	21.1	5.9	14.1	2.4	2.9	21.1	2.9	0.0	.7	1.5	17.4	9.7	.2	2.4	11
(12) long walls parallel to another	leg	.7	2.4	1.1	11.7	.7	7.9	16.1	6.4	6.4	3.7	37.2	5.3	.4	37.2	12
(13) member of a sentence	leg	4.2	2.2	2.2	1.5	.4	.4	13.2	15.2	6.6	27.1	8.8	16.7	1.3	8.8	13
(14) overreach	fox	.7	2.0	2.2	3.7	12.8	2.4	5.9	1.8	59.4	4.2	3.3	1.1	.4	2.2	14
(15) part of a surgical bandage	leg	2.6	1.3	.4	.9	.9	5.1	7.5	17.0	22.7	24.4	11.0	5.3	.9	11.0	15
(16) phantom	eye	2.0	.9	39.6	11.4	3.7	12.3	14.7	.2	1.8	11.9	.4	.9	0.0	14.7	16
(17) rudder	foot	1.8	1.8	.4	3.5	1.1	2.6	4.0	26.6	27.9	14.3	15.8	0.0	0.0	26.6	17
(18) spasmodic distortion of the mouth	dog	7.9	12.5	2.6	8.8	20.0	10.6	1.8	.4	.4	5.5	.7	28.2	.4	7.9	18
(19) the upper millstone	donkey	2.6	11.2	1.8	8.6	2.0	.9	4.4	5.9	5.5	48.2	1.5	6.2	1.1	11.2	19
(20) windlass	donkey	3.1	14.1	2.0	12.1	4.0	5.7	5.5	1.8	33.4	4.2	7.7	4.2	2.2	14.1	20
(21) a wood louse	donkey	13.4	1.8	21.1	3.5	10.8	24.7	4.6	2.2	2.0	3.5	2.9	8.1	1.3	1.8	21
(22) the worst throw at dice	dog	3.5	8.4	.2	1.5	2.2	57.9	13.4	2.0	9.5	.2	0.0	.9	.2	3.5	22

314

Returning to the main purpose of the experiment we may conclude that over three fourths of the causation of the twenty-two Greek usages lies within the history of Greek life and language; or at least outside of the common mentality of European man, not to say of homo sapiens. We may also conclude, from the wide variation found even under the close restrictions of this experiment, that if a person seeks to name a fact by adding a new meaning to some old word many words may be suggested by the fact that would be acceptable to him.

If these students had been asked to write words to mean "act or deed," "agent or servant," and so on, very few of them would have written any one of the twelve test-words for any one of the twenty-two facts. Of 55 students asked to do so for "spasmodic distortion of the mouth" none wrote any one of the twelve.

VI. LOST MEANINGS

Obviously if people cease to think of the fact expressed by a certain meaning of a word, that meaning will die out from the language. Many meanings relating to astrology, feudal customs, hawking and the like have become obsolete for this reason. If a new way of expressing a fact becomes popular, it may come to all minds ahead of the old way and inhibit its use so often that the old way is forgotten by many and rejected as out of date by those who remember it. A word's associations with persons may discourage its use. If indecent or impious or low-class persons come to favor a usage it will thereby be disfavored by those who wish to be respectable. If pompous and pedantic persons come to favor a usage it will be disfavored by those who wish to appear simple and unassuming.

We may supplement these obvious facts by comparing the obsolete meaning of a word with its primary meaning in modern English, and comparing also its added live meanings with its primary meaning.[18] The obsolete meanings are more often literal, pedantic, and dull than the "live" meanings are. The added live meanings are more often lively and interesting. The former are more often general; the latter more often special. The former more often have to compete with some new word or added meaning that expresses the fact in question. The former probably more often confuse or blur the total impression made by the word than do the latter, though the difference here is surprisingly small.

There are also customs of discarding meanings that have certain patterns, each covering a considerable number of words. For example, verbs made by en- plus an adjective tend to discard meanings other than the simple "make ——." *Enable, endear, enlarge* and *ensure* have lost fifteen such meanings, and kept only three such, all of *enlarge.*

Many dull, pedantic, general, ineffective and confusing meanings, however, are not lost, and some meanings satisfactory in all these respects *are* lost. Indeed if we exclude losses because the facts to be expressed have vanished from our civilization, a majority of losses of meanings cannot be explained by any set of rules. One does not go far in examining the live and lost meanings of words to find sets like those of *balk* and *bastard* that are insoluble without allowing a large margin to human caprice. Many meanings have merely gone out of fashion like women's *coifs, hoopskirts,* and *bustles;* men's *trunk-hose, stocks,* and *beards;* houses' *turrets* and *baywindows.*

Many meanings now in full standing, and rated neither "rare" nor "archaic," and relating to facts which will be as important a hundred years hence as now, will doubtless become obsolete in the next hundred years, but no prudent philologist or psychologist would expect much success in predicting which meanings they will be.

---

[18] The statement in this and succeeding paragraphs are based on such comparisons which I have made but will not report here.

CHAPTER XX

The Psychology of Labor *

MOST of us have been taught to think of labor as a necessary evil which men are bribed to carry on with wages or profits, much as we have been taught to think of east as where the sun rises and west as where it sets, or of two and two as making four. Man is cursed with labor since Adam; the less he has of it the better. Freedom from productive occupations is the Eden we all crave. Shorter hours and higher wages are the two rails on which the world's workers move toward welfare. We may perhaps concede that labor has a value for health and morality, and that we shall enjoy heaven better for having toiled on earth. But intrinsically, from the simple selfish point of view of the laborer, labor is, we have been taught, a cloud whose only silver lining is wages. To keep the world going so many tons of coal must be mined, so many bushels of wheat raised, so many yards of cloth woven; and the world labors to produce these rather than go without them. Labor is, we have been taught, a suffering endured only because it prevents the greater suffering of lacking what the wages or profits would have bought. Labor laws, labor disputes (at least on the surface), and welfare schemes for laborers reflect and in the main confirm this view.

It is, however, an unsound and dangerously incomplete view of the psychology of labor. A sound and adequate view of human nature in its relation to labor must take into account all the important facts about productive labor, not merely the fact that much of it to many persons is objectionable. It must

* This chapter is reprinted, with a few minor alterations, from *Harper's Magazine*, (May, 1922), Vol. 144, pp. 799–806.
317

consider all the conditions and results of labor as well as the contents of the pay envelope.

First of all, activity of body or mind is not intrinsically objectionable to human beings. On the contrary, if the activity is within the individual's capacity in quality, quantity, and duration, so as to be done without strain, it is intrinsically desirable. We avoid labor nearly or quite as often because we wish to do something else as because we wish to do nothing. Boys and men leave their farm chores to do more violent activity in hunting. The lawyer stops thinking of his brief in order to think harder in a chess game. The housewife abandons the family mending to do fancy embroidery.

Nor is productive labor intrinsically more objectionable than the same activity undertaken for sport. Human nature has no predilection for the useless as such. On the contrary, the child would prefer to have his mud-pies edible, the hunter would prefer to secure a useful trophy, the lawyer would enjoy his game of chess no less if by some magic it made two blades of grass grow where one grew before. Indeed it adds somewhat to his enjoyment if he thinks of it as valuable mental training or a healthful mental relief.

In fact there is hardly a gainful occupation that is not used as a cherished pastime by some men or women. Rowing a boat, driving a team, maintaining a garden, driving, overhauling and repairing an automobile, managing a farm, and breeding livestock, are cases easily observable. Sawing logs has been the sport of famous and infamous men. Digging ditches and bookkeeping are the recreations of some known to the writer if not to fame.

Many men and women would, if they sought happiness with wisdom, continue their productive labor even if they were given ample wealth. This is admittedly true of the eager inventor, the zealous musician, the captain of industry, the man of science and many others whose productive labor is what they would wish to do in any case. We admit it because the facts show that they work regardless of wage or after the need of profit ceases. It is to some extent true of almost all men. Probably three out of four chauffeurs would really much rather drive a car than live as, say, the King of England does. The locomotive engineer may bewail his hardships and ostensibly yearn to sit on his porch smoking a pipe, but his real longing may be for the work he is paid to do.

The economist will here object that our illustrations are from highly skilled labor and do not justify the generalizations. Most labor, he may assert, is out-and-out objectionable to the laborer. Farm work, mining, factory work, routine clerical work, selling and domestic service are fair specimens of the great bulk of labor; and these, he will claim, are essentially unpleasant, not to say intolerable. Who would for month after month milk cows, or dig holes, or hammer a drill, or operate a punch press, or wheel boxes, or copy names, or wash dishes or scrub floors, except for a money reward?

Doubtless the economist would not. Doubtless it would be a great sacrifice to him to milk cows and clean stalls for a year. If by a miracle he were to be doing it, and if I insisted that he was being paid for what he would fairly well like to do in any case, he would rightly scorn my sense of fact and logic. But he is not the one who is doing it. If the one who is doing it is a person strong in body, dull in mind, who hates being forced to think, decide, or step outside his beaten track of routine, who enjoys the company of animals, and feels a certain sense of mastery and pride in being a good milker, the economist may well be wrong. To such a one milking cows and cleaning stalls may be no more objectionable than talking and writing is to the college professor. The work of chambermaid in an institution would doubtless be one hundred per cent objectionable to the economist, but it is very nearly one hundred per cent satisfactory to certain feeble-minded girls and women, though they get no wages of any sort for it. They would mourn having their bed-making taken away from them as a prima donna mourns her retirement from the stage or a president of this country his failure of nomination for a second term!

A woman of limited intelligence may feel the same satisfaction in empting a slop jar without spilling the slops on the floor that the economist would feel in making or refuting arguments in favor of the gold standard.

If the labor of the man sailing an airship is not all bad—a necessary evil to him, endured for wages, neither is the labor of the chauffeur driving his chosen car; nor that of the taxicab driver; nor need be that of the motorman; nor that of the man on the truck; nor that of the man on the tip cart; nor even that of the day-laborer pushing his wheelbarrow load of bricks! There is no necessary gap. Doubtless more men would drive a motorcar for enjoyment than a wheelbarrow, but some men get genuine satisfaction from pushing the wheelbarrow. Labor is not all bad, a nasty pill sugar-coated by wages.

Wages and profits are rarely the only reward for labor. Many workers work to some extent for love of the work. Still more are paid in part by the approval their skill and achievements receive. Some are paid in part by the sociability of the workers or the friendliness of the boss. In fact almost every fundamental human appetite may be gratified to some extent by productive labor.

We should not think of the laborer as leaving most of his human nature behind him when he goes to work, and becoming then a single-hearted devotee of money. We should consider all the instincts and habits, some of them deep hidden, that move him as truly when he works as when he rests with his family or plays with his friends or fights or votes or marries.

There are five fundamental trends in human nature which specially deserve our consideration. The first is the satisfyingness of activity physical or mental at which one can succeed. Man tends to do something when he is wakeful as truly as to cease action when sleepy,—to be busy after rest as truly as to rest when fatigued. Continued idleness is seductive when accompanied by sociability, or stimulation by novel sights and sounds, or a sense of superiority to those who cannot afford to be idle, or opportunity to display one's power or wealth, but mere idleness *per se*, as in a sanitarium or a jail, is attractive only to exhausted bodies or minds. The labor problem is not so much to bribe men from idleness to activity, as to induce them to be active in ways that are advantageous to the community.

The second is the satisfyingness of mastery. To have other human beings step out of the way, bend the knee, lower the glance and obey the command, is worth more than fine gold to most men and to many women. It would be an interesting study to ascertain whether a plumber has a helper, a farmer a hired man, a waiter a bus-boy, and so on, simply because these helpers really increase efficiency, or partly because the plumber, the farmer, the waiter thus has someone on whom to gratify his craving for mastery.

The third is the satisfyingness of submission—*to the right kind of man.* Contradictory as it may seem, it is as natural for human beings to submit to the person whose size, looks, voice, prowess, and status make him an acceptable master, as to exercise mastery themselves where they can. The same man who enjoys mastery almost to the point of tyranny over his employees may enjoy submission almost to the point of servility, to some business giant, or to some hero of baseball, or even to his wife. The strength of this tendency to submissive loyalty varies, being much greater in some men than in others, and greater in general in women than in men. The same man who excites ready loyal submission in some may thus excite rebellion and attempted contra-mastery in others; and some men may never as workers find a foreman whose power over them is not a constant irritation.

Probably the present work of the world cannot under present conditions be done without a balance of dissatisfaction because there is too much need for submission and too little chance for mastery for the great majority. Roughly speaking, labor has to be too submissive to suit human nature. But not all of the submissiveness is annoying; and the two trends, though often opposed, need not always be. If Jones appeals to Smith as a thing to be mastered, and Smith appeals to Jones in the same way, both cannot be satisfied. They are not necessarily and inevitably opposed, however. If Smith appeals to Jones as a great man whose smile produces thrills of delight, whose nod is a benediction, whose commands are unquestionable, both may be happy.

Next to be considered is the satisfyingness of company and cheerfulness. Man is by nature gregarious and fond of human happiness about him. He likes to have human beings around him, and to have them smiling and laughing, rather than peevish and sad. The department store and factory are actual reliefs to many girls whose home life is essentially a complaining mother and crying children. Many a young man gets enjoyment from the bustle of the office very similar to that for which he pays at the amusement park or on the excursion steamer.

Last and most important is the satisfyingness of the feeling that one is somebody of consequence, who is or should be treated respectfully by his community, which we may call the love of approval.

Besides these outer signs of approbation, man reacts to his own inner image of himself. If men neglect or scorn him, he may derive some satisfaction from concluding that they do not appreciate him properly. Religion often is a comfort by its assurance that in the sight of God and in a future life he will have a station above those rich and successful in this.

Now this hunger for consideration, approval and eminence is one of the great moving forces in human life. Under present conditions in America it deserves to be ranked along with the primary motives of physical hunger, sex, the craving for physical safety, and the intolerance of bodily pain.

The New England housewife did not sand her floors, and polish her kettles, and relentlessly pursue dust beneath beds and in far corners for wages. Her husband would in most cases have paid her more to be less tidy! She cleaned her house so that it might force glances of admiration, ready or unwilling, from her friends and foes. Women devote an enormous amount of labor to dress and other personal adornment; and a large percentage of this is not a matter of sex attraction but simply to win a general diffuse approval, chiefly from other women. We have the testimony of Carlton Parker that a miner will, not exceptionally but almost as a rule, sacrifice wages for the sake of setting up his blasts in such a way that other miners passing by will admire his skill in using so few drill-holes, or the like.

It may be accepted as axiomatic that labor which adds to the laborer's sense of worth and consideration by those whose opinion he lives for has a plus over its money wages, and that labor which detracts therefrom has a lack which wages or some other considerations must supply.

In general the reward for labor is not only the power to buy food, shelter, clothes and whatever else money will buy which comes as a money wage, but the degree of gratification given to each and every human craving by the job itself. The evil of work to the worker is not only that he has to work so long for so little, but that he may have to strain his powers at work for which he is not fit, submit to rule that is humiliating, lose caste in his world, and in general be thwarted in the fundamental impulses of his nature.

He comes to a job not simply as an operator of the X.Y.Z. machine, but as a man. The job brings to him each week not only a pay envelope, but forty or more hours of life, whose desirability may vary almost from heaven to hell. We must consider both him and the job in an adequate way.

More than this, we must, if we wish to understand a labor problem, consider the total situation of which the job is a part. Human nature tends to attribute to any obvious external fact, such as a locality, or a person, or a job, whatever feelings have been associated with it, regardless of whether it is really their cause. Thus a workman, really upset by the illness and peevishness of his wife, may think that his work is too hard, his machine not properly adjusted, or his foreman unfair. It makes a difference to the laborer, just as it does to his boss, whether his home is comfortable to him, whether he can digest his food easily, whether the community in general is peevish and miserable.

A factory does not and cannot live to itself alone. Its jobs acquire merit or demerit from total community conditions. Sagacious employers realize this. It is a main reason why they so abominate the presence of the mere agitator, professional or amateur. The mere agitator, they claim, does nothing of any value to the workers, and does much harm to both the employers and the employees by replacing a general peacefulness and content and good feeling, by irritability and suspicion.

The behavior of the owner's family or the manager's family, though it has no causal relation to any condition of the job itself, may soothe or irritate the workers. Transportation conditions very often come to be felt as part of the job. If a worker has to go a long distance and stand up and travel in unpleasant company, he tends consciously or unconsciously to figure this in on the job. Even though he may be led to blame it exclusively on the greed of the traction companies, the effects of it carry on to his work.

Finally there is to some extent a different labor problem for each laborer. What is objectionable and what is attractive in each job, and in the general community conditions associated with that job, will vary enormously with individuals. Partly by inborn nature and partly by the circumstances of training, individuals vary in physical strength, in acuity of vision, in the endurance of the eye muscles, in love of order and system, in neatness, in memory, in whatever trait may be in question. The postman's walk and burden would be physically a pastime to one and a daily fatigue to another. The work of a clerk in a bank or an insurance company is as easy as knitting to certain young women of sturdy visual apparatus and a passion for arranging items, but it would be a form of torture to others. To hear a signal over the 'phone and report a letter and six figures like N 314297 would, after training at it, be objectionable to some men only by its monotonous ease, but it would require an almost intolerable strain of attention from others.

Dirt, monotony, noise and solitude vary in their annoyance to individuals from zero or near zero to an almost insupportable agony. The conflict of personalities in trading varies from an agony to the joy of living. Politeness, attentive consideration, and winning persuasiveness as required of the salesman would be as ashes in the mouth to most miners, engineers and cowboys.

There is also large variation in the public opinion whose approval is so large a factor in man's tolerance of his work. The opinion of Cedar Street that John Smith the barber has done very well counts more to John Smith than the opinion of all polite literature that the barber's is a rather servile trade. There is, of course, a general sensitiveness to the diffuse approval of the world as it filters through to all communities. And this is of great importance. But each locality and social group has its special public opinion. The man whose abilities qualify him to be an unskilled laborer or machine hand usually has been born and bred in a group who do not in the least scorn him because he is an unskilled laborer. By them he is never made to feel a failure because he is not a professional man or expert tradesman. He is esteemed within his group as the tradesman is within his. Similarly a successful plumber usually feels no more degradation at not being a sanitary engineer than the average doctor feels at not being a Pasteur or a Lister. A plumber lives in a plumber's world. The prizefighter cares as little for the economist's scorn of his intellect or the moralist's scorn of his trade as they care for the prizefighter's scorn of their puny blows—probably less. The prizefighter lives in a prize-fighter's world.

It seems certain that the acceptance of the facts reviewed here will help to improve the management of labor by employers and by workers themselves. By reducing what is really objectionable in labor—rather than by reducing labor indiscriminately, by attending to its immaterial as well as its material rewards, by considering the total situation as it influences the worker rather than the job just as it appears in the company's scheme for production, and by studying men as complex individualities, we may hope to get more and better work done with more satisfaction to all concerned.

This seems certain, because we find actual improvement now in cases where men base their action on these facts, and because we find difficulty where they are neglected. A brief mention of such cases may prove instructive.

Some of the objectionable features of labor may be mitigated, and in some cases, eliminated, at no cost. Work that is either too far above or too far below the worker's ability involves in the one case painful strain, and in the other irritating boredom. A shop manager would not use a wood-saw to cut steel or on the other hand run it at half-speed. Wise employers who spend time in studying their personnel as well as their machines, uniformly report that the study is profitable.

Needless personal indignities inflicted on workers by foremen, works policemen, and others who have an official status of mastery make work a misery to the sufferers and debauch the inflictors of the affront. From the day that a boss, small or great, sacrifices the welfare of the concern to gratify his craving for personal power, he begins to lose in value to the concern, and probably will lose more and more rapidly. Carlton Parker related as typical of industrial disputes a case where some women employees in a garment factory were sent away from the passenger elevator to the freight elevator because it was being used by some woman buyer. This led to one of the most bitter strikes of the season. Yet all that was required was to ask the operatives to wait, or request them in a decent way to waive their privilege for the time.

Sex affronts to women employees, common as they are, seem worse than needless. Men will in the long run keep their minds on their jobs much better if they understand that any annoyance of women employees means summary dismissal. Any high executive who has not the self-control to set a proper example should consult a psychiatrist.

It should be understood that it is not the actual infringement of personal rights and dignity that is the main trouble. It is the rankling memory of them for weeks afterward and the daily bitterness of expected tyranny. It should be understood further that the elimination of needless personal tyranny does not imply any foolish idealization of workers or treatment of them with refinements of courtesy which they would interpret as signs of weakness or fear. The distinction indeed is not between a harsh and a gentle treatment, but between bossing them in the interest of the concern and bossing them out of sheer thoughtlessness to gratify the craving for personal mastery. The welfare of the business should be the master of the shop.

The immaterial wages which the whole man receives in addition to the pay envelope which the "economic man" receives can be increased at little or no cost. A large concern operated a workmen's clubhouse itself at considerable expense. It was rather a failure, little use being made of it. The policy was changed to one of payment by the workers for the club privileges, and it became a success. The men were glad to pay for self-respect. A factory superintendent who went through the war and post-war periods without labor troubles attributes his success in large measure to a number of simple rules about treating workers as men and women. For example, the doorman is chosen partly for his cheerful voice and smile. He greets each worker, by name if he can. The foremen take pains to learn the name of each new worker and exactly how to pronounce it on his or her first day. They are instructed to call workers by their names always, inquiring in case they forget. Soon everyone who has contacts with the worker calls him or her by name. The "Here You" and "You over there" and "You on Number 12" are never heard.

Contrast this procedure with that of a company which kept men waiting in the rain without cover long past the time announced before hiring any of them; and left a score of them so waiting long after the jobs advertised were filled, before informing them that they were filled.

How far business and manufacturing concerns should go in providing gratification for the fundamental trends of human nature is a matter for study and experiment. Other things being equal the worker will enjoy his work better in proportion as this is done, but the other things may not be equal.

Here are a few sample problems: Should each job be given dignity by a title, so that the youth can say I am "Second assistant operator on No. 43" instead of "I am a machine hand"? Should each driver drive the same team or truck not only to place responsibility better and reduce accidents, but also to enlist whatever loyalty and affection he may feel toward something he lives with as his, and give room for his instincts of ownership and mastery? How far should the craving to "belong to" something be gratified by social and athletic clubs connected with the concern? How much of an argument for turning over a share in the management of the shop to its workers is found in the satisfaction of the craving for personal dignity and importance which accrues thereby? Would it be silly to put the name and title of each clerk in a bank or office on his desk, so that he could be addressed by name by whoever cared to do so? Would it be utterly silly to do this in a department store? What is the proper use of rivalry between individuals, and between departments? What is the golden mean between a sullen gloom which depresses all workers, and such cheerful sociability that work is neglected?

From an impartial consideration of the total setting of labor in the community and nation, every worthy interest should gain. Labor is part of a total life which it affects, and by which it is affected. Other things being equal, good schools and churches and hospitals and parks and a friendly community life are good for labor. General peace, decency and happiness help us to work and to like our work. On the other hand, vice, disease, and quarrels of all sorts cut both our productivity and our enjoyment. Every crook who leads an easy life, every loafer, rich or poor, who has public esteem, degrades labor. Every false economic prophet who hides essential facts misleads labor.

Other things being equal, the American worker will be efficient and happy in proportion as the general life for him, his parents, his wife and his children is desirable.

This desirability should however be such as fits their actual natures, not necessarily such as a philanthropist or social philosopher might choose. Model cottages designed to suit the subtle refinements of highly cultivated tastes may be less desirable to me than the crude home which I choose for myself, and help to build. We should beware of the library full of admirable books which nobody reads; and of the high school which only the rich can afford to attend.

Perhaps the greatest gains of all are to be expected from the adjustment of labor to individual differences in abilities and tastes, and from such education of individuals as will fit them for the world's work. A perfect fit of work to workers cannot of course be guaranteed. There may be more dirty work than men who do not mind dirt can do easily, more monotonous work than men to whom monotony is inoffensive, and the like. It does not appear, however, that this will happen frequently unless we set up fantastic ideals for the young. The excess seems more likely to be of difficult intellectual and executive jobs over men with the ability to handle them.

At least we can do much better than now, when vocational guidance is a mixture of casual reports of some friends about their jobs, irrational prejudices and fantastic expectations derived from story-books, all operating on ignorance both of the world's work and of one's own powers and temperament. At least employers can realize that a job is never really filled until the employee is found who fits that job in the sense of being able to do it reasonably well and get reasonable satisfaction from it. Anything short of that is a makeshift.

So far the gains illustrated have been such as required action by employers and the public rather than by the laborers as such. It seemed more convenient to present the facts in this way, but there is no implication that these psychological studies of labor as a total fact, including all its evils and all its rewards for all sorts of individuals, should be made chiefly by employers and by the public. On the contrary, it seems highly desirable that workers should provide for the scientific study of work, and for hopeful enterprises to improve efficiency and enjoyment in work as well as to attain and maintain fair hours and wages. Many of the best friends of organized labor are hoping that it may increasingly become the source of impartial knowledge of labor in all its aspects.

CHAPTER XXI

Science and Values *

A WISE custom recommends that this address be upon some topic in which substantial recent advances have been made and about which your retiring president is especially competent to speak. I have, nevertheless, chosen a topic about which very little has been learned in the past decade and in which I am not expert. The reason is that the topic is important for workers in all sciences, and is especially important now. You will all agree that wisdom in the wants and valuations which are the prime movers in human affairs has not kept up with knowledge of the brute facts of human nature, much less with knowledge of the lower animals, plants and inanimate nature. Foes of science are asserting, and some of its friends are admitting, that science is incompetent to improve the judgments of value and esteem which rule men. On the other hand, certain alert students of government, law and morals are suggesting that what is needed in the treatment of questions about good and bad, right and wrong, useful and harmful, is the matter-of-fact curiosity of science. So I invite your attention to some facts of the psychology of values, as I see them.

The facts about valuation have been much discussed under the title of "Ethics" and "Esthetics" by thinkers of philosophic temper. In spite of the great acuity and scope of their intellects, their efforts to devise general theories of the good or of the beautiful or of what men ought, and what they ought

* Address of the retiring president of the American Association for the Advancement of Science, St. Louis, December 30, 1935. From Science, Vol. 83, (Jan. 3, 1936), pp. 1–8.

not, to enjoy have been unsatisfactory to philosophers as a whole, and rather mystifying or empty to men of science. Nor do they seem to profit by the general advancement of knowledge. Aristotle's solutions seem as good as Hegel's. Being extremely able men, they often propose ideas of great interest and influence, as do great poets and great theologians. But in cases where these ideas concern matters of observable fact, the observations and experiments of working scientists have often disproved their brilliant conjectures. To become a disciple of any of them in other matters is then risky. Their royal roads to knowing what is the right thing for each creature to do in each set of circumstances by learning what "The Good" is do not fulfil expectations.

Among the doctrines upon which they do show a high percentage of agreement is one which, though obviously true when taken advisedly, is likely to be a barrier to useful thought about valuation. That is the doctrine that the science (or super-science or meta-science) of ethics can be sharply distinguished from such natural sciences as biology, anthropology and psychology, since it is a normative science, telling what should be or must be, instead of describing what is and predicting what will be.

This doctrine is useful as a reminder that judgments that health, honesty and herrings are valuable differ from judgments that the Klebs-Loeffler bacillus causes diphtheria, that cheating in school children is negatively correlated with intelligence or that herring eggs will become herrings only under certain conditions. But it may do harm by encouraging us to argue and worry unprofitably about whether law, government and education can be sciences and what sort of sciences we should try to make them be. It may also frighten workers in the sciences of man away from observations of and experiments with values, and restrict them to studying only those parts of a man which he uses as materials and tools to satisfy his wants, neglecting the wants themselves.

VALUES VS. MERE EXISTENCE

Just what is the real and operative distinction between judgments of value or worth and judgments of fact or existence? Do the former concern categorical imperatives which are not amenable to the observations and experiments and predictions and verifications of the natural sciences? Must they be revealed by religion or deduced from some theory of a moral universe above or outside of the world of natural events?

My answer is that, on the contrary, judgments of value are simply one sort of judgments of fact, distinguished from the rest by two characteristics: They concern consequences. These are consequences to the wants of sentient beings. Values, positive and negative, reside in the satisfaction or annoyance felt by animals, persons or deities. If the occurrence of X can have no influence on the satisfaction or discomfort of anyone present or future, X has no value, is neither good nor bad, desirable nor undesirable. Values are functions of preferences. Judgments about values—statements that A is good, B is bad, C is right, D is useful—refer ultimately to satisfactions or annoyances in sentient creatures and depend upon their preferences. Competent students judge the existence of things by observations of them; they judge the values of things by observations of their consequences.

Values appear in the world when certain forms of preference appear, when certain animals like or dislike, enjoy or suffer, are contented or unhappy or feel pleasures or pains. They apparently precede learning and knowledge, which work chiefly in their service. Chicks or rats are indeed in a sense more confirmed moralists than civilized men. They pursue what is good, fit and proper to their minds with a whole-hearted devotion. Their duty is often their pleasure also.

In civilized man the variety of the valued and disvalued increases greatly. There are many scales of merit, many points of view from which and in respect to which persons, acts, things, events, can be regarded as desirable or the reverse. One thing may have a score of different positive values and a dozen negative ones. The inborn values of sweet tastes, unimpeded movements, rest after exercise, exercise after rest, courtship and love, and so on, are worked over into an enormous structure by the family, school, neighborhood, church, books, laws, and other man-made forces. Man acquires multifarious customs and traditions about values. Thus certain acts are good or right because they satisfy the tribal gods; others are so because they minister to the happiness of ancestors long since dead, others are right, one knows not why. Opinions about values become diverse and conflicting.

In assigning values on the basis of consequencees, we may and do attach various weights to the consequences for ourselves, our friends, white men, black men and yellow men, sane, insane and idiotic men, dogs, horses, tigers and snakes, living men, the spirits of dead men and men yet to be, the God of our fathers and other gods, in case we recognize such at all. We also attach weight to remote and indirect consequences, for example, by way of the example set to others. There is also a large margin of guesswork, especially about what the consequences will be for the satisfaction of men of the distant future and men unlike ourselves. Opinions about consequences are also largely second-hand and conventional. The ratings by consequences are, however, always justified in the end by satisfactions or annoyances for some sentient being, if they are justified at all.

ALLEGED ABSOLUTE OR TRANSCENDENTAL VALUES

We can choose whose satisfactions we shall give weight to and what sort of persons we shall esteem; the two amount to essentially the same. But if sane and intelligent, we rarely attach value to something which makes no differences, directly or indirectly, to the satisfactions and annoyances of any sentient beings.

When certain moralists and theorists who are sane and highly intelligent give us the notion that they assert that certain qualities and acts can have an absolute intrinsic value, regardless of any satisfaction or annoyance to any sentient being, they or we (or both) are probably confused by analogies or verbal subtleties. It is to be observed that the qualities and acts alleged to be thus justified by their mere nature are easily justifiable as ministrants to real desires and aversions.

The commonest cases of alleged absolute values, irrespective of any satisfaction or annoyance to any sentient being, are truth, beauty and the development or perfection of human powers.

The truth, in the sense of those ideas about reality which correspond to it, enable us to predict it and lead us to adapt ourselves to it and to wants which are satisfiable by it, is a pure good. Anyone can possess it at no cost to anyone else and often to their enrichment; an increase in the amount of it available for men or in the amount of it possessed by an individual is, in and of itself, an aid in the satisfaction of other wants, and interferes with none of them. Whatever is an essential conflict with it is bad. Whether it has any more absolute warrant for commanding our regard we need not inquire, since even by the most empirical and utilitarian, or by the most metaphysical and supernaturalistic, theories it is valued as among the highest things a man may seek.

Beauty in the sense of that which causes unselfish, impersonal and noble enjoyment, free from exaltation of one at the expense of another's degradation, from use by one at the expense of another's deprivation, from taints of bestiality, meanness, stupidity, and the like, also ranks very high in any reasonable scheme of values. To make or to enjoy a poem that is fine satisfies good or at least innocent wants in the poet and his readers, without, in and of itself, reducing the satisfactions of any one else.

Creating and enjoying truth and beauty are samples of the class of satisfiers which involve positive satisfactions for some without subtraction from, and often with addition to, those of others. Enjoyment of the happiness of others is a third member of this class, and good health is a fourth. Other things being equal, such are obviously on the average better than what may be called the possessive or exclusive satisfiers, such as eating, ownership, supremacy or victory, where the satisfaction of one involves the deprivation of others. They are also samples of the dignified, as opposed to the trivial or mean satisfiers, such as chewing gum, scratching one's head or watching a dog-fight. They have fine consequences and fine affiliations; and these are enough to guarantee them without assuming any absolute or transcendent quality in them.

The doctrine that the perfection of human powers furnishes a general criterion and rule for valuation was probably invented and maintained because of the belief that there must be some one adequate universal criterion, and the fact that to be perfect, to be the best of a certain sort or series is very often good. Since some powers, such as to deceive, defraud, terrify and torment, are obviously better restrained than developed, the limitation, harmonious, is often inserted. Powers whose perfecting is undesirable can then be excluded as being out of harmony with those which the theorist thinks are better.

There need be no one universal criterion, and the idea of perfecting is of little real value save as a suggestion that the good life of any creature depends upon what kind of creature he is. The addition of "harmonious" brings the practical applications of the doctrine back to a calculus of actual wants and satisfactions of sentient beings and their interrelations.

Values then reside in satisfactions and annoyances of sentient beings. In so far as these lie within the natural world of men and animals, they are amenable to scientific study. In so far as we think reasonably, not by prejudice, wishful delusion or chance, we judge the values of things, events and relations by their consequences. We also sometimes judge them indirectly by their affiliations. The theory and technique of estimating the value of a thing by its affiliations—

by what it goes with—is important, but I lack time to explain, illustrate and justify it, and to show its proper uses, dangers and limitations. The value of any given fact to any given group is, in so far forth, a natural fact like the smell or taste of any given chemical to any given animal. Values are not banished entirely from the realm of science into some exalted sphere. Facts, principles and laws about values differ from facts, principles and laws about time, distance, area, volume, mass, temperature, chemical constitution, memory, dreams, knowledge, prices, diminishing returns, laws, customs, myths, taboos, family organization, and so on, not fundamentally and utterly, but in the very important features which I have described.

They are amenable to the methods of science. But they are often much harder to determine, since they depend upon knowledge about sentient beings, present and future, their wants, the right weights to attach to each of these, and the consequences of the act or fact in question to each of them. As a result, there is a very wide variation in the common-sense knowledge which science starts with and seeks to improve. The variation in the weights given, often unconsciously, is especially influential. In the actual genesis of moral judgments one of you may, and probably does, weight the satisfaction of himself and a dozen of his family and friends above those of all the worms in the world; but some St. Francis or Brahmin may not. The saint may weight the satisfactions of any other Christian as equal to his own, but the average sensual man does not. The abstract thinker may give substantial weight to the satisfactions of the human species in 3000 A. D., but these vanish in the valuations of most men. Such habits and attitudes acquired and used in ordinary life are hard to exclude when one tries to judge impartially as if he were a trustee for the welfare of the world or a purely scientific solver of the world's problems.

THE ASSIGNMENT OF WEIGHTS

Assuming that all human beings, present and future, are to be considered, how should an impartial student, a trustee for the welfare of all, assign weights? His criterion will be, as always, the consequences.

If the satisfaction of a certain want (say for food, or for power, or for approval) in A bids fair to cause great benefit to all men, whereas the satisfaction of the same want in B bids fair to cause little, he will weight A's want much more heavily than B's.

When it is not feasible to learn what the consequences of weighting one person's satisfactions more than another's will be, our trustee for humanity will do well to weight the wants of good men more than the same wants of bad men, since there is a probability that the gratification of wants will cause both to maintain or increase their customary activities.

Goodness and intelligence are positively correlated: so he will for the same reason do well to weight the wants of intelligent men more than the same wants of dull men.

He will do well to weight the wants of the men of 1950 above the same wants in the men of 2050, unless he has reason to suppose that the latter will be better men than the former, for there may be no men in 2050, and if there are, they may, some or all, lack the want in question. He will, however, give far more weight to the men of 2050 and 2150 than statesmen do or than most philanthropists have ever done.

Ethics, politics and philanthropy have been guilty of neglecting individual differences, partly because doing so simplifies all problems, and partly because of the retention of theological and sentimental prejudices in favor of the similarity and equality of man.

No egalitarian system of weights can be just or wise. More weight should be given to the wants of superior men than to the wants of inferior men. What able and good men want is much more likely to be better for their community or nation or race or the world as a whole than what stupid and bad men want. Providing for their wants will presumably enable them to do more of what they want to do; and this will improve the world and its customs for future residents. Other things being equal, it should lead them to have more offspring, and this will improve the world by increasing its percentage of good men.

It is of special importance to attach great weight to the wants of those individuals who have eminent abilities in the impersonal activities of art, science and the management of men. What such persons want will be largely time and freedom to do their work in, tools to do it with and conditions enabling them to do their best. They will doubtless sometimes want what is not good for their work for the world; but their judgment will on the whole be a good guide when knowledge of consequences is lacking.

It seems probable that the harmful vagaries of men of genius in the fine arts would have been much reduced if their cravings for untrammeled expression in art itself and for approval of their real merits had been more fully satisfied. It also seems at least possible that the ruthlessness and selfishness of some men of genius in business and government would have been reduced if they had been given power more and been less required to extort it by force. Even if these creators continue to seek occasionally eccentric, ignoble or ruthless satisfactions, it will still be an excellent bargain for the world to attach great weight to their wants as a whole. The world's greatest folly has been its treatment of those who are most superior to it in intellect, originality, sensitiveness and humaneness. Its most prudent investment is to find them out early, and give them whatever they need to do their perfect work. One good clue to what they need is what they themselves desire.

HUMAN WANTS

The work of a science of values, a realistic ethics, is to learn what men do want and how to improve their wants, and to trace the consequences of acts, events, ideas, attitudes, and so forth.

What are the fundamental and dependable satisfactions of life for man? A leading psychiatrist answers, "Love and security." But a student of boy's gangs may think that "Conflict and adventure" is as good an answer. The philanthropists of the early and mid nineteenth century thought that men would be satisfied if they and their children were without hunger and pain, able to read, with regular work ten hours a day and freedom to think and vote as they liked. Cynics of the twentieth century doubt whether people in general really want liberty and culture as much as beer and excitement.

I have no satisfactory answer, and no time to state the provisional answer which anthropology, psychology, sociology and the other sciences of man suggest. I shall instead report one small bit of evidence concerning what the inhabitants of this country want.

We do know fairly well how the population of this country spent their incomes in 1929. Using the figures given by Lynd and supplemented by Dr. Ella Woodyard, we have 17 billions for food, 8 billions for clothing, 6½ billions for automobiles, and so on through thirty items like a billion and a half for laundry, cleaning and dyeing, over a billion and a half for tobacco, to three quarters of a billion for death and burial.

The payment for food satisfies chiefly hunger, appetite and the want for sweet and savory tastes, but also in part the craving for social enjoyments, for the approval and esteem of others, for protection against disease. Payment for physicians is chiefly for protection against disease and pain, but also helps to satisfy the more general cravings for security, comfort, self-respect and the approval of others. Laundry bills represent the satisfactions of self-respect and social approval, protection against disease, pleasures of sight and smell, and others also.

By the aid of a consensus of psychologists, I have divided each item of our people's expenses among the wants to which it probably ministers, and then combined the results into a list of wants and the amounts paid for the satisfaction thereof. The outcome will suffer from whatever constant errors afflict psychologists to-day, but this inventory of wants satisfied from income is at least a step in the right direction. I shall not present it in detail, but only by samples. According to it:

Our bill for food is spent as follows: 56 per cent to satisfy hunger; 15 per cent to gratify the pleasures of taste and smell; 10 per cent for the pleasures of companionship and social intercourse, including courtship; 3½ per cent for the approval of others, and smaller percentages for protection against disease, protection against cold, enjoyment of the comfort ·of others and the pleasures of vision.

Our bill for clothes is spent (according to the psychologist's distribution): 41 per cent for protection against cold, heat and wet; 6¾ per cent for protection against animals and disease; 12½ per cent for the approval of others; 7 per cent for self-approval; 10 per cent to gain pleasure in courtship and sex activities; 8 per cent for other social intercourse; 6 per cent for pleasures of vision; 3½ per cent to win mastery or domination over others, and 2 per cent to win their affection.

The 700 million dollars for cosmetics and beauty parlors is spent about one seventh for the pleasures of sight and smell, one fourth for the pleasures of sex and courtship, one third to gain general approval from others, one eighth to have inner-self-approval, and about one tenth to secure mastery or domination.

When the entire annual budget is thus transformed item by item into a budget for the satisfaction of human wants, payments for sensory pleasures, security, approval of others and the pleasures of companionship and sociability (includ-

ing romance and courtship) are in each case close in magnitude to the amount paid for freedom from hunger. In fact, we
pay more to maintain self-respect and the good opinion of
others and avoid scorn, derision and shame than to keep
our bodies fed and free from the distress of hunger.

We pay more for entertainment (including the intellectual
pleasures and the sensory pleasures of sight, sound, taste
and smell) than for protection against cold, heat, wet, animals, disease, criminals and other bad people, and pain.

Less than one third of what we spent went for wants which
must be satisfied to keep the human species alive and self-
perpetuating. The rest went chiefly to keep us amused and
comfortable physically, intellectually, morally and especially
socially.

Relatively little is paid for the satisfactions of the intellectual life. The psychologists consider that the payments for
private schools, books and magazines are often for prestige,
power and other practical satisfactions, and do not credit
the theaters and movies of 1929 with much intellectual appeal.

The psychologists do, however, pay us the compliment of
crediting us with spending twice as much from good will to
man as from fear of criminals and other bad men, and of
spending at least as much to win the affection of our fellow
men as to have the pleasure of bossing them.

In tracing the consequences of ideas, acts, laws, customs,
inventions, and so on, both the biological and the social
sciences have somewhat neglected the inner or mental wants
of men. Nourishing food, hygienic housing, medical care,
relief from bodily pain and fatigue have, quite naturally, been
emphasized. But inner peace, contentment, a sense of personal worth, surety of friendship and affection, the absence
of fear, the presence of a good conscience and other states of
mind are also real and important.

Many features in religions, caste systems and other folkways which seem undesirable to us did have the merit of
satisfying some of these deep inner needs. If we abandon
such folkways on the ground that they are deceptive and

unjust, we should replace them by something true and just which gives equal comfort, dignity and flavor to the inner lives of men. Doubtless it is better to be a dissatisfied Socrates than a satisfied pig; but also it is worse to be a dissatisfied coolie than a satisfied coolie. Most discontent is not divine. Not once in ten thousand times will becoming dissatisfied cause a coolie to become a Socrates. Some inner conflicts, miseries and rebellions are good, if not for the man's soul, at least for his work for the world. But many are not good for anything.

Theoretically, men should face the facts of the world, including all their own weaknesses and follies, make a reasonable adjustment and then live serene in the faith that they are doing their best and that all the good in all the world should and will support them so far as it can. But how can they be taught to do this?

THE IMPROVEMENT OF WANTS

The desires and aversions of men can be changed as truly as their ideas and habits, though not as much or as easily. The same forces of repetition and reward that strengthen tendencies to think and act operate upon tendencies to like and dislike. If a certain attitude can be made to occur in a person in connection with a certain situation, and if he is led to regard it as fit and proper in that connection, he will "learn" to take that attitude to that situation just as he learns to think "ten" in response to "seven plus three." In strengthening good wants and in attaching desire to good objects, there are, however, difficulties and limitations which are absent in the more neutral unprejudiced sphere of ideas and skills. Experiments in changing wants, interests and attitudes do not justify the fond hopes of certain doctrinaires in sociology and education, but they do guarantee that, if sound methods are used, men can be taught to find satisfaction in useful work, healthful and noble recreation and the welfare of others, to a degree that the world has never seen.

What is known concerning the inheritance of moral traits

in man and the lower animals encourages us to hope that the inborn cravings of men may be improved at no cost to other goods.

TRACING CONSEQUENCES

The consequences of events, especially of the ideas and acts of men, to the satisfactions of mankind, need study by all the sciences of man and nature.

Non-scientific estimates are sadly untrustworthy. The national prohibition of the sale of alcoholic liquors did not have the consequences which millions of people expected who worked to attain it. Who knows what its consequences would have been if the work that attained it had been quadrupled to secure its enforcement? Among all the consequences, beneficial and ruinous, blessed and dire, which were expected from the granting of votes to women, which were real? People accept guesses and follow the unconscious logic of hope and fear in estimating consequences, perhaps because they feel that good intentions are the important requirements.

People also naïvely expect that everything will stay the same except what is changed by direct action upon it. Nine persons out of ten, and possibly ninety-nine out of a hundred, assume that the general features of civilization which are stable in their experience will remain so. Roads, schools, policemen, houses, beds, payment for work, a chance to buy what you want if you have the purchase price and a hundred other commonplaces of our social order will continue like the sunshine or rain. So they think.

To think anything else is almost a psychological impossibility for the ordinary man of this country today. He does not realize that these features of his life depend upon an extremely complex structure of ideas and acts of rulers and ruled, employers and employed, parents and children, borrowers and lenders, and are kept in condition by an equally complex structure of customs and laws. He has no more fear that any act of his or anybody else will stop railroad trains from running than that it will stop the sun from shining. Lay-ing a tax on incomes is to him like digging a ditch that diverts the rain from one place to another. He does not have the slightest fear that it will have any effect on the amount of income. Why should he? To do so he must reason, and reason against habit and experience. Only exceptional minds do that.

Scientific ethics must rely largely on economics, political science, sociology, psychology, education and biology in studying the values positive and negative of all sorts of activities; for example, paying prisoners full wages for their work, keeping criminals under surveillance by parole officers instead of incarcerating them, legalizing divorce when both parties desire it, encouraging birth control by the weakly, dull and psychopathic, taking property by force from the rich and giving it to the poor, trying to make one's own community or nation wax rich and strong at the expense of others by tariffs and quotas, and other moral or semi-moral issues, where action is now unfortunately being taken largely as a result of the emotional interests of enthusiasts or the selfish interests of special groups.

This lays a heavy burden upon these sciences, and cautious workers will be reluctant to take it on. Questions about consequences to human welfare are often confused by conventional interpretations of welfare; one is tempted away from fundamental inquiries which are really important to superficial questions which seem important to the public; the basic facts are often lacking; devising ways and means to secure trustworthy observations is very difficult; even after heroic labors, the solution may have a disgustingly wide margin of error.

So science has been rather willing to leave values alone. So psychologists rarely study the causes of happiness, economists recoil from all wants save those expressed in money prices, students of education deal with the consequences of school work upon abilities, but not, save rarely, upon desires and satisfactions. So we all have left and still tend to leave decision about consequences to humanists—to philosophers, sages, men of affairs, historians and literary men.

Some of the humanists would gladly accept the responsibility, being confident that science should leave such decisions to them. They distrust the activities of the social sciences and especially their entry into the field of human values. It is better, such a humanist will assert, to listen to the seers and sages and to follow the dreams of inspired artists and moralists than to poke about in the schools, streets, market-places, prisons and asylums, or collect statistics, or drag human aspirations into the laboratory.

We may reasonably think that it is better to do both. We should admit that Thucidydes reports a better description of liberty than the average Ph. D. candidate in political science today would give. If we had to choose between reading Sophocles and Euripides and reading the most scientific family budgets, we would reject the science. We would have science gladly learn and gladly teach what able men have thought about the consequences of various forms of conduct, but we would also have it test and experiment, regarding nothing as outside the scope of science.

Much of the scorn of certain humanists for the efforts of modern science seems to be due to the fact that the observations and experiments of scientific workers make dull reading. A cardinal virtue of these humanists is to be interesting; many of them are literary men to whom success in entertaining cultivated persons is a duty, as well as a source of pleasure and pride. It is partly because of this that we can not trust the humanist alone. We must be suspicious of interest as a guide in any tracing of consequences. The talent for selecting what has a literary appeal may well be wrapped tight in a napkin and buried deep while one is doing scientific research.

We must consider one final objection to using the methods of science in the world of values. Science, according to a very popular view, deals with a fatalistic world in which men, their wants and ideals, are all parts of a reel which unwinds year by year, minor whirls in a fixed dance of atoms. Values can have no place in such a world, and efforts to attain them by science must fail.

The truth of the matter, which is rather subtle, may best be realized by considering what I have elsewhere called the paradox of science, which is that scientists discover "causal" sequences and describe the world as one where the same cause will always produce the same effect, in order to change that world into a form nearer their heart's desire. Man makes the world a better home for man and himself a more success-ful dweller in it by discovering its regular unchangeable modes of action. He can determine the fate of the world and his own best, not by prayers or threats, but by treating it and himself by the method of science as phenomena, determined, as far as he can see, by their past history. The only safe way he finds to gratify human wants and fulfil human aspirations is by learning the regular predictable modes of action of na-ture, especially those which relate to these wants and as-pirations. The more fully he can turn the world into a progres-sion of events devoid of chance, unswerved from its onward march by any magic, the more he can control it. If man should know himself as fully as he knows the chemicals he puts into a test-tube, so that he could predict the exact reaction he would make to any situation, he would be better able to con-trol and improve his own future than any race of men or gods has ever been.

A deterministic world of science is the least fatalistic world there can be. A world entirely ruled by the wishes of deities external to it would be utterly fatalistic. It would present a far more hopeless determinism than the determinism of sci-ence, for human access to and influence upon those forces external to nature would be difficult and of doubtful avail, whereas the nature we live in and are parts of we may hope to influence.

The solution of the paradox lies in this last fact. Men are parts of nature. They and the scientific knowledge they ac-quire and the choices they make are on the reel, in the dance of atoms, among the marching events. Their wants and aspirations can determine nature's future because they are determined by nature's past. Everything that man is and does influences nature. Any ideas men have influence it. The knowledge of it as a complex of the regular "determined" sequences described in the so-called "laws" of science is the force that man can use most advantageously in changing men and the rest of nature to fit human wants. If and as the world is determined, there is hope of controlling it in the interest of human values. Every regularity or law that science can discover in the consequences of events will be a step toward the only freedom that is of the slightest use to man, and an aid in the good life. If values did not reside in the orderly world of nature, but depended on chance and caprice, it would be vain to try to increase them.

Are there any valid reasons why the methods of science should be abandoned in favor of either philosophical arguments or intuitional conclusions when one passes from facts of existence to facts of value? We have found none. It is certainly undesirable for men of science to restrict their thinking to what is and will be, leaving to propagandists and reformers and talkers the decisions about what ought to be. Is any group of thinkers qualified to study the wants of mankind, the consequences of acts and events, and the improvement of human valuations without reliance on the facts and methods of anthropology, psychology, sociology, economics, government and other sciences of man? Can science avoid the responsibility of trying what impartial curiosity and honest work can accomplish in this field of controversy and prejudice?

The world needs the insights and valuations of great sages and dreamers. It needs the practical psychology of men of affairs, leaders in business, government and education. But it also needs scientific methods to test the worth of the prophets' dreams, and scientific humanists to inform and advise its men of affairs and to advise them not only about what is, but about what is right and good.

CHAPTER XXII

Darwin's Contribution to Psychology *

PSYCHOLOGY, as you all know, means the science of mental, as opposed to physical, facts—the study of thoughts and feelings, as opposed to physical objects. But the science of mental facts may mean to different individuals and at different times very different things; and to understand Darwin's contribution to it we must for a moment consider some of them.

To most of the writers on psychology of the first half of Darwin's century, it meant naming, describing, and classifying our states of mind and our so-called mental powers. For instance, the most important writer of this sort of psychology in Darwin's youth was James Mill. His son held the same position during Darwin's maturity. I quote almost at random from a book written by the former and edited by the latter, *The Analysis of the Phenomena of the Human Mind.*

> "When we have an idea, the having the idea, the being conscious of the idea, knowing the idea, observing the idea, are only different names for the same thing. They mean the being conscious in a particular way. But the being conscious is to take notice of the consciousness. To be conscious and not to take notice, is the same as to be conscious, and not conscious. The notice is the consciousness and the consciousness is the notice."

Darwin nowhere makes mention of this book, and, so far as we know, never read it. Had he read it, and been asked about, say, this passage, he would probably have said modestly that he was not at all sure that he understood what it was all about.

* Address delivered June 21, 1909, during the Summer Session of the University of California, and published in the *University of California Chronicle,* Vol. XII, No. 1, pp. 65–80.

About a year after the publication of the *Origin of Species* there appeared the *Psycho-Physics* by Fechner, a book in which experiment and elaborate measurement were put to service in support of psychological theories. The theories in this case concerned the relation of mental states to the physical events which caused them. The book was one of the chief beginnings of present experimental psychology. It, too, Darwin nowhere mentions and almost certainly never read. In fact, Darwin never felt any great interest in the inner life of the mind—in thoughts and feelings studied for their own sake. And he would have doubted his competence to observe or argue about them.

At the time of the publication of the *Origin,* too, Ibsen was doing his first successful work and training himself for those later plays, each of which, by the insight of the artist, is a masterpiece in the psychology of human motive and passion. George Meredith was already writing his wonderful psychological novels. But such psychology as Ibsen's or George Meredith's would have been, I will not say beyond Darwin, but entirely apart from him. He was too simple and direct to enjoy and, possibly, fully to understand subtle analyses of the complex passions, conventionalities, and conflicts in human nature.

But psychology, at least today, means more than such reflections as Mill's, such measurements and speculations as Fechner's, and such insights as Ibsen's or Meredith's. It means the study of intellects and characters in all their relations to the bodies which possess them. Human psychology shares with physiology, anthropology, and sociology the study of all human nature and activity. Psychology in general shares with zoölogy the study of all animal nature and activity. Now in the activities and the behavior of man, as of any other animal, Darwin was interested. He was preëminently a naturalist. Only when the mind played a part in the general economy of life—only when it could be studied from the outside by careful and impartial observation of its effects, did he feel special interest or show special capacity in studying it. It was to psychology as the science of human and animal behavior that he contributed. Just what his contribution was is our question for this hour.

He made four important direct contributions to psychology. First of all, he showed in the *Origin of Species* and in the *Descent of Man* that the instincts and the moral and aesthetic capacities of man are subject to variation and natural selection. Again and again he gives concrete evidence that the mind, like the body—the behavior of an animal, like its structure—is the product of a long growth, not a sudden creation. Intellect and character have a natural, not a miraculous, history. The mind is to be derived as well as described.

It is somewhat amusing to note that the implication that our intellect and character are descendants from those of non-human animals did not provoke so much resentment as the implication that our bodies came from their bodies. To many eminent divines the idea that their bodies should be related, even at a distance of a thousand centuries, across a thousand cousinships, to the bodies of apes was so repugnant that they took its falsity for granted without the slightest investigation. Yet they showed far less irritation at the hypothesis that their minds and manners were bound to the apes by the same link. Perhaps this notion was so utterly preposterous that they did not even understand it.

Darwin's second direct contribution to psychology was made in connection with his doctrine (of sexual selection) that the attractiveness of certain qualities in one sex to the other sex selected those qualities for survival regardless of any further utility. It consisted in a fund of data regarding the attractions and aversions manifested by animals, including man.

The fact of sexual selection is probably subordinate to natural selection as one minor outcome of it—not coördinate and independent as Darwin seems to have thought. The attractions and aversions which he inferred from the structure and movements of animals probably do not in all cases exist. And the semi-aesthetic feelings ascribed to the animals by him are almost entirely not what he supposed them to be, or at least not what he led others to think he supposed them to be. But after a generous allowance for these imperfections, there remains a body of valuable observations of animal behavior and a stimulus to the study of a very important biological and psychological problem.

Darwin's third direct contribution to psychology was an account of the bodily expression of the emotions, which is still, after nearly forty years, the most distinguished study of this topic. I cannot in a brief description or by quotations give an adequate idea of the wealth of detailed observations and the carefulness in theorizing which characterize this book. Its most striking doctrine is that certain acts, which were in our ancestors ordinary acts aimed to produce an effect on something or somebody, have left, as slight relics of themselves, acts of emotional expression. Thus, the uncovering of the teeth, especially of the canine teeth, preparatory to biting an antagonist has dwindled into the snarl of anger and the sneer of scorn. But Darwin did not overstrain evolution as an explanation of the ways in which emotions and bodily conditions are related each to the other and to the cause of both. If you will read his accounts of weeping, blushing, shaking the head for negation, and the muscular turmoil of rage, you will be convinced of his breadth of view and fine sense of fact throughout. For instance, he gives full attention to the law of habit and to what is now called the diffusion of the motor impulse.

Darwin's fourth contribution was his study of the mental development in infancy of one of his sons. This, the first of the psychological biographies of babies, is also one of the best. It is characteristic of Darwin's modesty that he did not announce that he had used a new method of research or advertise the importance of child psychology. On the contrary he did not intend to publish this study at all and did so only years later to meet a need aroused by Taine's similar study.

One special aim of this biography of a baby by its father was to ascertain the resemblances of the mental life of infancy to the mental life of the lower animals, an inquiry which has since been made the chief business of one whole school of psychologists, led by the American, G. Stanley Hall.

There is a type of prejudice which would readily make capital out of this fact—that a man of science experimented on his own child—and which would call attention with a sneer to the evolutionist seeing in his own child only likenesses to the lower animals. It is the direct object of this lecture to display the influence of Darwin's work, not the dignity, gentleness, and quiet heroism of his life; but I venture to read to you a letter written after the death of one of his children. It is perhaps too intimate for quotation on an occasion like this, but it is right and fitting that with Darwin, as with Lincoln, we should join to esteem of his work, honor and affection for the man.

> It was delightful and cheerful to behold her. Her dear face now rises before me as she used sometimes to come running downstairs with a stolen pinch of snuff for me, her whole form radiant with the pleasure of giving pleasure. Besides her joyousness, she was in her manners remarkably cordial, frank, open, straightforward, natural, and without any shade of reserve. Her whole mind was pure and transparent. One felt one knew her thoroughly and could trust her. . . . In the last short illness her conduct was in simple angelic. She never once complained; never became fretful; was ever considerate of others, and was thankful in the most gentle, pathetic manner for everything done for her. When so exhausted that she could hardly speak she praised everything that was given her, and said some tea was "beautifully good." When I gave her some water, she said "I quite thank you," and these, I believe, were the last precious words addressed by her dear lips to me.
>
> We have lost the joy of our household and the solace of our old age. She must have known how we loved her. Oh, that she could now know how deeply, how tenderly, we do still and shall ever love her dear, joyous face! Blessings on her!

It would well repay us to return to a more adequate study of Darwin's psychological work, but the rest of the hour must be reserved for his still more important indirect contribution through his more strictly biological work.

First of all, of course, Darwin gave psychology the evolutionary point of view. Psychology had studied the human mind by itself alone and had taught that our minds were all made after one pattern mind, which worked as it did for no intelligible reason, but just because it did. Darwin showed psychologists that the mind not only is, but has grown, that it has a history as well as a character, that this history is one of hundreds of thousands of years, and that the mind's present can be fully understood only in the light of its total past.

Psychology has by no means fully mastered this lesson. Human learning is still too often described with total neglect of animal learning. But each decade since the *Origin of Species* appeared has shown a well marked increase in comparative and genetic psychology. Of our own countrymen, for instance, William James, Stanley Hall, and John Dewey have consistently worked at psychology on a genetic basis. Psychology has also been careless in *applying* this lesson. The ostensible followers of Darwin have sometimes shown far too little of his industry in mastering facts and of his caution in making inferences from them. The kind of thinking that considers the pleasure humans take in swimming fully explained as a relic from the minds of our ancestors who were fish, or that accounts for human coöperation in industry by reference to ants, bees, and wasps, may take the name, but has not the spirit, nor, in reality, the method of Darwin. But, side by side with such extravagant speculations and unnatural history, careful observations and experiments have been made with reference to animal learning, to the mental powers of primitive man, and to the mental evolution of the human species.

Only those of expert acquaintance with the recent history of psychology would appreciate a list of the psychologists who have thus been Darwin's followers, or a review of the investigations which they have made; but you will all perhaps be interested to know the present status of the doctrine of mental evolution,—the present belief concerning the genealogy of human intellect and character.

I must warn you that we shall be dealing with the battle of investigation at its very outposts, hearing the latest returns, but not knowing how far they will be finally confirmed; and that very many of my statements may be amended by later and better work. But I can only report what, with present knowledge, seems to me the course of development of the human intellect. Of the development of human character, I cannot, for lack of time, speak at all. And for the same reason, I must begin our mental history, not at the very beginning, but half way in its course, with the fishes.

You know that starting from this point our bodily descent is roughly as follows: fishes begat amphibia; amphibia begat reptiles; reptiles begat mammals; some early mammals begat the primates; some early primates begat man.

The existing fishes have intellects of a sort, in the sense that they can learn,—can so change their natures as not to do the same thing in the same circumstances. The unfit object they first tried to eat, they later reject; the unfit place they first went to, they later avoid. The nature of their learning will be clear from a simple but typical instance.

If the common Fundulus of the New England coast is confined by a wire screen at one end of an aquarium upon which direct sunlight shines, it reacts to the situation by swimming toward the shaded end of the aquarium. When it pokes its head against the screen, it changes direction, swims alongside the screen, and then again toward the shaded end. It will thus in the course of time swim at nearly every square inch of the screen. If now a small hole has been left in the screen, say in the upper right-hand corner, the fish will, in the course of such instinctive swimmings toward the shade and changes of direction, swim through the hole and reach the shaded end, where it will remain in physiological peace. If the experiment is repeated again and again, say at intervals of twenty minutes, the fish will make, sooner and sooner, fewer and fewer of the useless darts at the screen, will make the appropriate movements of swimming to the right, rising up, and swimming through the hole. Whereas at the first trial it spent five or ten minutes in getting out, it will now spend less and less time. Eventually, after many trials, it will have eliminated all the futile movements,—will, when confined by the screen, swim to and through the hole directly in five or ten seconds.

The fish has learned to respond to that particular situation in an adaptive way. It has modified its behavior to suit the situation. Its learning consists in the stamping in or strengthening of the connection between that situation and the particular response of swimming to and through the hole, and the weakening and final elimination of the connections between that situation and the movements which resulted only in the perpetuation of the unsuitable situation. Sensitiveness to a situation, a variety of responses, the selection of the fit one and its association with the situation, are the four essentials of its learning. No "ideas" or "thinking" of the human sort are necessary to account for it.

Such learning by directly connecting certain responses with a situation and disconnecting certain others from it, was undoubtedly characteristic of the fishes of long ago who were our forefathers. They learned, but they learned without thinking about the situation or thinking beyond the situation. They learned very few things.

The amphibians and reptiles, which come next in the line of descent, show the same sort of intellect, the only known difference being that in general they can be sensitive to more kinds of situations, can make more kinds of responses, and can connect the latter with the former in more ways.

In the case of the mammals, other than the primates, special studies have been made of dogs, cats, rats, mice, racoons, and guinea pigs, which agree in finding this same learning by the direct selection of one response for association with a situation as the main component of the animal's intelligence. With it there are, possibly, obscure traces of the life of ideas, of thoughts of things past and to come, of things bound to the actual present situation only by connections made in the animal itself. But the early mammals, who are in the direct line of descent to man, probably progressed beyond the reptiles only by being able to learn more and different habits, not by learning them in a more human way.

In the monkeys, which have been studied somewhat elaborately by four psychologists, the same learning without thought, the same responding to the situation of the moment without recalling the past or foreseeing the future, the same trial and success method, is the rule. The monkey in general does not call up ideas, select the idea that seems fit, and act upon it. He acts impulsively, not intellectually, doing not what he thinks of doing, but what he feels like doing. But he feels like doing an enormous number of things; and at times, when one of those things is notably successful, he drops his previous behavior and adopts the successful act so suddenly that he *seems* to have formed not a habit, but a notion.

It is safest to doubt that having ideas, thinking about things instead of poking, pulling, biting, clawing and chattering at them, plays a large rôle either in existing primates or in the early primates who came between the mammals in general and those mammals whom we would accept as brother-men.* But there can be no doubt that in the number of kinds of situations to which they respond, in the number of responses they make, in the number of connections they can make between situation and response, and in the love of mental activity for its own sake, the primate group—the present monkeys, chimpanzees, gorillas and the ancestors of them and of us— are far in advance of other mammals and in a line that leads straight to the human mind.

For the demonstrable intellectual difference between the year old baby and the monkeys is not that he has many ideas while they have few or none. He, too, has few or none. It is that he responds to more things and in more ways. He differs from the monkey as the monkey differs from the dog and as the dog differs from the fish.

The arousal of the human yearling by all sorts of sights and sounds, and his varied, incessant manipulations of all sorts of objects, seem a random, futile play. They do not seem to pre-

---

* [In the forty years since this was written more evidence has accumulated that the primates, and perhaps other mammals, do have the rudiments of ideas.]

serve him or the species. But it is this behavior, which we significantly call "monkeying with" things, that produces ideas. By responding to one thing in so many contexts and with so many acts, the little child comes to respond to it by no act at all, but by thinking it, having an idea of it. By extending the animal learning far enough, it of itself produces ideas, and ideas produce all the rest.

When once the mind begins to function by having free ideas, all the phenomena of reasoning soon appear. The adult seems to differ enormously in intellect from the year-old baby. And in practical efficiency he does. But the psychological factors of an adult intellect are all observable in the average child of three. Roughly speaking, between his first and third birthdays a child becomes intellectually a full human being.

How slowly or how abruptly the changes came from early ancestors not intellectually above the present primates to our nearer ancestors possessing, like two-year-old children, free ideas of at least the common objects around them and their own common bodily acts, no one has attempted to estimate. It was a radical change in its consequences; but psychologically it would require only an extension of instincts and capacities already present in the primates. It could well have come, according to pure Darwinian principles, from small variations repeatedly selected. Thus in mind, as in body, man is a part of nature. His intellect is no new creation, but a simple, though extended, variation from the general animal type as found in our nearest physical relatives, the primates. Among the minds of animals that of man is chief, but also kinsman; ruler, but also brother.

The second great influence of Darwinism upon psychology was its stimulus to the study of the concrete particulars of intellect and character in individual men. You will remember that the voyage on the Beagle aroused in Darwin a permanent interest in the variations within species and in the gradations of species one into another. You will also remember that during most of his life thereafter he studied the variations of animals and plants from the type of the species, especially under the varying conditions supplied by domestication. His work turned the emphasis from the type to the variations from it. Biologists could no longer think of the animal and plant kingdom as a collection of replicas, occasionally imperfect or defaced, of originals made in some supernatural mint. Just as there is continuity, gradation, change little by little, as we pass backward to more and more remote ancestors, so within each species and between many species there is continuity, gradation, change little by little, as we pass sideways to more and more distant cousins. Psychology adopted somewhat reluctantly the new point of view. It used to speak in terms of the mind,—a pattern mind, possessed by all men. But now it studies "minds" rather than "the mind," and makes the differences which distinguish human individuals as significant as the likenesses which mark us as members of one species, and does not doubt that our common humanity goes with a very wide range of variation. Moreover, these intellectual and moral variations among men show as a rule continuity, gradation, change little by little.

Language encouraged us to think of men as grouped into clean-cut classes, good and bad, intelligent and stupid, quick and slow, and the like, and the pre-Darwinian psychology, in cases where it did get away from the doctrine of a single pattern mind, usually jumped to the equally false popular view of two or three or more patterns still distinct, with gaps between. What psychology would not do was to think of intellectual and moral traits along continuous scales, as physical science thinks of length, temperature, weight, or density. But this is just what it must do to get insight into or control over the facts. And this it is now doing as a result partly of the general emphasis on quantitative methods in all sciences and partly of the special emphasis on variability and continuity in living things due to the work of Darwin.

The last line of influence from Darwin's work that I shall try to describe is the least definite, but perhaps the most important of all —his influence in making psychology a natural

360   A CONNECTIONIST'S PSYCHOLOGY

science—in depriving teleological or supernatural causes from
their last remnant of power in the minds of scientific men.

Primitive thinking explains events of every sort by supposing that someone wishes the event to take place. The wind
blows because Poseidon wishes a storm. It thunders because
Zeus wishes to show his wrath. The crop is good because
Demeter so decides. Primitive thinking tries to control events
by wheedling or bribing someone, just as a little child teases
his mother to make a snow storm or to stop the rain. Men soon
learn, in certain very easy cases, that this explanation by someone's wish, by personal design, does not work. The succes-
sions of day and night, for instance, are easily seen to be regular, and to neither need nor heed the wishes of men or gods.
The sun does not stand still at any one's caprice. Only a fool
will hope to delay its setting by sacrifices or to hasten its rising
by prayer. You may still beseech some person to speed to its
mark the stone that you throw, but you would not expect him
to hold suspended in air the stone you drop.

The progress of common knowledge first, and of the refined
knowledge which we call science, later, gradually repudiated
the caprices of persons—of gods, goddesses, fairies, and elves
—as explanations of one physical event after another. The
movements of the stars, the behavior of all bodies in motion,
the action of heat and light, the affinities of the chemical substances,—as fast as men learned enough, personal wants were
forced to abdicate rule over each of these. Magic and begging
were abandoned as means to control them. But every case was
a struggle, and even the most thoughtful, the most scientific
men were not converted to natural causation with all their
hearts and minds. As a rule, even they kept all the superstitions they could. At a time when they would not have sung
an incantation to make water boil quicker, they would have
chanted formulas to make base metals change into gold. After
they had ceased to pray someone that fire might leave wood
unharmed, they would still pray that the wind might change.

By Darwin's time men of science had, of course, given up
the cruder forms of belief in the regulation of nature by per-

sonal caprices; but they kept a refined form of it in the case of living matter. For they did not see any natural way by which the varieties of animal and plant life could have come into existence with all their adaptations to the world in which they existed. They had gradually become thorough naturalists in their astronomy, physics, chemistry, and, last of all, in their geology; but they did not see how to rely on nature alone in biology. They still reasoned, like primitive men or babies, that animals and plants were as they were because someone had chosen that they should be so. They could not find within nature any cause for the specific forms which living matter wore. Men of science before Darwin, his grandfather among them, had proposed causes inherent in the natures and surroundings of animals and plants themselves. But the forces they invoked were not adequate. So for species and adaptation science still accepted a cause outside of nature in the time-dishonored form of someone's personal wish.

Darwin showed a natural way. He found within nature forces able to have produced species and their adaptations. The wish for birds with the feathers of which men may keep themselves warm or dry was shown to be as unnecessary to explain the birds' existence as the wish for water is to explain the combination of oxygen and hydrogen, or the wish of the gods to play marbles is to explain the spheroidal form of the earth and moon.

And Darwin's work did not suffer the caprice of persons to be considered a cause of mental events, of human psychology, of the history of men and nations. These also are to be understood, not by divining the intentions which they might possibly serve, but by examining them and the natural world of which they are a part. These, also, are to be controlled, not by devices to change someone's intentions, but by straightforward work with nature itself. Science and true religion now teach man to be throughout, in psychology as in physics, honest with nature and with himself. No excuse is left for hoping and fearing instead of thinking—for teasing and bribing instead of working. Our intellects and characters are no more subjects for magic, crude or refined, than the ebb and flow of the tides or the sequence of day and night.

Thus, at last, man may become ruler of himself as well as of the rest of nature. For, strange as it may sound, man is free only in a world whose every event he can understand and foresee. Only so can he guide it. We are captains of our own souls only in so far as they act in perfect law so that we can understand and foresee every response which we will make to every situation. Only so can we control our own selves. It is only because our intellects and morals—the mind and the spirit of man—are a part of nature, that we can be in any significant sense responsible for them, proud of their progress, or trustful of their future.

I have tried to make clear Darwin's direct contribution to the body of knowledge about human nature which we call psychology. This included a proof that the instincts and intelligence of animals and men are subject to variation and natural selection; a body of facts concerning human likes and dislikes and their evolution; an account of the expression of the emotions which is after nearly forty years unequalled; and one of the first studies of the mental development of man during infancy.

I have tried to show also that indirectly, through the revolution he brought about in biology, he made, or helped to make pyschology genetic, comparative, and concrete. He brought men of science to see that intellect and character grow, that their present nature is a result of their whole past history. He taught men of science to study the concrete individual differences which are of so great significance not only to the course of mental evolution, but also to the practical conduct of life.

To all human thinking and conduct Darwin taught two great principles. The first is the principle of evolution, of continuity,—that each succeeding segment of the stream of life, each successive act in the world drama, is the outcome of all that have gone before and the cause of all that are to come.

The second is the principle of naturalism,—that in life and in mind the same cause will always produce the same effect, that the bodies and minds of men are a part of nature, that their history is as natural as the history of the stars, their behavior as natural as the behavior of an atom of hydrogen. If there were time I could show how this same contribution has acted to transform our views of all human institutions, of the state, the church, education, and every feature of civilization, and our treatment of every practical concern of life.

Gladstone and Lincoln lived in the thick of human business, and devoted their exceptional talents to the affairs of state. Each led a great nation, one through a generation of steady development, the other through the nation's greatest crisis. Darwin, making experiments in his quiet garden at Down, seems utterly remote from such leadership of men. Yet so far as such subtle problems can be calculated, we must conclude that Darwin will in the end have had the greatest influence upon social institutions, even upon government itself. For, in the long run, the only cure for national ills and the only foundation for progress is science, sure and verifiable knowledge, directing a good-will toward men. And this good-will itself can be aroused and increased only by use of the facts and laws of science. Even now, in the treatment of subject races, in legislation for criminals and dependents, in the care for public health, and in the new view of the family, we may see the influence of Darwinism beginning to spread to statesmanship and social control.

I venture to prophesy that when, a hundred years from now, men again celebrate the work of Darwin, there will be no more doubt of his transformation of the world's activities than of his transformation of its thinking. If the chief art of reason is life, so also the chief duty of life is science, the search for truth. The best citizen is the one who advances most the common good. The surest, perhaps the only sure, means of advance is increase in truth. To the search for the truth Darwin gave an intellect of wonderful fairness and care, and a life of perfect devotion.

Index

Abbreviation as a cause of linguistic changes, 310
Abilities, 155 f.
Abstraction, 113
Achievement, satisfyingness of, 320
Adults and children compared with respect to word associations, 94 f.
After-effects of a connection, 13 f. *See also* Rewards and Punishment
Age at entrance to a given grade in high school, resemblance of siblings in, 207
Age at entrance to Columbia College, resemblance of brothers in, 205 f.
ALLPORT, G., 279
Analogy, 109 f.
Analytic Processes, 108 f.; subtler forms of, 113 f.
ANASTASI, A., 311
Animals, experiments with, 2, 3, 4, 41 f.
Annoyers, 18. *See also* Punishment
Approval, 322 f., 325
Arithmetic, 165 f.
ARMSTRONG, A. C., 1
Assimilation, 109 f.
Association, by contiguity in time, 63, 73, 305; by sensory affiliations, 85 f.; by instinctive tendencies, 87; by contrariety, 88 f.; by similarity, 122, 305
Associations of ideas as evidence concerning personality, 261, 267. *See also* Trains of thought
Attention to parts and features as a means of analysis, 113 f.
Autobiography of E. L. Thorndike, 1 f.
Aversions, reports of, 238 f., 244; obsessional strength of some, 246
AYLESWORTH, M., 53

Babble-luck theory of the origin of language, 284 f.; criticisms of it, 291 f.
Backward spread of the influence of a satisfier, 29 f.
Beauty, value of, 335
Belief, measurements of, 141 f.
Belongingness, 62 f.; zero of, 68
BENTHAM, JEREMY, 246
BERGSTRÖM, J. A., 226
BETTMAN, S., 226
BOAS, F., 7
BOLTON, T. L., 226
Bow-wow theory of the origin of language, 280 f.
BREGMAN, E. O., 181, 220
BRETNALL, E. P., 16
BURGERSTEIN, L., 226
BURNETT, C. T., 135

CALKINS, M. W., 137 f., 151, 152
CARNAP, R., 294
CARROLL, LEWIS, 302
CASON, H., 79, 80
CATTELL, J. McK., 3
CATTELL, R., 196, 205
Child psychology, Darwin's contribution to, 352 f.
Children and adults compared with respect to word associations, 94 f.
COBURN, C. A., 48
Comparative psychology, debt of to Darwin, 354
Complexity, of mental connections, 81 f.; of the behavior due to genes, 185 f.
Compound words, 303
Computation, abilities involved in, 170 f.
Conditional reflex, 63
Confirming reaction, 16 f., 34 f., 78 f.

365

(1)